Charter Schools

Charter Schools

Creating Hope and Opportunity for American Education

Joe Nathan

Jossey-Bass Publishers • San Francisco

FIRST PAPERBACK EDITION PUBLISHED IN 1999.

All individuals quoted and identified have been quoted and identified with their permission.

Excerpts from Joe Nathan's columns in the *St. Paul Pioneer Press* are reprinted by permission of the *St. Paul Pioneer Press*.

Excerpts from Albert Shanker's columns in *The New York Times* and an American Federation of Teachers press release are reprinted by permission of Albert Shanker.

Substantial discounts on bulk quantities of Jossey-Bass books are available to corporations, professional associations, and other organizations. For details and discount information, contact the special sales department at Jossey-Bass Inc., Publishers (415) 433-1740; Fax (800) 605-2665.

 Manufactured in the United States of America on Lyons Falls Pathfinder Tradebook. This paper is acid-free and 100 percent totally chlorine-free.

Library of Congress Cataloging-in-Publication Data

Nathan, Joe, date.
    Charter schools : creating hope and opportunity for American
education / Joe Nathan. — 1st ed.
       p.   cm. — (The Jossey-Bass education series)
    Includes bibliographical references and index.
    ISBN 0-7879-0263-2 (acid-free paper)
    ISBN 0-7879-4454-8 (paperback)
    1. Charter schools—United States. I. Title. II. Series.
LB2806.36.N38 1996
371—dc20   96-35609

FIRST EDITION
HB Printing 10 9 8 7 6 5 4 3 2 1
PB Printing 10 9 8 7 6 5 4 3 2 1

The Jossey-Bass Education Series

Contents

Acknowledgments

Many people contributed to this book.

First, thanks to the pioneering educators, parents, and students in charter schools around the nation who shared their dreams, ideas, questions, and concerns with me. I hope this book is useful to them and to others committed to young people.

Many people have generously shared their insights. Special thanks go to Ted Kolderie, John Ayers, Jeannie Allen, Sue Bragato, Joan Buckley, Yvonne Chan, Andrea DiLorenzo, Frank Dooling, Suzanne Donovan, Jim Goenner, Jim Griffin, Howard Fuller, Eric Hirsch, Toni Haas, Jude Hollins, Peggy Hunter, Wayne Jennings, Rhonda Lauer, Debbie Lazarus, Lynn Lavely, Margaret Lin, Alex Medler, Paul Nachtigal, Eric Premack, Pam Riley, Jon Schnur, Darryl Sedio, Ted Sizer, Sarah Tantillo, Bill Windler, and Cindy Zautcke, and to legislators Ember Reichgott Junge, Mindy Greiling, Becky Kelso, and Matt Entenza.

I also thank the trustees and staff of the Annenberg Foundation, the Blandin Foundation, the Bradley Foundation, and the General Mills Foundation, all of which helped support this research. Thanks go also to University of Minnesota presidents Nils Hasselmo and Mark Yudof, who provided encouragement and financial support so that the Center for School Change can continue its work. My deep appreciation goes to G. Edward Schuh and John Brandl, who have served as deans at the Hubert H. Humphrey Institute of Public Affairs. They provided critical advice and assistance.

Many people shared information they had gathered. Thanks go especially to Jon Schroeder, Ted Kolderie, Jeannie Allen, and Eric Hirsch for providing valuable information. Research assistants Stella Cheung, Jennifer Power, and Monishae Mosley worked hard and carefully at gathering information about charter schools. Thanks for their cheerful, diligent efforts.

The Center for School Change staff in Minneapolis helped in countless ways. Deb Hare, Betty Radcliffe, and Jerry Langley-Ripka dealt with many critical details. Their patience and good humor made this a much better book. Vicki Nelson, Doug Thomas, and Terri Anderson share a deep commitment and special insight into what can help young people and communities. Thanks to Nancy Smith for her excellent efforts to bring people together and help them understand the marvelous possibilities for having an impact on youngsters—to understand, in the words of Sitting Bull, "what life we will make for our children."

Thanks to Lesley Iura and Christie Hakim at Jossey-Bass Publishers for their interest and encouragement.

Elizabeth, David, and Laura Nathan asked important questions and reminded me to include student views. JoAnn Nathan has shared more than twenty years of encouragement, advice, challenge, and support. JoAnn, who is a public school teacher, is a daily inspiration.

My thanks to all these people. I apologize for any mistakes that may have crept into the book. They are my responsibility.

J. N.

Preface to the Paperback Edition

"I'm a convert to the charter movement." That's how Kent Matheson, superintendent of the Flagstaff, Arizona, public schools put it, surprising the two hundred or so school administrators who had gathered in Boise, Idaho, to hear a debate about the value of charter public schools. The program organizers thought I would present the pro-charter side and Matheson would present the "con" position. It didn't work out that way. He and I agreed that the charter movement was a fundamental, important, and positive change.

That was one of the most intriguing, encouraging days I've spent in the two years since the first edition of this book was published. Matheson's rethinking helps illustrate some of the changes the charter idea has produced over the last couple of years. The next few pages offer a brief update on the charter movement's growth, evolution, and challenges.

Almost every day, people call or write with important, thoughtful questions about the charter school movement. Parents wonder, "Do you know of charter schools in my neighborhood (or city or area or state) that would help my children?" Educators ask, "How can I start a charter school? Do you know of charters that are looking for educators to work in them?" Journalists have their own questions: "Can or will charters improve achievement? What happens to other public schools when charters start? What are good charter schools to visit?" This book was written to help answer these and many other questions.

Perhaps my biggest challenge is to convey the positive impact of the charter movement on thousands of students, educators, and families. How can I reach out, in these words and pages, to tell you about students who are doing far better in school, about parents who were frustrated but are now delighted by their children's school, or about teachers who say the charter movement has given them the opportunity to be the real professionals they've been trying to be for fifteen to twenty years?

No one change will solve all the problems of American education. But it is important to understand the charter idea. The Flagstaff experiences illustrate one of the central ideas of the charter movement: the movement is not just about making opportunities for people to create new, potentially more effective public schools; rather, the movement represents a dramatic change in the way states offer public education. The new approach says that there can be more than one source of public education in a community. The idea, in part, is to encourage and stimulate improvement in existing schools and school districts.

Charter Accomplishments

The charter movement certainly faces challenges. But before discussing these, here is a list of the movement's seven key accomplishments over the last couple of years.

1. *The movement has grown significantly, both in numbers of states with charter legislation and in numbers of charter schools operating.* Thirty-three states and the District of Columbia have now adopted some form of the charter idea. The movement has expanded from one state in 1991 to thirty-three states in late 1998, with eight new states in the last two years.

The number of charter schools also has grown steadily, from one school in 1992 to about eleven hundred operating in the 1998–99 school year.

And a number of states have strengthened their charter laws because of positive experiences with the concept. For example, in 1996 Minnesota allowed up to 30 charters; Texas allowed up to 20 state-sponsored charters; California allowed up to 100. Minnesota now has no limit on the number of charters it permits. California will permit the creation of up to 250 charters in the next year and up to 100 more in each succeeding year. Texas now permits the state to sponsor up to 120 charters, along with an unlimited number of charters if the schools are designed to serve mostly students who have not succeeded in traditional schools. Georgia originally did not allow educators and parents to create new charter schools, only the conversion of existing schools. In 1998 the Georgia legislature authorized the creation of new charters. In 1998 Wisconsin decided to permit the city of Milwaukee, as well as the local district, to sponsor charters—a move that one Milwaukee school board, which is cited later, reports had an immediate, positive impact.

2. *The movement has attracted veteran community activists like Rosa Parks, the civil rights legend, who recently requested permission to start a charter school in Detroit.* As the *New York Times* reported, "More than 40 years after Rosa Parks refused to give up her seat to a white passenger on a bus, the opening salvo in what became the Montgomery, Alabama, bus boycott, she is trying to set up one of the first charter schools in Detroit."[1] It is deeply gratifying for people who lived through—and in some cases participated in—the civil rights movement to be on the same side of an issue as Rosa Parks.

Some of the nation's finest charters have been started by inner-city community activists working with talented educators and dissatisfied families. A front-page *New York Times* story noted that some of these activists are working hard to get states to adopt charter laws: "From New Jersey to Massachusetts and Pennsylvania to Minnesota, Texas and Colorado, minority legislators and advocacy groups from the inner cities have been forging powerful alliances with conservatives to enact legislation that authorizes the charter schools."[2]

3. *The movement has unleashed caring, talented, committed educators around the nation.* These folks know they can make a positive difference in the lives of young people. One of them is former Arizona Teacher of the Year, Karen Butterfield. She attempted unsuccessfully to carry out many of her ideas within the structure of her Arizona school district. One of those ideas was intensive collaboration with a local museum. So she established a charter school at the museum. The local superintendent says that Butterfield's school is excellent, and has helped stimulate improvements within the district.

Florida has hired former National Teacher of the Year, Tracey Bailey, to head its Office of Public School Choice and Charter Schools. Bailey has called the charter movement a terrific opportunity for educators.

4. *The movement has attracted the interest and bipartisan support of Congress.* This has led to millions of federal (tax-payer) dollars going to help start charter schools. Federal charter start-up funding has grown steadily—to more than $50 million a year.

That funding is a mixed blessing. It has helped many people start charter schools across the nation but has also led to some unfortunate things. For example, at one midwestern charter school one of the creators told me they were going to run the school entirely on federal money for the first year because the district did not want to commit any funds to the program. In some states, the state government has given out fairly large charter-planning grants with no expectation that the planning would lead to the creation of schools.

5. *The movement has encouraged many families who felt that their children could do better in school with a different kind of learning environment.* All over the nation I've heard from parents who say, as a California parent reported, "It's like I have a new child. He is so enthusiastic, so eager to go to school. It's a smaller school, where people know and care about each other."

This parent's enthusiasm is echoed in several studies in which parents give higher grades to the charter schools than to the previous schools their children attended. For example, a national study of charter schools asked parents to compare the charter school with the school their child previously attended. More than 60 percent of these parents rated the charter school as better in such key areas as class size, individual attention by teachers, school size, quality of teaching, extra help for students, academic standards, accessibility and openness, and discipline.[3]

A University of Minnesota study asked charter school parents to assign a grade to the school. About 90 percent of the parents gave the charter school an A or B. The University of Minnesota study noted that another national poll, given the same year, found that about 65 percent of parents nationally give their children's school an A or B.[4]

6. *The movement has improved student achievement in many communities.* The evidence continues to grow that charter schools can improve student achievement. These changes have been measured in various ways, including by traditional standardized tests. A 1998 study examined thirty-one charters in ten states. The study, which

I helped conduct, found that twenty-one of the charters had clear evidence of improving student achievement. Some examples:

- Community Day Charter in Lawrence, Massachusetts, serves 132 students in grades K–5; 70 percent are students of color; 69 percent qualify for free or reduced-cost lunch. During its first two years, using the Metropolitan Achievement Test, students in grades 2 through 4 averaged improvements of 1.3 to 1.5 grade levels per year. In other words, they made more than a year's gain for every year they attended the school.
- Addison Elementary School in Marietta, Georgia, enrolls seven hundred students, grades K–5. About 15 percent of the students are students of color. Data from the Iowa Test of Basic Skills over three years show that students make an average gain of 1.35 years each year they attended the school.
- Before converting to charter status, SABIS International Charter School was one of the lowest-performing schools in Springfield, Massachusetts. The school enrolls 750 students in grades K–9; 61 percent are students of color; 54 percent qualify for free or reduced-cost lunch. Sixty-two percent of the students scored *below* grade level when the school opened. Two years later, 62 percent scored *at or above* grade level.
- Fenton Avenue Elementary had been known as a "hellhole" school before converting to charter status. It enrolls 1,295 students, grades K–6. More than 97 percent of its population are students of color; over 95 percent qualify for free or reduced-cost meals. Test scores improved consistently, with growing numbers of students meeting or exceeding national norms. The California State Department of Education named Fenton one of California's Most Distinguished Schools, and in 1998 the Los Angeles school board renewed its charter.
- Pueblo Colorado's School for the Arts and Sciences enrolls 416 students in grades K–12; 50 percent are students of color; 44 percent are eligible for free or reduced-cost lunch. The school used a Portfolio program developed by the American College Testing Program to assess student achievement. ACT readers compared samples of student work. Ninety-one percent of the students with at least two years of work made "highly significant improvement" in science, and 57 percent

made "highly significant improvement" or "significant improvement" in language arts. The Pueblo school board unanimously renewed the school's charter in 1997.[5]

These are only a few of many examples that could be cited. Evidence is growing that charter schools can improve the achievement of all kinds of students, that is, students of all races, incomes, and achievement levels. Improved achievement is one major reason the charter movement continues to grow. Even though not all charters improve achievement, part of the idea of accountability in the charter movement is that ineffective schools will be closed.

This is no longer just an idea. The Minnesota State Board of Education did in fact close a charter in 1998 because it did not improve student achievement. It's vital for the charter movement to continue to insist on rigor.

One of the contributions the charter movement is making to American education is the effort being made in many places to develop thoughtful, appropriate evaluation programs. Because accountability is a key part of the charter approach, student assessment is critical.

7. *The movement has stimulated a variety of improvements in some districts.* As noted earlier, Kent Matheson, superintendent of the Flagstaff schools, described a number of improvements in his district that "might not have happened, or came about much more rapidly, because Arizona has a charter law permitting people to go to the state, as well as the district, to obtain permission to create a charter school." He had been the Washington State Superintendent of the Year before moving to Arizona.

Matheson said that when the charter law first passed, he was "bristly and angry. I have a completely different attitude now." Matheson described changes that had taken place in the district that were due, in part, to the charter movement:

- Set up a new magnet middle school emphasizing fine and performing arts, science, and technology and will soon start a new magnet elementary school
- Invited business leaders in to help judge senior high school student presentations

- Became more welcoming to parents, in part because families have more options
- Became more active in explaining to community groups what is happening in the schools
- Changed to full-day kindergarten at eleven of the district's twelve elementary schools

Another superintendent said, "Wouldn't the district have done these things without the charter law?" Matheson replied, "I don't think we would have responded as much without a strong charter law. The law was a very strong motivating force making us want to compete."[6]

Another example of competition's power comes from Wisconsin. For some years, Milwaukee has contracted with small alternative schools to work with students who have not succeeded in traditional secondary schools. These schools have asked to receive most of the money that their students generate from the state. Milwaukee school board member John Gardner, a union activist for more than twenty-five years, has advocated strongly for these schools. But he found a great deal of district office resistance to responding to what he considers a very legitimate request—giving these schools most of the money their students generate. In 1998 the district offered the schools about $5,700 per pupil.

Then the Wisconsin legislature authorized the city of Milwaukee to sponsor charter schools. The city said it would provide $6,100 per pupil to these schools. The district responded, offering $6,214 per pupil to the schools, along with a three-year contract, which the schools had requested for several years.[7]

Many people working in schools know how hard it can be to negotiate with a central office. The Flagstaff and Milwaukee examples show the value of having more than one organization sponsoring public education in a community.

University of California graduate student Eric Rofes traveled to twenty-five districts in eight states, interviewing officials about the impact of the charter idea. He visited states with different kinds of laws. Some had weak laws, permitting only local boards to sponsor charters. Some had stronger laws. Rofes reported that in twelve of the twenty-five districts, there was either strong or moderate impact from charter schools. Thirteen districts reported mild or no impact.

His research helps show the importance of laws that permit other entities as well as local districts to sponsor charter schools:

> States which had policies that provided for the chartering of new schools only through the local district showed significantly less evidence of reform effects from the development of charter schools than did states which allowed for multiple sponsors. . . . District personnel on at least five occasions in this study acknowledged— sometimes begrudgingly—that charters had served to jump-start their efforts at reform. While they initially opposed charters and the chartering had been accomplished outside their authority, they felt that district schools ultimately had benefited from the dynamics introduced by the charter school.[8]

So the charter idea has not only expanded opportunity and increased achievement, it has helped promote district reform efforts, encouraging existing schools and districts to improve their programs. That is a key goal of the charter movement.

Two award-winning educators currently working with the U.S. Department of Education offer a final example of the charter movement's broader impact. Deborah Meier and Paul Schwarz have won widespread acclaim for their work with youngsters in East Harlem, a low-income section of New York City.

During the summer of 1998, Meier and Schwarz met a Los Angeles teacher who was starting a charter school there. As they noted "She had great enthusiasm, high hopes and enormous energy. . . . She has been teaching for ten years and she told us that she had never been so excited about the beginning of school."

In a September 1998 letter, Meier and Schwarz announced that the U.S. Department of Education would hold a meeting in the fall to discuss three issues.

1. What is it about charter schools that makes them so exciting, so attractive to so many people?
2. What disincentives to charter like school change currently exist and might have the effect of driving public school educators to private enterprises or of stifling their professional creativity?
3. What incentives could be built into "regular" public school systems and policies that would capitalize on the strengths of teachers and principals and parents and local community folk that

have been tapped into the charter school movement (creativity, hope, redesign, flexibility, autonomy, local accountability)?[9]

Charter Challenges

Over the last couple of years, charter schools and the charter movement have faced serious challenges. The movement's growth shows that the challenges can be met. But they must first be considered.

Internal Issues for Charter Schools

Many charter schools struggle with these key issues: *evaluation, governance, funding,* and *facilities*. Over the last few years reformers have learned a great deal about each issue. Following are a few brief comments; more detailed discussions of these topics appear later in the book.

1. *Evaluation:* Having real, measurable accountability for improved achievement at the school is a new idea for most people involved in education. Despite all the rhetoric about accountability, the reality is that most schools in most states continue to operate and receive funds, regardless of whether achievement improves or declines.

The study cited earlier about charter schools that had improved achievement also showed that some schools and their sponsors had not agreed on clear goals and evaluation methods before the schools opened.[10] Charter contracts should include clear, measurable goals, along with a description of how progress toward those goals will be assessed. And contracts should include some indication of how much progress will be expected if the contract is to be renewed.

The charter movement, along with public education in general, needs continued work on the evaluation issue. This is one of the central ways in which the charter movement will be judged and is discussed more extensively later in the book.

There are tough questions about the most effective ways to measure gains in student achievement, and equally tough questions about how much progress should be expected before a school's contract is renewed. Priscilla Wohlstetter and Noell Griffin concluded after interviewing charter school operators in three states that there is "a continuing dispute over standards for student performance. . . ."[11]

Some schools and sponsors have done a good job of resolving these questions. The Colorado and Massachusetts departments of education have been particularly effective in this area. Sample contracts now are available from many state-based charter resource centers and from Internet web sites. (See Appendixes A and C for places to contact.)

2. *Governance:* One of the central differences between a successful and unsuccessful charter is its ability to govern itself efficiently and effectively. When charter advocates gather, this is one of the first things that comes up. Many of us have not been trained to run meetings. People who start charter schools often are driven, passionate folks with very strong views. Learning to work together, to delegate, and to decide has been very difficult for some charter schools, which have excellent ideas about how to work with youngsters. Dealing effectively with governance is vital for charters.

3. *Funding:* In many states, charter opponents have been successful in producing political compromises that result in charter schools receiving less money than other public schools and districts. This is especially true in states with strong charter laws in which charter schools are not part of an existing district. A Minnesota study, for example, found that charter schools receive an average of $1,000 less per pupil than other public schools.[12]

Charters often receive state average funding rather than the proceeds of local property tax referendums. And charters often receive far less in start-up funding than other public schools. Generally, when school boards decide to open a new school, they go to the district's voters, pass a referendum, and obtain start-up funds to pay for books, chairs, desks, computers, and so forth. Charter schools cannot do this.

Of course, there are funding issues across public education. Some wealthy districts receive far more than other districts because of their wealth in property tax. But clearly, charters are a part of the financial debate. It is ironic that some states have higher expectations for charter schools than traditional schools in terms of improving student achievement but provide charter schools with less per pupil.

4. *Facilities:* Directly related to the funding issue is the question of buildings. Some charter schools are developing alliances with social service agencies, museums, and businesses to share space. A number of marvelous examples are given later in the book. But many charters have difficulty finding an appropriate building that meets applicable code requirements.

Many communities in this country have problems with their school buildings. Public education has put money into other things, and there are significant variations among communities in the amount of money generated by property taxes.

External Challenges for Schools

Why do many people who see themselves as defenders of public education have such low expectations of public schools? That's a central question that is emerging, according to critiques of the charter movement.

Low Expectations for Schools and Students. Some members of the "academic left"—often university professors or those who work in think tanks—insist that we really cannot expect schools to significantly increase the achievement of students from low-income, limited-English-speaking, or otherwise challenging backgrounds. A major national education publication ran a column by a North Carolina professor who insisted, "Education by itself is a weak treatment." He criticized the high expectations many people have of schools and insisted that schools by themselves could do little to overcome students' problems.[13]

This is a common view among educators. One award-winning professor wrote me that "school reform is a con job" promoted by businesses and conservative politicians to detract attention from helping families, improving health care, finding good jobs, and reducing crime.

My Answer. Some of the nation's strongest charter school supporters also are working hard on societal problems. This includes people like Rosa Parks, liberal U.S. senator Paul Wellstone (D-Minnesota), and President Bill Clinton. Wellstone, for example, recently called the charter idea "a marvelous innovation which is spreading throughout the country."[14] In the same speech he described ways we can and should help strengthen families and make inner-city neighborhoods safer. In a 1997 speech in California, President Clinton said he would like to see all public schools operate like charter schools.[15]

The charter movement can help solve our nation's problems. It clearly is not a distraction from other societal problems. There are many problems outside schools that we need to work on. But those problems should not serve as excuses for failing to address problems inside the schools and in the public education system.

Years ago researcher Ron Edmonds asked, "How many effective schools serving inner-city students does it take for us to agree that schools can make a big difference in the lives of youngsters?" Edmonds spent years studying and documenting characteristics of schools, and his research showed that public schools can make a major difference for all kinds of students, a finding that is still relevant today.

Researchers have studied the impact of teacher expectations on students. Those whose teachers thought they would do well in school did significantly better than those whose teachers thought they would not. Expectations matter. Results depend in part on expectations. High expectations help produce high results—low expectations, low results. Generally, we'll get what we expect—from students and from schools.

Low expectations are one of the key challenges the charter movement faces. It is easier to make excuses than to make progress. It is easier to blame families and students than to insist that we can do better, much better.

Difficulty of Measuring Improvement. Some argue that we do not know how to measure improvements in student achievement. Richard Rothstein says that the idea "that we can hold schools accountable for results is a myth." He argues that "there is no consensus about how to assess educational outcomes objectively."[16]

My Answer. It is true that there is no consensus—no general agreement—about how to determine whether students are learning more and whether a school is making progress. But many states and school districts have agreed on how to measure these things.

And we may not need universal agreement to make progress. Many historians believe that a majority of people living in the English colonies did not support breaking away from Great Britain. Nevertheless, the American Revolution was successful. Did we have universal agreement about ending slavery? Was there a consensus about expanding voting rights to women? Was there a consensus regarding the goals of Dr. Martin Luther King? Of course not. Yet we were able to move ahead. And the charter movement can move ahead without a consensus.

Other Opposition. Opposition of the types I have mentioned remains intense and powerful. Along with members of the so-called academic left, opponents include some members of education groups who are deeply concerned about the shift of power and money that the charter movement represents. They do not like charter schools receiving what they consider to be "their money." And some opponents say they like it as long as only local school boards can authorize charter schools.

My Answer. School districts already have the power to create new schools. The charter idea is not just to create new schools but to provide school districts with new, strong incentives to improve. That means, as Eric Rofes points out, permitting multiple groups to authorize charters.

Americans are pragmatic people. We support things that work. We don't trust monopolies because we've found they often take customers for granted. We pay taxes and legislatures allocate those taxes. But we pay for the education of children, not for the preservation of a particular system. Some school administrators, some teachers union members, and some superintendents are coming to understand that.

The list of believers in charter schools is growing. The number of young people who are doing better in school is growing. The number of educators, parents, and community members who are able to create schools that make sense—and make a difference— is growing.

The charter movement represents central American values: responsibility, opportunity, choice. America has grown steadily under the guidance of those principles. There have been big bumps in the road. As a nation we have made mistakes but we have learned from them and made progress. That is happening with the charter movement. It is growing. It is learning. The charter movement is bringing new hope and opportunity to American students, families, educators, and communities.

Minneapolis, Minnesota   *Joe Nathan*
October 1998

Preface

One can resist the invasion of armies
but not the invasion of ideas.
Victor Hugo

The charter idea is part of a two-hundred-year effort in this country to expand opportunity, especially for those who are not wealthy and powerful. Many charter school advocates come from the same worldview as people like Susan B. Anthony, Dr. Martin Luther King, Jr., and Cesar Chavez, people who spent their lives working with and for people who had little power and influence.

This is a book for people who believe, or would like to believe, that schools can help youngsters. All kinds of youngsters. Young people from troubled families. Young people who are angry and alienated. Young people who are bright and bored. Young people who feel lost or frustrated in large schools. People—educators, parents, community leaders, policy makers—who believe that schools can make a difference in the lives of youngsters will get support here.

Charter proponents readily agree that significant problems in this society are producing troubled families and challenging youngsters. It is vital to work toward a more just and a fairer society that will prize all youngsters and strengthen families. But acknowledging enormous problems *outside* schools does not mean that educators cannot do a much better job at helping youngsters *inside* schools. That is what effective, talented educators have long believed. The charter public school movement gives them the opportunity to carry out their dreams.

The charter school idea is about the creation of more accountable public schools, and the removal of the "exclusive franchise"[1] that local school boards presently have. Charter schools are public, nonsectarian schools that do not have admissions tests but that operate under a written contract, or *charter,* from a local school board or some other organization, such as a state school board. These contracts specify how the school will be held accountable for improved student achievement, in exchange for a waiver of most rules and regulations governing how they operate. Charter schools that improve achievement have their contracts renewed. Charter schools that do not improve student achievement over the contract's period are closed. The term *charter* comes from the contracts given to European explorers, which specified expectations and responsibilities of both the explorer and his sponsors.

The charter idea is not just about the creation of new, more accountable public schools or the conversion of existing public schools. The charter idea also introduces fair, thoughtful competition into public education. Strong charter laws allow these schools to be sponsored by more than one type of public organization, for example, a local school board, a state school board, or a public university. Evidence shared later in this book shows that when school districts know families can get public education from more than one source, that competition helps produce improvements.

Humility also is important. Educators, parents, and legislators have heard about a *lot* of ideas in education intended to revolutionize the system. The charter concept will not solve every problem, cure every ill. But it will help many, many people. In fact, as we will see, it already is helping thousands of youngsters, families, and educators.

In 1991, there was not a single charter school in the nation. By mid-1996, almost three hundred were operating. In 1991, Minnesota passed the nation's first charter school legislation. Less than five years later, twenty-five states have adopted some form of charter legislation. About half of these laws are strong and will give the charter concept a real test.

Today, from the *New York Times* and the *Washington Post* to the *St. Paul Pioneer Press* and the *Seattle Times,* the charter school idea is a front-page story. Such mass-market magazines as *Time, Newsweek,* and *U.S. News & World Report* have featured stories about charter schools. The idea is spreading more rapidly and attracting much more attention than the usual educational reform. In his 1996 State of the Union address, President Clinton asked "each state to let teachers form new schools with a charter they can keep only if they do a good job." The day following this speech, U.S. Secretary of Education Richard Riley visited a charter school in Minneapolis, where he proclaimed the administration's strong support for charter schools and announced that the administration would ask Congress for $20 million in start-up funds for charter schools. Congress responded by allocating $18 million, more than tripling the amount it had authorized in 1994.

Is the current interest in charter schools justified? What does the charter school idea include, and why is it spreading so rapidly? Why have so many political leaders, liberal and conservative, Republican and Democratic, endorsed the idea? Can charter schools meet public expectations for them? What are the key similarities and differences among the twenty-five charter school state laws that have been adopted? What controversies have charter advocates encountered in passing charter school legislation? What motivates and worries people who oppose charter programs? How much do we know about charter schools at this point, some five years after the first charter school was established? Who starts them? What kind of students attend them? Are these schools actually helping students? Are they having much impact on other schools, public or private? This book offers answers to these and other important questions.

Support for charter schools is coming not only from the parents who feel their children are not receiving the best education possible in today's public schools but also from teachers, especially those who entered the profession believing they could change kids' lives. This country's public schools employ many talented, committed educators. Unfortunately, these excellent teachers often are frustrated by a system that does not value their skills. They are disappointed by an administrative bureaucracy that sometimes stifles their creativity and by parents who object to proposed reforms and do not want their children to participate. They discover that it is difficult to remove mediocre teachers from public schools. As the frustrations mount, energetic, enthusiastic teachers become bitter, burned-out teachers. Some give up. Some close their classroom doors and do the best they can with their own students. Many report that they would not advise their children to enter their profession.

The charter school movement gives real power not only to parents and children to choose the kind of school that makes sense for them but also to teachers to use their skills, talents, and energy. Along with this opportunity comes responsibility—the responsibility to demonstrate improved student achievement as measured by standardized tests and other assessments. Hundreds of charter schools have been created around this nation by educators who are willing to put their jobs on the line, to say, "If we can't improve student achievement, close down our school." That is accountability— clear, specific, and real.

Powerful opposition has not stopped the charter school movement from growing; legislated in only one state in 1991, charter schools are currently allowed in half the states. The movement has grown because it makes sense to people across the entire political spectrum. Advocates for youngsters and families from the inner city and among the rural poor have testified in favor of charter school legislation and have helped start charter schools serving these students. Democrats like President Clinton, Secretary of Education Riley, and Senator Paul Wellstone, perhaps the most liberal U.S. Senator, have endorsed the charter school concept. Conservatives from President George Bush to House Speaker Newt Gingrich also support charter schools.

Perhaps the support is so broad because the idea makes sense and seems fair. According to a Gallup poll, 65 percent of Americans think public school choice is a good idea.[2] It seems reasonable to expect schools to improve their students' educational achievement. Moreover, because charter schools are public schools, they do not have admissions tests and do not charge tuition. It seems fair that schools receiving public funds should not be allowed to pick and choose among students and should not be allowed to charge tuition beyond what the state provides. Charter schools are nonsectarian and so avoid the deep emotional controversy about separation of church and state that has split this nation and produced enormous debate but almost no adoption of the school voucher idea.

Audience

Charter Schools is intended for school administrators and teachers who are already active in a charter school, thinking of starting a charter school, or working in a district that is or will be granting authorizations to these schools. It is also intended for members of school boards at both state and local levels. Finally, it is designed to inform and assist parents and community members who are involved with an existing charter school, are in the process of planning such a school, or are simply considering whether a charter school is appropriate for their children or their community.

Overview of the Book

Charter Schools is a book about parents, policy makers, and educators coming together to make a difference. To help them succeed, this book describes the history of the charter school movement and the patterns that current charter school advocates may find themselves repeating; offers examples of existing charter schools, enabling legislation, and community reaction; and presents guidance for charter school developers and operators.

The Introduction describes the key elements of the charter concept and shows how it differs from school voucher systems, magnet schools, privatization efforts, and the school-site management trend. The points emphasized in the Introduction are those that were discussed during the development of, and debate about, the nation's first charter school bill. The Introduction also covers issues raised during discussions at a national state legislators' conference, in a dozen state legislature hearings, at meetings of state boards of education, and in a U.S. congressional hearing.

Part One (Chapters One and Two) presents the background necessary to an understanding of the charter school movement. Chapter One tours a number of charter schools. It examines who started them, discusses why, and describes how they are working with youngsters. One of the most important lessons of this tour is the enormous differences found among charter schools in almost every conceivable way—site, curriculum, philosophy, and ages of students, to name a few points of divergence. Yet in one critical way, all these schools are the same. All must show improved student performance on standardized tests and other measures, or they will be closed. This is called accountability. It is missing from today's public education in almost every state. It is part of the reason some people are intrigued and some feel threatened by charter schools.

Chapter Two examines the history of the concept and its genesis among teachers and parents who wanted different, more effective public schools. It also reviews the intense political battle that produced the nation's first charter school law in Minnesota in 1991, explaining the effects of the many compromises that were made. Similar battles have taken place in almost every state that has discussed charter school legislation. This chronicle illustrates how legislation gets shaped, how advocacy shifts opinions, and why it is important for people who work directly with children and those who advocate for young people from low-income families to be involved themselves in charter school legislative battles, which may otherwise be dominated by powerful interests whose first priority may not be children's needs.

Part Two (Chapters Three and Four) examines some specific challenges facing charter schools and their potential role as competitors who improve the performance of the entire public school system. Chapter Three discusses both the opposition and the occasional support that charter schools encounter from school boards. When local boards know they face real competition, a number have encouraged district educators to create new schools and programs under the charter school concept. Chapter Four looks at the current general opposition to charter schools from the teachers' unions, and the union efforts to block or water down legislation so that the charter school concept does not get a real trial, the exceptions to that opposition, and the opportunities that unions should see for their members in charter schools. Indeed, some unions see charter schools as an opportunity to help them realize the goal of empowering teachers.

Part Three (Chapters Five, Six, and Seven) offers guidance for people who want to start or are starting charter schools. This section relies on information from a survey of 110 charter schools around the nation, what I have learned in my visits to several dozen of these schools, and what I have learned during twenty-five years of helping people start innovative public schools in urban, rural, and suburban areas. Chapter Five looks specifically at the preliminary steps of getting started, such as understanding your state's charter school legislation and developing a plan. Chapter Six examines ways for you to promote the charter school concept and your school in particular, begin to recruit students, involve the community, and answer some typical questions from critics. Chapter Seven suggests how to manage the actual running of the school in such areas as hiring the right faculty, managing the school's business affairs, evaluating student performance, and finding a physical facility.

Part Four (Chapters Eight and Nine) looks backward and forward simultaneously. Chapter Eight describes lessons learned so far from the charter school movement. Because only a few charter schools are more than three years old, the research is limited. However, some information is available to tell us whether charter school students are learning more and what impact charter school legislation is having on other public schools. So far, much of the information appears to be positive. Chapter Nine looks ahead to the future of charter schools. How much can we hope for from the charter movement? How might charter proponents use the lessons of the last twenty-five years of school reform? And what are the central tasks for charter schools if they are to avoid the limited impact that is the fate of most innovations?

Finally, three appendices offer specific resources. Appendix A lists current charter school legislation and state-specific contacts in the twenty-five states that have charter school laws. Appendix B lists people and organizations, including on-line resources, of general assistance to charter school organizers. And Appendix C contains a model for charter school legislation.

Over the years I have spent as a professional public school educator, I have heard a lot of claims, proposals, and promises. It is easy for many of us to be critical, cautious, and cynical about new proposals or to dismiss them as purely theoretical. But *Charter Schools* was not written in an ivory tower. I have visited charter schools all over the nation. I've testified in more than a dozen states on the issue. I have spoken to, interviewed, and debated with state legislators, educators, parents, union leaders, administrators, and school boards who have had differing views of charter schools. I have reviewed hundreds of documents about charter schools, written by proponents, researchers, and opponents. And, last but not least, I have heard from more than two thousand parents, educators, students, journalists, businesspeople, school board members, and legislators who have called me or written to me over the last five years to ask for information about the charter school concept—

some excited; others curious; a few worried or upset. The contents of this book reflect that experience and that research.

I admire the courage and commitment of many people involved in the charter school movement. I am encouraged by developments in many states that have charter laws. However, there are still many important problems and challenges that charter proponents must acknowledge, face, and resolve. It is not enough to criticize the current system. Charter school proponents must learn from previous, not always successful efforts to start new schools.

Charter Schools outlines these problems and challenges as it offers background, examples, and guidance to those interested in the potential of charter schools. It will be of use to those who want to start charter schools, to those who want to write strong charter school legislation, and to those who care deeply about public education and want to learn new ways to strengthen this vital, troubled institution.

Minneapolis, Minnesota   *Joe Nathan*
August 1996

| **A New Choice**

Charter schools are public schools, financed by the same per-pupil funds that traditional public schools receive. Unlike traditional public schools, however, they are held accountable for achieving educational results. In return, they receive waivers that exempt them from many of the restrictions and bureaucratic rules that shape traditional public schools. The charter school movement brings together, for the first time in public education, four powerful ideas:

- Choice among public schools for families and their children
- Entrepreneurial opportunities for educators and parents to create the kinds of schools they believe make the most sense
- Explicit responsibility for improved achievement, as measured by standardized tests and other measures
- Carefully designed competition in public education

This chapter explains the basic principles of the charter idea and then contrasts them with other reform concepts such as school site management, magnet schools, and vouchers. Individual charter schools have many differences in the students they attract and their curricula and approaches to learning. Some would be considered conservative; others are liberal. Some defy easy philosophical description. But despite these differences at the individual level, it is possible to define what the charter school movement is and what it is not.

The Charter School Strategy

The charter school concept is about *an opportunity,* not a blueprint. Here are the key elements of a model charter school strategy (summarized in the sidebar, p. 2).

Model Charter School Strategy.

1. Teachers, parents, and other community members can create new schools or convert existing schools by authority of a charter granted by an authorized sponsor.
2. Charter schools are responsible for improved student achievement.
3. In return for accountability for specific results, the state grants an up-front waiver of virtually all rules and regulations governing public schools.
4. The state authorizes more than one organization to start and operate a charter public school in the community.
5. The organizers, usually teachers, parents, or other community members, can approach either a local board or some other public body, to be the school sponsor.
6. The charter school is a school of choice.
7. The charter school is a discrete legal entity.
8. The full per-pupil allocation should move with the student to the charter school.
9. Participating teachers should be given support to try new opportunities by having their status protected.

1. *Teachers, parents, and other community members can create new schools or convert existing schools by authority of a charter granted by an authorized sponsor.* These charter schools are public schools and retain key elements of public education. They must be nonsectarian. They cannot charge tuition. They cannot employ admissions tests, and they must be open to all kinds of students. They cannot discriminate against students on the basis of race, religion, or gender. They must use buildings that meet health, accessibility, and safety regulations.

2. *Charter schools are responsible for improved student achievement.* The charter that each school must negotiate with its sponsoring agency must designate areas in which students will learn more—will increase their skills in reading, writing, math, and other academic areas—and how that learning will be measured. Most schools use a combination of standardized tests and other measures (see Chapter Seven) to evaluate student progress. All charter schools measure the basics: reading, writing, and mathematics. However, they vary in the additional skills and competencies that

they measure. Charters typically have terms of three to five years. Schools that fail to achieve the contracted improvements are closed by the sponsoring organization.

3. *In return for accountability for specific results, the state grants an up-front waiver of virtually all rules and regulations governing public schools.* Aside from the basic regulations mentioned in the first item in this list, charter schools should be exempt from state regulations about how schools operate.

4. *The state authorizes more than one organization to start and operate a charter public school in the community.* As former newspaper reporter, editorial writer, and director of the Twin Cities Citizens League Ted Kolderie wrote in an extremely influential memo, the state should withdraw the "exclusive franchise" it has given public school districts up to now.[1] Local school districts should be able to sponsor charter schools in addition to continuing their traditional public schools, but other publicly accountable groups such as the state board of education, a city council, a county commission, or a public university also should be able to sponsor public schools in the form of charter schools.

5. *The organizers, usually teachers, parents, or other community members, can approach either a local board or some other public body, to be the school sponsor.* People with innovative educational ideas should have several places they can go to get supervision and sponsorship for a charter school. Imagine people who want to open a new restaurant, gas station, hardware store, or restaurant having to get permission to open the new business from their competitors. It would be tough, right? That is why it is vital for people who want to establish a charter school to have the option of gaining permission and sponsorship from an organization other than the local school board.

6. *The charter school is a school of choice.* It is actively selected by the educators who work there and by the families whose children attend it. No one should be *assigned* to work at or to attend the school.

7. *The charter school is a discrete legal entity.* The enabling legislation should let the school founders choose any form of organization available under general state laws. The charter school has its own board. Its teachers should have the opportunity to organize and bargain collectively; however, this bargaining unit should be separate from and not bound by any district bargaining unit.

8. *The full per-pupil allocation should move with the student to the charter school.* This amount should be roughly the average amount spent in the state per pupil or the average in the district from which the student comes. If the state provides extra funds for any purpose—to help districts with school buildings or to educate students with disabilities or from low-income families, for example—these funds also should follow the students.

9. *Participating teachers should be given support to try new opportunities by having their status protected.* The state should explicitly permit teachers to take leave from their public school systems and retain their seniority when they wish to try teaching at a charter school. The state also should allow them to continue participation in local or state retirement systems. Charter school teachers should be able to be either employees or partners, to organize a professional group under which they collectively own and operate the school or to choose any other method of organization available to nonsectarian groups.

Various people have contributed to this model charter school strategy. As noted later, some of the elements were extensions of other ideas, such as public school choice and school site management, that were widely discussed in the 1980s. But it was Ted Kolderie who urged that several key points be included: permitting multiple potential charter school sponsors, making schools accountable for results, and giving charters independence from local collective bargaining agreements.

American Federation of Teachers vice president Adam Urbanski supports public school choice because, when students and their families have educational choices, "educators have additional opportunities, if [they] want them, to develop distinctive programs. Teachers are able to use their skills, talents, energy and philosophy to create the kind of program they believe makes sense. Families have more high quality options." Urbanski further observes that "parent and teacher empowerment are not necessarily in conflict. In fact, the two can complement each other."[2]

Rosanne Wood, a Tallahassee, Florida, public school educator who helped develop the innovative school where she is now principal, a school judged by the state department of education to be one of Florida's best high schools, believes that "more choices allow schools to have a theme or focus instead of an 'all-purpose' curriculum that attempts to meet all needs with one approach. . . . [T]he more choices we have, the fewer programs we'll need for problem students because fewer students will have problems. We'll have more students with 'schools that fit.'"[3]

Urbanski, Wood, and other committed educators constantly battle the idea that equal educational opportunity means everyone must have the same kind of school. As one insightful teacher once said to me, that approach calls for "identical education, not equal education. Some youngsters do better in a very traditional school. Others flourish in a Montessori program, or a more innovative school, or in a school which stresses an area which interested them, like performing arts."

It is the equity issue that makes Charles Glenn, director of the Massachusetts Bureau of Educational Equity and a central figure in the case that desegregated Boston schools, describe himself as a "convert to choice." He has acknowledged that school choice programs could "exacerbate racial and social class separation and thus work against educational equity." However, he believes choice also can be used "to strengthen public education. . . . [C]hoice can do much to promote equity. It does so by creating conditions which encourage schools to become more effective, it does so by allowing schools to specialize and thus to meet the needs of some students very well rather than all students at a level of minimum adequacy, and it does so by increasing the influence of parents over the education of their children in a way which is largely conflict free."[4]

These educators see public school choice as giving them the chance to create distinctive schools that do not have to try to satisfy everyone and so can do a better job of satisfying a specific group of families. They see choice as an expansion of opportunity for youngsters, families, and educators.

Differences Between Charter Schools and Other School Reforms

School choice is a powerful tool, something like electricity. Carefully used, choice and electricity do good things. But badly used, electricity and school choice create more problems than they solve. The details of choice programs are critical to their success.

School Vouchers

The charter school concept is significantly different from proposals for vouchers. Under a school voucher system, families would be
given certificates (vouchers) for a set amount of money. They
could then use these vouchers to pay tuition at their choice of public, private, or parochial schools. Numerous voucher proposals
have been put forward.[5] However, virtually all have been defeated,
either by state legislatures or in popular referendums.

Why has the charter school concept been so much more attractive than voucher proposals to state legislators? The charter
school concept differs from the voucher concept in four key ways.
First, charter schools must be nonsectarian. Voucher proposals,
however, usually allow voucher funds to go not only to public
schools but also to private and parochial schools, resulting in public funding for private and parochial schools. Public funding for
parochial schools in particular raises fundamental, deeply emotional and contentious issues of separation of church and state. By
insisting in the enabling legislation that charter schools be nonsectarian, policy makers avoid this controversy.

Second, in most states, the charter school legislation does not
allow schools to pick and choose among applicants on the basis of
previous achievement or behavior, whereas most voucher plans say
participating schools can choose students any way they want. But
that seems extremely unfair to the public schools that would be
competing with the private and parochial schools under the
voucher plan, because public schools generally must accept all
kinds of students. This difference in admission policies is a key reason charter schools have been more acceptable politically and with
the general public than vouchers.

Third, voucher proposals usually permit private and parochial
schools to charge additional tuition beyond the state allocation
they receive via the voucher. Conversely, charter schools cannot
charge any tuition beyond what the state provides. Again, this appears to many policy makers to make the competition between
charter and other public schools fairer than that proposed between
public schools on the one hand and private and parochial schools
on the other under a voucher system.

A final difference between charter school and voucher proposals concerns explicit responsibility for documenting improved student achievement. To keep their charters, charter schools must demonstrate that their students are improving their skills and expanding their knowledge. Schools supported by vouchers would have no responsibility to document higher student achievement.

Magnet Schools

Many of the issues just discussed also differentiate charter schools and magnet schools. Magnet schools are public schools with specialized curricula designed to attract particular students from throughout a school district. They are often part of an urban district's desegregation program, intended to bring together students of different races. Unlike other public schools, however, many magnet schools have admissions tests: a large national study found that more than half (54 percent) of secondary magnet schools and about a quarter (24 percent) of elementary magnet schools have some kind of admissions test.[6]

Moreover, many magnet schools spend more per pupil than other schools in their district. A set of articles published by the *St. Louis Post-Dispatch* noted, for example, that for the 1986–87 school year, magnet elementary schools in St. Louis spent $5,590 per student, 42 percent more than the $3,858 spent per student at other St. Louis elementary schools. Magnet middle schools spent an average of $6,915, 25 percent more than the $5,507 expended in other middle schools. And magnet high schools spent $7,602 per pupil, 27 percent more than the $5,403 spent in other city high schools.[7] A survey of magnet schools in Chicago, Philadelphia, Boston, and New York also revealed that magnet schools often were given extra resources.[8]

In contrast, it is a key element in the charter school strategy that charter schools will receive the same as, and no more than, the state per-pupil average spent on education. For charter school advocates, the issue of financial equity is critical: if charter schools are to demonstrate the value of school choice and show the worth of innovative teaching methods, they must be able to do their work and improve students' learning for the same average amount spent per public school pupil in the state.

Accountability is the third key difference between magnet and charter public schools. Magnet schools are not required to demonstrate that student achievement has improved. Charter schools, with their contracts for results, are.

Privatization

There also are important differences between the charter school concept and the idea of hiring private companies to run public schools, an idea sometimes called privatization. Several commercial educational companies have asked local school boards to give them contracts to operate public schools with designs, concepts, and in some cases, curricula the company has developed.

One of the central objectives of the charter school movement is to empower classroom teachers, administrators, and parents, giving *them* the opportunity to create the schools they believe will help youngsters. The corporate model for public schools does exactly the opposite—the corporation develops the ideas for teaching and then hires teachers to implement those ideas. But when teachers are hired simply to carry out a plan someone else has designed, teacher insight, creativity, and talent may be lost because teachers will have little motivation to use these qualities.

A few state charter school laws allow for-profit companies (in addition to nonprofit groups, parents, and educators) to create charter schools. In Boston, for example, the Edison Project is creating a school called the Boston Renaissance Charter School, using a curriculum the company developed. But in this project, the company has had to conform to the charter school legislation requirement for evidence of student achievement. Taking responsibility for improved student achievement is central to the charter concept and always required by charter school contracts. But it is not central to privatization and is not necessarily a part of contracts between school districts and private companies. In some of the contracts between school districts and the company Educational Alternatives, Inc. (EAI), for example, the contracts have stipulated that the company would help raise money to support innovation in the school or that the company would save taxpayers money. But several EAI contracts have made no promise to improve student achievement.

School Site Management

A responsibility for results also is one of the key differences between the charter school concept and proposals for school site management, also sometimes known as school-based management or shared decision making. School site management proposals derive from the belief that schools will be more effective if important decisions are made by faculty (in some cases with parent and student involvement). Thus, some people have promoted delegation of responsibility from central offices or even states to schools, where decisions affecting responsibility can be shared.

Delegation of responsibility is not necessarily a bad idea, as long as it is not merely delegation of authority with no accompanying responsibility. However, very few site management programs include any consequences, either positive or negative, for schools. This is a bit like giving a teenager increasingly more freedom without any consequences for his or her irresponsible actions. Improving education and increasing student achievement depends in part on educators' believing that what happens to students will have a direct impact on their school's funding. This kind of accountability is not a part of most site management plans.

Not surprisingly, the results of site management have not been especially encouraging. When a site council is dominated by educators who do not see the need for changes, for example, reforming a school can remain extremely difficult. In too many places site management has become the tyranny of the traditional. One large analysis of research on school site management concluded that "there is virtually no empirical and statistical evidence" to show an impact of site-based management on student achievement. "The studies that have some numbers and some controls provide no significant support to the proposition that school based management will increase achievement."[9]

Charter school advocates agree with the rationale for site-management—that critical decisions about budget, personnel, curriculum, and instruction should be made by people at the local school site. However, charter school legislation takes the critical next step and delegates accountability as well as decision-making authority. The people who make decisions at a charter school know they are responsible for what happens with the school's students.

Rewards and Consequences

Trying to increase standards for all, some states, such as Kentucky and South Carolina, have made accountability for results a part of their school reform program. They have tried to encourage that accountability by establishing rewards and consequences. South Carolina compares schools enrolling similar students and rewards schools with cash payments when they do the best job of increasing student achievement and parent involvement. The state can remove administrators if a school does not show increased student achievement after several years. Kentucky's school reform program includes cash payments to schools that make progress on state-mandated tests.

However, neither state has made entrepreneurial opportunities for teachers or school choice for families a part of its reform package. In fact, the Kentucky school reform architects have pushed state schools toward a single model of elementary education. Much to the chagrin of some educators and parents, the Kentucky plan mandates that elementary schools move toward a continuous progress primary model. Such an educational approach will result in an educational system that is great for some youngsters but much less helpful for others (the very situation charter schools are designed to overcome). It is a serious mistake not to tap into the creativity and energy of Kentucky and South Carolina teachers and parents. These people, like their counterparts around the nation, could create marvelous, distinctive schools if given the chance. But this school reform approach will not provide them or parents or students with the kind of opportunity that is central to the charter school concept.

Part of the reluctance of South Carolina and Kentucky legislators to build in options for school was due to that region's experience with segregation. One way that some states tried to avoid desegregation was to create "freedom of choice" programs. Thus, the idea of school choice has a negative connotation for many Southerners.

However, Southern leaders such as President Bill Clinton and former U.S. Secretary of Education Lamar Alexander have urged their states to develop effective school choice programs. Clinton was the first Southern governor to propose, and Arkansas the first Southern state to adopt, cross-district public school choice. Clinton has remained a strong proponent of public school choice, including charter public schools. As the president understands, public school choice can have many benefits for educators, parents, and students.

The charter school concept is unique. It is not the same as a voucher system, the magnet school concept, privatization of public schools, school site management, or a system of rewards and consequences that must try to operate within all the traditional rules for public schools.

Needed: Public Schools That Do a Better Job

Of course, the idea of allowing groups of parents and teachers to create the kinds of schools they think make sense is not a panacea for educational ills any more than allowing people to vote in elections has solved all the problems of this or any other nation. But the charter school concept does apply the principles of opportunity, freedom, and accountability, the key principles that have helped this country grow, not into a land of perfection but certainly a country respected around the world for many of its achievements. Public education plays a vital role in this country, in both our economy and our democracy. And charter legislation can help our public education system operate more effectively.

Most people believe that public schools can, and should, do a better job of helping youngsters learn. Readers will not find pages of statistics in this book comparing student achievement in this country and other lands. There is a great debate in this country about which statistics, which studies, and which reports make the most sense. Some studies show U.S. youngsters doing relatively well; others show them doing relatively poorly. Depending on which tests are used, U.S. students are doing better, about the same, or not as well as they were twenty years ago. Frankly, all this is beside the point.

What really matters is this: some public schools are able to help young people overcome troubled families. Some public schools are able to encourage, stimulate, and inspire youngsters. Achievement on tests improves in these schools. Equally important, youngsters graduate from these schools believing that they can, and should, help this country be a better place.

The charter school concept springs largely from the desire of many people for higher student achievement and greater, more positive educational results in public schools. That is in part why politicians as different as Bill Clinton and Lamar Alexander both support the charter school idea—they see it as a way to increase student achievement.

For many years, parents, business leaders, and internal and external critics of the educational system have urged public schools to focus more attention on student achievement. Many readers will be familiar with the criticisms of current student achievement made in *A Nation at Risk,* the now famous report published in 1983.[10] But this report was only the latest in a long line of criticisms that U.S. schools did not have high enough academic standards. In the 1950s, for example, critics of the status quo included Arthur Bestor, who wrote *Educational Wastelands,* and Navy admiral Hyman Rickover, who wrote *Education and Freedom.*[11] Rickover sounded much like some critics writing in the 1980s and 1990s when he remarked that education "is even more important than atomic power in the Navy, for if our people are not properly educated in accordance with the terrific requirements of this rapidly spiraling scientific and industrial revolution, we are bound to go down."[12] Some critics have urged the nation to pay more attention to the needs of youngsters from low-income families, charging that the public schools, particularly those serving inner-city youngsters, amount as Jonathan Kozol put it to "death at an early age."[13]

Parents' Frustrations

Parental and public frustrations with the present system are widespread. A Public Agenda Foundation study found that 61 percent of Americans say academic standards are too low in the their own local schools. Parents routinely complain that their children are being allowed to "slide through," without developing strong skills.[14] The public is right! Recent reports from the National Assessment of Educational Progress show that relatively few seniors have attained proficiency in key academic areas. For example:

Only 18 percent of 12th graders in 1992 had attained the proficiency level in mathematics.[15]

Only 36 percent of 12th graders in 1994 had attained the proficient or advanced level in reading. This was a drop from 40 percent in 1992.[16]

Only 28 percent of 11th graders in 1990 attained the proficiency levels in persuasive writing.[17] As researchers from the Educational Testing Service noted, "although they appeared to be able to understand the assignments and present their points of view, students were generally unable to support their ideas."[18]

Another Public Agenda study also asked people around the country to select the area of government responsibility (crime, foreign policy, elections, welfare, or public education) that "most urgently needed change." Participants put public education in a first-place tie with welfare reform. As the Public Agenda Foundation noted, "Most Americans simply do not want to 'live with' the status quo."[19]

Parents from around the country write regularly to the Center for School Change, asking for help with school issues. Here are just a few samples from letters received over the last six months from parents who believe in public education but are frustrated.

> Some of the teachers at our junior high school are terrific. But others hand out A's for mediocre work. Our students are learning that poor quality work, handed in on time, is rewarded with good grades.

> The English and social studies teachers at our school seem to be in love with worksheets. My son breezes through them, but he's getting bored. And he doesn't remember much of what's on the worksheets.

> Some teachers motivate and challenge the students. We are very grateful to them. Others don't seem to care. They've used the same lecture notes for years. Students turn in assignments but don't get much, if any feedback from some teachers. We talk to the principal who says there is little he can do.

My tenth-grade suburban daughter routinely gets A's or B's for essays and reports that have awkward sentences and misspelled words. Other parents have similar concerns—but her teacher seems pleased that the students are turning in their assignments.

A lot of the students graduating from our son's high school can barely read. I discovered this one day when I heard one of my son's twelfth-grade friends trying to read the sports page. It was awful.

At one recent meeting in an inner-city school, parents presented the school's principal and a school board member with materials distributed by one of the school's teachers that had numerous spelling and grammatical errors. But the school board member told the parents there was little the board could do unless the teacher committed a crime. More letters from parents:

My fifth-grade son is bored. When I talk with the teacher, he tells me to give my son comic books to read when he finishes early.

When I called to ask the Superintendent how the money in the bond issue was going to be spent, he said the school board hadn't decided yet. When I said that I wanted to know before deciding how to vote, he told me that I should have faith in the school board to do the right thing.

I am a parent as well as a substitute teacher in a well-regarded suburban district. I've see many things that stunned me. In one advanced high school class the regular teacher told me that the students won't listen for more than a few minutes, so I should not try to talk for more than 5 minutes. The teacher told me that the best way to proceed was to allow the students to talk to each other.

Another teacher in this affluent suburban district makes money by selling pop, cookies and candy from her refrigerator, which students may eat and drink in class. I was told that they could do what they wanted so

I spent 35 minutes walking the aisles making sure that they at least were not being too loud. . . .

Some teachers, more than you think, have simply abdicated the role of disciplinarian. They take the posture that if the students choose to listen, that's good, but if not, the teacher has fulfilled his or her role by presenting the material.

I am the parent of a handicapped child, and boy could I tell you stories. Some of the teachers seem to care about my son. Others seem to blame me for his being paralyzed. It was the result of a disease, I didn't cause it. I don't understand why some teachers are so cruel. I am trying to do the best I can.

I am a parent and an aide in our kids' [inner-city] school. Perhaps you can explain something to me. Why do some of the teachers rush out almost every day, almost beating the kids out the door? They don't take home student papers or projects. These same teachers often get to class just before the students. Other teachers are very conscientious, helping students before or after school. When I ask the good teachers about the other ones, they just shrug their shoulders.

Parents are not the only ones who are frustrated when faced with an unresponsive bureaucracy and ineffective teachers.

Teachers' Frustrations

Teachers often encounter intense bureaucracy. Jessica Siegel, for example, was a New York City writing and journalism teacher who found ways to save money and produce a better student newspaper by hiring printers near her inner-city New York high school, only to be told that school district rules did not allow her to use these small neighborhood printers. Samuel Friedman, who tells the stories of Siegel and other educators, comments, "A good teacher is ground down to mediocrity over weeks and months and years, and a good teacher who tries to resist learns that the millstone is an implacable adversary."[20]

In another specific example, a group of social studies teachers teaching a high school course on current issues wanted to purchase course materials over a five-year period rather than use all the course money in the year it was allocated. District officials insisted all the money had to be spent in six months. The teachers responded that perhaps purchasing texts all at once for five years of an ancient history class made sense but that purchasing materials all at once for five years of a current issues class probably was not a wise use of funds. Ultimately, the teachers and district compromised: half of the money was to be spent the first year, and the remaining dollars spread out over four years. In the second year, there was a budget crisis, and the remaining funds were withdrawn. Teachers who had tried to make better use of tax funds and do a better job felt punished for trying to be more responsible and for trying to make effective use of tax funds.[21]

Herb Kohl, an award-winning inner-city public school teacher and author, speaking for many educators, has written, "No one checked on what I was doing, and no one really cared as long as my class wasn't disruptive."[22] Urban, rural, and suburban teachers encounter some colleagues and administrators who share their vision. But too often, colleagues are tired, bitter, and overwhelmed, and they have already given up.

The public school system often is unnecessarily bureaucratic and unresponsive, like many other monopolies. Sometimes administrators seem aloof or disinterested. Sometimes labor-management agreements seem to discourage committed teachers or parents. Too often, people encounter rules such as the one recently adopted in one school district stating that teachers can be asked to go to meetings before or after school for only twenty minutes a month. Administrators who require teachers to attend meetings beyond that time must pay them for the additional time.

The frustrations are not confined to urban schools. A major national study of rural schools found similar problems. Despite their smaller size, they appeared to be what researchers called "a troubled house." The study found that "too often small districts appear to be manifesting . . . relationships of an impersonal, bureaucratic society."[23]

These problems are not going to be solved by a new superintendent or a new school board. They are central to a system where funds come to the district regardless of whether graduation rates or student achievement improves.

The Entrepreneurial Spirit in Education

Most people believe that our public schools can and should do a better job of helping youngsters learn. And clearly, some public schools do this job. There is a long list of reports about these schools and a fair amount of research about what happens in them. People like James Comer, Robert Slavin, Sy Fliegel, Deborah Meier, and Hank Levin have written about how to create and sustain these schools.[24]

We ought to have more schools that help youngsters grow and develop. This is not to deny the enormous problems in our society that contribute to poor achievement in school. It is not to assume that even the most effective public schools will succeed with every youngster. But many Americans, liberal and conservative, Republican and Democrat, believe the public schools can do better.

One of the great strengths of this nation is the opportunity it gives to practical visionaries. Do you have an idea for a new product or service? If you can convince someone to loan you the money to test your concept, both you and the world may benefit from your idea. Entrepreneurial opportunity allowed Henry Ford to design new ways to produce cars. It allowed Steve Wozniak and Steve Jobs to found Apple Computer. Large successful companies know they must actively encourage new ideas if they are to survive in the competitive marketplace. Look, for example, at 3M, the international company that produces such products as Scotch tape and Post-It notes. 3M believes that if it is to maintain its position, 30 percent of its revenue must come from products that were not invented four years ago. Like other cutting-edge companies, 3M maintains an extensive new products and services division.

But the entrepreneurial approach has generally not been available to public school teachers and parents. Yes, teachers have been able to do what they wish in their own classrooms, as long as it does not alter what other teachers can do. But teachers or parents who had ideas about new ways of organizing an entire school were out of luck. Most school districts have not had a policy of encouraging educational visionaries who want to create a new approach to elementary, middle school, or secondary education.

The charter school approach creates entrepreneurial opportunity. Charter schools give the people who work in them daily a real incentive to care about the quality of teachers and teaching. These schools change the environment in which teachers work, so there are rewards for progress with students and consequences if there is no progress.

The charter school movement attempts to promote widespread improvement in public education both by allowing people to create new kinds of schools and by encouraging existing school systems to improve in order to compete effectively with these new schools. It seeks to change the basic ways public education is offered in this country. Public schools should not continue to receive tax funds regardless of how well they perform; funding should be tied to student achievement.

Dan Daly is an example of a teacher who wants to improve public education. He is also president of the Minnesota Association of Alternative Programs, a group of options to traditional public schools that over the last five years has grown from serving 4,000 students to serving more than 40,000. Daly teaches in a school serving primarily troubled, challenging teenagers. A charter school advocate, he knows firsthand the troubles families have and the problems youngsters bring with them to school. Yet when asked what advice he had for fellow public school educators, he smiled and suggested, "Less blaming, more changing."[25] The best teachers do not doubt that there are major problems outside schools, in communities, neighborhoods, and families and that these problems affect students' willingness and ability to learn. But they do not use those problems as an excuse for poor achievement and lack of growth inside the school.

The charter movement is really about hope and possibility. It is for people like Janet Fender, a 2nd-grade public school teacher near New Castle, Delaware, who sees Delaware's charter school legislation as "a chance of a lifetime"; Yvonne Chan, who directs an inner-city charter school in Los Angeles that has increased student achievement and saved more than $1 million by doing its own purchasing rather than going through the public schools' bureaucratic business office; secondary school teachers Nancy Miller and Kim

Borwege, who cofounded a charter school on the main street of LeSueur, Minnesota, that has attracted a national television network news crew; Rexford Brown, who founded and directs PS1, an award-winning Denver inner-city charter school; and Richard Farias, who directs a community center in Houston, is an advocate for Hispanic students, and is working with the Houston Federation of Teachers to create a new charter school under a Texas charter law that he calls "the perfect vehicle for us to do what needs to be done."[26]

Thousands of educators now are working in charter schools around the country, and interest in founding new schools is strong. New Jersey adopted its charter school legislation in January 1996, one of the strongest laws passed so far. Within five weeks, the state department of education received over 120 telephone calls requesting an application.[27] Almost four hundred people attended a May 1996 meeting for potential charter applicants.

It is one thing to have an interesting idea like charter schools. It is quite another to translate that idea into reality as these people are doing, into organizations that truly have an impact on other people. Chapter One offers a tour of several charter schools, illustrating what talented people can do when given the chance. Chapter Two outlines the history of the charter school concept and describes the passage of the nation's first charter school legislation.

Part One

Introducing
Charter Schools

| A Tour of Charter Schools

You will find one charter school in a former grocery store, another in a low-income housing project, another in a former post office, and yet another in a former VFW post. Some charter schools share space with other organizations—a YMCA, a city recreation center, or a business. Some are located in actual school buildings, but you would never assume from the outside that school was going on in some of the places where charter schools have found homes.

Some charter schools work with elementary youngsters; some with secondary. Some were operating before charter school legislation was adopted and were converted to charter status; others were established after a state legislature passed a charter school law.

Likewise, you'll find different educational philosophies among charter schools. So there is no one curriculum blueprint, no single organizational plan.

But there is one common denominator: charter schools know that they are responsible for improving student achievement. So the schools focus on what needs to be done in order to increase achievement. They do not make excuses. They do not ignore problems children bring to school with them, but they look for and generally find ways to "hook" youngsters, to encourage, incite, and inspire them. People organizing charter schools believe that public schools can and should make a clear, measurable positive difference.

Theories, political battles, and legislation are interesting. But in the end, what matters most in education is what happens to young people day to day. So it is important, before going any further, to describe what is happening in several charter schools around the nation. This chapter describes charter schools in three of the states with the most charter school experience: California, Colorado, and Minnesota. The examples illustrate the range of ideas and differences in guiding spirit that are characteristic of people who establish charter schools (see sidebar below for an overview of some specific charter school characteristics).

A National Snapshot of Charter Schools.

A 1995 survey of 110 charter schools in seven states (California, Colorado, Massachusetts, Michigan, Minnesota, New Mexico, and Wisconsin) revealed the following key features:

- About 27,500 students are enrolled in all 110 schools.
- Mean size is small, 287 students.
- Two-thirds are designed to serve a cross-section of students.
- One-half serve "at-risk" students.
- Educational philosophies vary widely: the most frequently cited academic focus is "integrated interdisciplinary curriculum"; the second is "technology"; the third is "back to basics."
- The most frequently cited reasons for chartering the school are "better teaching and learning for all kids," "running a school according to certain principles and philosophy," and "exploring innovative ways of running a school."
- Leased commercial space is the most frequent location.
- Biggest barriers to start-up are lack of funds, other financial issues, and problems with physical facilities.
- Most frequently used student evaluation methods are standardized tests and student portfolios, parent surveys, and student demonstrations of mastery.

Source: Data from A. Medler and J. Nathan, *Charter Schools: What Are They Up To?* Denver, Colo.: Education Commission of the States, and Minneapolis: Center for School Change, 1995.

City Academy

You will miss City Academy if you look for a traditional public school building.[1] The first charter in the nation to have its contract renewed meets in a formerly underused city recreation building on the east side of St. Paul, Minnesota. It is a low-income racially diverse area, with many troubled families. But Milo Cutter and Terry Kraabel, who founded City Academy together in 1992 after teaching in other public schools, simply refuse to focus on problems or to offer excuses. They are two of the most optimistic, upbeat people I have ever met. When I asked Cutter, "What does it mean to be the first charter public school in the country to have your school reviewed and your contract renewed?" she smiled and replied, "It means we can continue our work." Her focus is on students, not on the national significance of the successful review and renewal or even on what it might mean in terms of increased attention to the school. In fact, she encourages reporters to visit other charter schools: "We appreciate the reporters' interest, but our first job is working with students, not talking with reporters. Our first priority is our students." Similarly, although she has been asked to speak throughout the nation and has been invited to assist the National Education Association in working with charter schools, she remains focused on the youngsters at City Academy.

Students

City Academy works with youngsters ages thirteen through twenty-one, though most of the students are sixteen to eighteen years old and the "only requirement [for admission] is that the student not be enrolled in any other school." The reasons the students are out of school vary widely, but their own most common explanations are "I didn't think anyone cared" and "I was too far behind." A few have been excluded from other public schools because they brought a weapon to school. They come from a low-income area of St. Paul and include Native Americans, Hispanics, African Americans, Asian Americans, and European Americans.

The school has a substantial waiting list and "could be twice or even three times" its present size of about sixty students if it wanted to be. But Cutter, Kraabel, and the board think the school's small size is a strength. Instead of expanding, they have encouraged the local district to create more secondary school options and have provided advice to many other people who are considering opening additional charter schools in St. Paul.

Students help develop the rules at City Academy. One of the first concerns is "respect"—among students and between students and teachers. A variety of reporters and visitors to school have noted the deep bond between the faculty and students. It is not an if-it-feels-good-do-it or an anything-goes environment. As one student explained, "It's more like the teachers are saying, 'We care a great deal for you. So we expect a lot, and we'll help you get there.'"

Educational Views

Cutter believes strongly in the educational value of small schools and is disturbed by the millions of dollars that school districts now spend to hire police and purchase metal detectors. As she puts it, "More and more youngsters don't fit in large schools. We know it. Now we have to do something about it. Metal detectors and police probably won't help many students learn math. We need smaller schools where teachers know the students well and expect them to learn." Violence has not been a problem at City Academy. As one student pointed out, "We know everyone here, and everyone knows what's going on. If there's a problem, students and the teachers make sure we talk it out. People listen to each other. And people aren't afraid."

The emphasis in teaching is on "seeing these youngsters' strengths, not just their problems." Both Cutter and Kraabel have a strong interest in active hands-on approaches and in using the youngsters' energy to help them learn. Kraabel enjoys helping youngsters learn via construction projects, where they see immediate, practical applications of the math problems he gives them. As I watched, he helped several youngsters who were building a wall check their measurements. There had been a slight mismeasurement, and a board would have to be removed and reattached. "We don't get into finger-pointing or blaming," Kraabel explained. "The kids just know it has to be done right. And they usually do it that way the first time."

Under an arrangement with the East Side Neighborhood Development Corporation and with support from state "Youth Build" funds, students are given a chance to help rehabilitate area homes. Under the supervision of a contractor and union workers, students have helped gut buildings and retrofit them for new occupants. The students also help their neighbors in many other ways, including shoveling snow for elderly residents.

Cutter and Kraabel checked with local colleges and employers as they developed their graduation requirements. City Academy's requirements focus on the skills and knowledge students will need in the future. Beyond learning the traditional three R's, each student develops a plan for what she or he will do after high school. That postsecondary goal becomes one focus for each student's work at City Academy, and the school offers various courses designed to help students improve their skills and work toward their goals. Cheri Rosenthal, a St. Paul special education teacher who works with some City Academy students, praises the school as a place "where you don't encounter red tape, and you can get things done."

On one bitterly cold January morning when I visited the school, the first person I encountered was a young woman I will call June (all student names are pseudonyms), age sixteen. June likes working on projects like tearing down walls and tuck pointing, and she was looking forward to a roofing job. City Academy teachers push "me to do my best," she says. "They really care, while at a large school it seemed like most of the teachers just wanted us to be there." She reports she is learning much more than in her previous large high school and summarizes her reaction to City Academy by saying, "It's way better here."

Raul, also sixteen, was introduced to City Academy by his probation officer. For him, the best thing about City Academy is the "real experience" he gets. Raul finds he learns more working on construction projects than sitting in classrooms listening to teachers talk, which was what he encountered in most classrooms at his former school, a large conventional urban high school.

Yang, age seventeen, praises City Academy "as a place where students get respect. It is the right school for me." Sixteen-year-old Yolanda calls it "a peaceful place." Fifteen-year-old Simone tells her friends, "If you are having trouble in high school, come here! You'll learn a lot more." Seventeen-year-old Mike says that City Academy's projects and active learning "help me learn more."

Administration and Evaluation

When its charter came up for renewal after its first three years, City Academy was examined carefully by several district administrators. The school already had received accreditation from the North Central Association of Schools and Colleges. The reviewers found that the school had "either met or exceeded" all the "requirements and obligations" stated in the law and its charter,[2] and in November 1995, the St. Paul Board of Education voted 7 to 0 to renew City Academy's charter for another three years.

The school operates on a somewhat lower per-pupil budget than other St. Paul public schools. City Academy has also had help from others. Northern States Power (NSP) has donated computers, provided start-up funds, and employed a number of City Academy graduates. Cutter says that without that start-up help from NSP and some help with a facility from the City of St. Paul, "City Academy would not exist."

Cutter believes that one of the school's wisest decisions was to hire Don Jacobson, a school finance and accounting expert who has contracted with several Minnesota charter schools to handle their financial records. The City Academy board, including the school's teachers, develops a budget. Then, "the expert [Jacobson] handles the details. This has allowed the teachers to do the work they do best, teach."

Facilities

The City of St. Paul leases space to City Academy in a formerly underused city recreation building. The gym and meeting rooms are used by neighborhood youngsters after school and on weekends, which meant that during the traditional school day, the building was virtually empty. Now City Academy uses the building's space during school hours. The lease allows City Academy "to focus the majority of its resources on program delivery rather than facility expenditures." Being located in a community facility also requires the school to maintain "ongoing communication and involvement" with the neighborhood.

Cutter is quick to acknowledge that programs like the City Academy are options and that families and educators need a variety of choices. But City Academy's structure and the faculty's commitment to young people make it a place people around the country are paying attention to and learning from. At a time when there is great concern for order in schools and for helping youngsters who are not thriving in large secondary schools, City Academy demonstrates that progress is possible.

O'Farrell Community School

Another charter school that has received a good deal of attention is the O'Farrell Community School found in San Diego.[3] A number of O'Farrell staff people have been invited to national meetings to discuss the school's work and asked to contribute to various school reform efforts; one, for example, has worked closely with the New Standards project, which is developing academic goals and more effective methods of measuring whether students are achieving those goals. President Bill Clinton announced the first federal grants to help start charter schools after visiting O'Farrell students and faculty.

Unlike City Academy, which did not exist before it opened as a charter school, O'Farrell was established as an innovative middle school in 1988, using buildings that had housed a public school closed seven years earlier. It converted to a charter school in 1994. As Robert Stein, O'Farrell's CEO (chief education officer) explains, the school was established with the principles of "restructuring, teacher and community empowerment, interagency collaboration and interdisciplinary teaching concepts."

Students

The O'Farrell Community School works with about 1,400 6th- to 8th-grade students. The student body is very racially and ethnically diverse. Approximately 36 percent are African American, 37 percent Filipino American, 16 percent Hispanic, 4 percent Asian American, and 8 percent Anglo. More than two-thirds of O'Farrell's students come from families eligible for free or reduced lunch.

Walking through the campus, a visitor is struck by several things. First, the school is a calm place. Students guide visitors around the school, and the young people smile and talk readily to visitors. There is none of the tension or the gang signs and wall markings often found at large inner-city schools.

Educational Views

O'Farrell's 1,400 students are broken up into families of about 150 students each, and each family gets the same enriched curriculum. Rather than rely on outside substitute teachers who may or may not know the students and the school's philosophy, each educational family also has its own "family support service teacher."

The curriculum addresses six major areas of challenge:

1. *Community service.* Students complete twelve hours of community service per year. The service is designed to develop youngsters' sense of altruism, broaden their awareness of career options, and develop strong citizenship values.
2. *Exhibition.* Students present an exhibition during the fourth quarter of each year, designed to demonstrate their strengths and ability to reflect and assess their own work and to document progress in other challenge areas.
3. *Research process.* Students show they know how to explore real-life problems, sustain an effort over a period of time to complete an important task, gather information using a variety of technologies, and demonstrate individuality in presenting their findings.
4. *O'Farrell presentation.* Students prepare a presentation of the O'Farrell philosophy and goals, aimed toward persons not yet familiar with the school. This project helps students develop a greater understanding of the school and pride in what the school seeks to accomplish.
5. *Academic performance.* Students are expected to demonstrate skills in reading, writing, and mathematics, according to various standards and methods of measurement developed in the school.
6. *The O'Farrell way.* Students are expected to behave in a manner that shows they know how to solve problems, resolve conflicts, work with others, and behave appropriately.

Walking into an O'Farrell classroom is like walking into a busy office. Students are working on a variety of projects, checking out their work occasionally with each other or with the teacher. They are not reading a chapter and answering questions in a book. But the teacher is clear about what she is trying to accomplish. Periodically, she reviews the skills and knowledge she wants youngsters to develop: "I want them to know where we are going and why. I also want to give them the chance to use their insight and ingenuity. And I want them to get experience working with other people."

While teachers work with the students, the school's council has made working closely with students' families a high priority. It has hired four social workers and a full-time psychologist.

Finally, O'Farrell is educating not only students but also prospective teachers, to help them understand charter schools. In the 1995–96 school year, twenty-seven student teachers from San Diego State University spent time at the school, either assisting regular faculty or carrying out student teaching assignments. Students and staff have also created an informational homepage on the Internet, at edweb.sdsu.edu/O'Farrell/O'Farrellhome.html.

Administration

Obtaining charter school status does not mean that O'Farrell Community School has cut off all ties to the local school district. It purchases some services from the district, and some of its teachers maintain membership in the local teachers association. In fact, one O'Farrell teacher and union activist has been asked by the National Education Association to assist other public school teachers who want to establish charter schools.

In addition, Stein has found that the school's independence from districts, unions, and the state is at times ambiguous, and that the charter law is frequently unclear. For example, important issues face California charter schools concerning average daily attendance funds and staff development days. It has been difficult to learn what a charter school's fair share of state educational revenues is so that each charter school can determine its own budget. Moreover, at times, district support for charter schools can appear more verbal than actual.[4]

O'Farrell's governance structure reflects its priorities. The council includes teachers representing each 150-student family, students, parents, and representatives of some of the more than twenty-five community agencies that work with the school. The chief educational officer, the top administrator, is on the council and has responsibility for being what the council calls Keeper of the Dream.

CEO Stein is a charismatic visionary educator, who readily acknowledges that the school's governing council does not always agree with him. He suggested that the council consider converting the school to charter status shortly after the California legislature first passed the state's charter law, but the council hesitated at first. However, it then became clear to the council that under the existing school district's labor-management agreement and under California public school legislation, the council did not have nearly as much control over its budget and selection of faculty as it wanted.

According to Stein, three incidents convinced the O'Farrell council that applying for charter status made sense. First, the local teachers union filed a grievance against O'Farrell because the school council had decided to convert counselor positions into teaching positions. Second, the local school district adopted a policy that sites could not use funds to rent off-campus facilities for retreats and meetings. O'Farrell had received a grant from the Stuart Foundation for such events and wanted to continue them. Finally, the school had constant conflict with state credentialing laws for middle school teachers. These incidents, along with "the continual fear of teachers being placed under union rules at the site,"[5] convinced the teachers and parents at O'Farrell to apply for and obtain charter status in January 1994. Stein reports that district officials were not "extremely enthusiastic" about the school's decision but that district officials understood why O'Farrell was asking for charter status.

O'Farrell has also had to make some staffing decisions that reflect its priorities. When the council made the decision to convert O'Farrell to a charter school, the council and the district agreed that O'Farrell teachers who did not want to be a part of the charter school could join another school in the district. Four of the approximately fifty O'Farrell teachers left the school at that point.

Facilities

O'Farrell uses the kind of one-story nondescript block buildings often used by Southern California inner-city schools. The buildings and school grounds, however, are clean and extremely well maintained. That is in part because students help take care of them, and as my student guide explained to me, "Because students we know are in charge of keeping the school clean, we keep it cleaner. This feels more like 'our' school."

Minnesota New Country School

Birth, whether of a baby or a school, brings a mixture of pride, pain, and pleasure. You can see all three when visiting a relatively new charter school like the Minnesota New Country School (MNCS) in LeSueur, Minnesota, in the beautiful "Valley of the Jolly Green Giant," about an hour south of Minneapolis.

The school was established by two teachers, Kim Borwege and Nancy Miller, and a technical director for a small private computer company. They all had considerable experience in using computers in teaching in the small town of Henderson, Minnesota. The teachers encountered a great deal of frustration and resistance, however, when their original public school was consolidated into the school in the nearby town of LeSueur. Many of the veteran teachers at LeSueur had less experience, and less interest, in making extensive use of technology an important part of high school.

After several years of trying to make changes at the local secondary school, Borwege and Miller went to the local school board to ask for a charter. The school board turned them down but expressed a willingness to continue the discussion. Frustrated but determined, the teachers continued to build support for a charter school in the community. Several months later, the school district held a strategic planning session, and a number of charter school supporters attended. Many LeSueur residents described the kind of school they wanted: one in which students demonstrated strong skills and knowledge before graduation, one that made extensive use of the community, and one that made thoughtful use of computers and other technology. It sounded a great deal like the charter school proposal. The strategic planning group agreed to recommend support for the charter proposal as one of the district's action steps. With this broader support, the teachers went back to the school board, which now agreed to give them a charter, with one very important provision: it had to be "revenue-neutral." It could not cost the district money, even though dozens of district students were going to attend. Some of the charter proponents gulped at this idea, but ultimately, they decided to accept the provision.

Students

The Minnesota New Country School serves about ninety-five students in grades 6 to 12. Students travel as far as fifty miles, from the towns of Northfield, Mankato, St. Peter, Maple River, and Le Center, to attend the school.

Educational Views

Minnesota New Country School does not have classrooms or even classes in the traditional sense.[6] Walking into any of the downtown storefronts that are its facilities, a casual visitor might think she or he was walking into a business office, except that the employees are teenagers. School goals, as mentioned previously, are to graduate students with demonstrated strong skills and knowledge, to make extensive use of the community in teaching students, and to make thoughtful use of computers and other technology. The school has developed a list of several hundred competencies that students must demonstrate before graduating, in basic areas such as writing, speaking, mathematics, and art and in applied areas such as developing a post–high school plan and working effectively in a team.

At any given moment, some MNCS students will be reading, some will be writing, and some will be working with a computer. The school has one computer for every two students, and its students have created their own homepage on the Internet (http://mncs.K12.mn.us/). Other students will be out in the community on a field trip or internship. The school's location in the middle of the town makes it much easier for MNCS students to get to apprenticeships and internships at places like the local radio station and chamber of commerce.

Faculty members move from student to student, reviewing progress, asking questions, and providing advice. Small groups of students meet with individual teachers to review the projects group members are carrying out. For example, two students worked with the local chamber of commerce on a project to compile a database of the local businesses. The project was designed to help students learn to conduct research and produce a clear written document useful to adults. The students' survey revealed a much greater number and variety of businesses operating in the area than anyone in the town had known about.

One major student project has attracted a great deal of attention beyond the school. It began the day students and a teacher were out in the nearby Minnesota River taking water samples, and the students noticed that a few frogs appeared to have two, three, or five legs rather than the typical four. They then looked more closely and realized there were hundreds of frogs with this mutation. MNCS students contacted the Minnesota Pollution Control Agency and other groups. A visit to the river by these agencies confirmed the students' observation and a possible serious problem. Frogs are very sensitive to environmental influences, and frog mutations may be a sign of large pollution problems in the river. The 1996 Minnesota legislature, after asking MNCS students to testify, passed a bill giving thousands of dollars to the Minnesota Pollution Control Agency to study the problem and to support cooperative research involving the agency and MNCS students.

One MNCS teacher cites this project to explain why she joined the charter school faculty: "After a few years of working in a traditional school, I realized that most of the teachers didn't agree with me about how to promote learning. I want students out in the community gathering information, testing what they read in books. It could take years to convince most of the teachers and the administration in a traditional public school that these ideas made sense. I wanted to work in a place where people agreed with me . . . where my energy would go into developing these kind of projects, not in arguing with other educators."

All twenty-one of the randomly selected students I talked with on a recent visit felt they were learning more than they did in their previous schools.

Elizabeth, age sixteen, likes "the freedom to work on a project for more than an hour at a time." She praised the school's size and "family-like atmosphere." Jack, age fourteen, finds that the school's many computers and individual or small-group projects mean students "don't have to sit and listen to endless lectures." Twelve-year-old Darren liked the way "the three R's are combined in projects that make sense. In my other school, I used to get in a lot of trouble for not paying attention to the teachers. But I've had no problems at all here."

Jim, age fifteen, appreciates the way the school's computers "allow me to move rapidly." Jim reports that he "sometimes was bored" at former schools. "That doesn't happen here." Fourteen-year-old Alice appreciates the "high academic expectations" and the way students are expected to help clean the school. Gangs in her former large secondary school frightened her, but at New Country School, "everyone knows everyone. We don't have fights, which I saw regularly in my former school." And eleven-year-old Robin likes "going out and experiencing" the historical sites such as the Traverse de Sioux treaty location and the local businesses where students learn about potential careers. Robin's mother likes the way that New Country School teachers use "active learning and projects, rather than worksheets and lectures."

Minnesota New Country School staff agree on the value of holding conferences with each student and parent in August, before school starts, along with two other parent-teacher-student conferences held during the year. The August meetings are designed to build a stronger working relationship between home and school, review the student and parent priorities for the year, and begin planning each student's program. Each meeting begins with a review of the student's summer. What were his or her major activities? What did the family do together? Were there any major changes in the family that the school should know about? Then the students and parents identify their priorities, given the school's overall expectations. What kinds of projects will the student work on in the first several months? How will the family help the school out? What kind of reporting to the parents will the school do, and how often will it occur?

MNCS staff find that this August conference is one of the most valuable ways they have of building strong working relationships with families and of answering parent and student questions before school starts. Indeed, the August conference idea has spread (such testing and passing along of ideas is a hoped-for function of all charter schools). A nearby school district, Mankato, heard about the August conferences at a meeting where New Country School staff made a presentation. One Mankato elementary school used the August conference the next fall. Then, all the district's elementary and middle schools decided to do it. Mankato officials report the same strong positive family and faculty response that NCS has found.

One of the Minnesota New Country School's major ways of reporting student progress is the school's Presentation Night, held in a community center every other month and attended by parents, relatives, and just plain curious members of the local community. During the school's first year, faculty asked students to make a presentation each month. Parents and community members praised the general idea; however, teachers, students, and parents alike felt that the pressure to make a presentation every month sometimes resulted in lower-quality presentations than were desired. Now the presentations are held every other month, giving students more time to prepare. So far, most MNCS people feel this change has been wise. Each student's presentation is videotaped, and his or her speaking abilities are assessed. Students get feedback about areas of growth and identify presentation skills that still need attention.

MNCS's extensive use of computers and other emerging technology has also influenced other schools. A local public school agreed to allow some of its own teachers to attend a summer workshop at Minnesota New Country School on use of educational technology. The workshop instructors included both MNCS faculty and students. That workshop was so successful that in January 1996, another group of local public school teachers went to an MNCS workshop. This session attracted an ABC television crew, which recorded the event for broadcast on the national news.

Administration and Evaluation

To meet its school board–imposed goal of being revenue neutral, the MNCS is paying the district for various bookkeeping services. It also pays the district for allowing MNCS students to participate in extracurricular activities or attend classes at the regular local high school.

The school also received start-up grants from several sources. The largest came from Community Learning Centers (CLC), a New American Schools project. (New American Schools is a national school reform program.) Wayne Jennings, director of the CLC program, was very impressed with both the ideas and the people involved in creating the charter schools. The experienced teachers had "the skills to carry out an ambitious, 'break the mold' program," he said, and he cited such strengths as the adviser-advisee program, the thoughtful use of technology including the homepage on the World Wide Web, and the periodic public presentations by students that attract a number of community residents as well as parents and relatives. He described one of these events as "a lot like a well-run science fair, except that it covers all kinds of subjects."[7] Grants also came from the Southwestern Minnesota Initiative Fund, the Center for School Change, and a local business that wanted the school's help in training its employees to use the Internet.

These grants were invaluable in equipping the school. Traditional Minnesota public schools have thousands of dollars from local property taxes with which to buy equipment when a new school is opening. Minnesota charter schools receive only the state per-pupil average; they do not receive state funds that go to local districts for building maintenance or the local property tax revenue, funds that can amount to $2,000 to $3,000 per pupil.

The founding teachers also decided to do without an administrator. This move freed thousands of dollars, some of which was used for technology, and some of which is being used to pay the teachers a somewhat higher salary than they would get from the local district. In return, MNCS teachers work a longer school day and a longer year than is stipulated in the local labor-management agreement. As at charter schools in states with strong charter laws, the teachers at MNCS develop their own working conditions rather than being bound by the agreement reached by the local school district and the teachers' bargaining unit.

Both student and faculty evaluation are receiving close attention. First, keeping records of student progress takes an enormous amount of time. Even though some of the record keeping is computerized, the staff are constantly looking for ways to streamline the process while also making the tracking of progress clearer and stronger. Second, faculty strongly believe in the importance of yearly evaluations. Each faculty member develops a personal growth plan. This plan, and progress on it, is reviewed periodically by a board evaluation committee, and that committee gives formal yearly feedback to each person. As one teacher explained, "We think it's critical for each of us to grow and learn, as we expect each student to do the same thing."

Facilities

Minnesota New Country School looks different from most schools. Its three buildings are former storefronts on LeSueur's Main Street. With parent and student help during the summer before the school started, the school founders reconstructed the storefronts to house the school. The school building is open at 8:00 A.M. and does not close until 5:30 or 6:00 P.M. Students often are in the building working on various projects early in the morning and late in the afternoon. The school is also open on Monday evenings for parent, student, and staff use. The school's large number of computers is partly the result of money saved by not hiring an administrator.

Rather than establish its own food service, the school contracts with the Welcome Inn, a Main Street café and neighbor, to provide lunch. Students are charged $1.70 and have their choice of six or seven options every day. Both the students and the café owner seem delighted by the arrangement. Students often complain about school food, but you do not hear complaints about the food from the Welcome Inn. Initially, there was some concern about the possible behavior of students who were going into a local café for lunch, but the restaurant's owner praises them as "friendly and responsible."

Academy Charter School

Academy Charter School is one of Colorado's most well-known charter schools.[8] Located in Castle Rock, a community about twenty-five miles south of Denver, a rapidly growing area between Denver and Colorado Springs, it was started in September 1993 by a group of parents who were not satisfied with the programs available in their district.

Parents were really challenging what the district was offering, and said they wanted something different. The district could have reacted defensively and refused to consider their ideas. But the superintendent, Rick O'Connell, and Pat Grippe, one of the superintendent's assistants, and the school board were willing to listen and to give parents the chance to create the kind of school they thought made sense.

Douglas County Assistant Superintendent Pat Grippe believes it's critical to involve parents. Grippe says the district also should have an attitude, a "philosophical base" that it would support choice for families among different kinds of schools. His experience is that "when families select schools they are more committed to them, and their students do better."[9] The district sponsors three charter schools, two of which feature the Core Knowledge Curriculum and one of which uses whole language, multiage classroom approaches.

Students

The K–8 school presently has 315 students. The youngsters represent the range of academic abilities in the district, from children who have been classified as disabled to those classified as gifted. About 14 percent of the students have some form of disability.

Educational Views

Walking into the Academy Charter School, you might see students building a model of the Parthenon with Lego blocks. You might see other students practicing a play they have written about ancient Greece, based loosely on some of the classical Greek plays. All students use some of the latest computer programs on compact disks (CDs) to study history, geography, and mathematics. The Lego blocks, student-written plays, and computer learning programs are examples of the eclectic approach used at Academy Charter School. One teacher calls it "pragmatic education." She says school staff believe content and behavior are important. They also believe it is important to use a variety of teaching and learning approaches, not just drill.

Academy Charter School combines innovative teaching techniques with some conservative ideas about curriculum. The school's parents and teachers believe in the importance of using phonics in teaching students to read. Teachers teach spelling and penmanship and emphasize the rules of capitalization and punctuation in students' writing. The school holds periodic spelling bees. It offers integrated art and music teaching and advanced-level math. Examples of students' writing, art, mathematics, and so forth are posted on the walls. The school almost exclusively uses the Core Knowledge Curriculum, developed by Professor E. D. Hirsch.

Academy uses the Saxon math program along with ability grouping. The school uses educational assistants to help every student move ahead. Sometimes groups of students work with an assistant or with a parent. The school teaches to an enormous range of student abilities. A visitor might find students of the same age whose math skills range from barely subtracting to performing algebraic functions, with all ranges of needs being met.

Like teachers at many elementary schools, Academy faculty think it is vital to encourage students to do their best and to praise their honest efforts. The student teacher ratio is 18 to 1. The school constantly groups and regroups students so that each student gets individual attention, and each youngster is challenged.

Administration and Evaluation

One of the most important parts of Academy is its governance structure. Although the school district oversees Academy through terms in the charter, the school functions independently with its own dean and governing board. The governing board is composed of seven parents who set policies and procedures. The dean is responsible for the day-to-day operations of the school and staff; the governing board is the final authority on long-range planning, broad educational goals, curriculum, hiring, and contracts. The parent-controlled governing board ensures that the school will be parent-directed and will represent the wishes and goals of the parents, not just the administrators. This responsiveness to parents was part of the school's original vision.

The school's accountability arm recently wrote and implemented a character development program that incorporates elements of ancient philosophy and literature with some of the moral and ethical standards set at the nearby U.S. Air Force Academy. In writing its own program, the Academy committee sought to sidestep some of the values clarification programs found at many public schools and use a more traditional, conservative approach requested by parents.

Academy Charter School started its fourth year in September 1996. The first year's progress report, using the Iowa Test of Basic Skills (ITBS), showed a 9 percent overall improvement in math, a 4 percent language improvement, and a 3 percent gain in average reading score. Test scores continued to improve, and in the spring of 1996, the Douglas Country School Board extended Academy's charter for another two years.

The school has been selected as a Colorado School of Excellence by the state department of education. It has also received several foundation grants. "I'd like people to view us as a model parent-run school of choice," says Karen Woods, one of the original teachers.

Facilities

From the outside, Academy Charter School looks like a store in a small one-story shopping mall. From this exterior, it is almost impossible to imagine what's happening inside. Parents helped convert this former grocery store, painting, hanging dry wall, laying carpets, and building walls as they did for the school's first home. The school's first facility also was in a shopping center but lacked connections between some of the interior spaces, lacked a playground, and was too near some railroad tracks. Parents and faculty looked for and found the current home.

Karen Woods is proud and amazed at what has been accomplished in the school's first three years. "What surprises me is how far we've come in such a short while. We know every child. We have a learning plan for every student, and we can really see progress." From spelling bees to CDs, the school has a unique atmosphere.

Hickman Charter School

Richard Ferriera has been a public school educator since 1969. He has been a 6th-grade teacher, a junior high school English teacher, a principal, and a district superintendent. Today, he spends 20 percent of his time directing one of California's more unusual charter schools.[10] Hickman is located about ninety minutes east of San Francisco, in the San Joaquin Valley.

Students

Hickman Charter School enrolls 550 students, grades K–8. Some of the students take courses in classrooms located in six separate sites. Some do all or most of their work at home. The home-schooled students' initial scores surprised Ferriera, who has spent his professional career in public education. He reports that students' scores on the California Test of Basic Skills average "in the 70th to 75th percentile of students nationally, which puts them 20 to 30 points higher than many of the public schools" in the area.

Some of the students have disabilities. The Hickman charter contracts with a regional education unit to work with these students for a portion of the day.

Educational Views

Hickman combines public and home schooling ideas, using a curriculum designed by the school rather than commercially available material. The only tangible items the school gives home-schooling families are these curriculum materials. The school has about forty instructors who teach classes in science, computers, writing, art, music, and physical education for students and many workshops for parents. The school also has six grade-level coordinators, who work with parents to plan and monitor each student's individual program.

Some critics of home schooling are concerned about parents' extremist viewpoints that may limit the range of ideas home-schooled students encounter. Ferriera says, however, that Hickman "wouldn't work with parents who have extreme views."

Impressed by the commitment of families with which the charter school is working, Ferriera has advice for other public school educators: "Don't be afraid to shift paradigms. . . . We educators have to admit the traditional classroom of twenty-five to thirty students sitting in desks simply isn't working for many, many students. We have to be open to carefully designed options which recognize students' learning styles and provide more individual attention."

Ferriera views Hickman Charter School as "a valuable option." The school's growth from 260 to more than 500 youngsters in two years shows that clearly there are other people who agree with him that this kind of school is a worthwhile choice.

Evaluation

At the beginning of the year, each student takes a screening test in reading, writing, and math.

Facilities

Hickman rents classrooms in schools in various school districts, including Stockton and Merced.

New Visions School

U.S. Secretary of Education Richard Riley visited New Visions School in Minneapolis the day after President Clinton commended charter schools in his State of the Union speech.[11] Riley likes the idea of charter schools and liked what he saw at New Visions. Since 1987, its founder, high school teacher Bob DeBoer, has been carrying out programs with young people who have some type of learning disability. He worked initially at an innovative Minneapolis public school, but gradually the local system restricted the school. For example, the district bowed to pressure from local principals who did not want to allow the school to hire an innovative educator and author who did not have an administrative certificate.

DeBoer and his wife have a daughter who was born with some disabilities. After her birth, he recalls, "I no longer had the luxury of objectivity." Professionals told him that his daughter would not be able to accomplish much, but he felt they were mistaken. Looking around the country, he found some people whose work intrigued him, and he began developing a program to help students with disabilities. Eventually, other educators became interested in his work, and he has conducted training workshops for hundreds of parents and professionals. His curriculum has been replicated in Minnesota, California, and North Carolina.

DeBoer applied to the Minneapolis Public Schools for a charter during the 1992–93 school year. Some university professors and people in what he called the district's "special education bureaucracy" opposed his work. So despite his superintendent's support, the local board of education rejected his proposal on a 4 to 3 vote. DeBoer's superintendent then recommended, and the board agreed, to give DeBoer a contract to work with a limited number of students.

At one point, the superintendent asked DeBoer whether he wanted to be a principal in the district. But DeBoer felt he would not have real control over selection of faculty or budget, and he felt it was critical to have that kind of control if his ideas were to get a real test. Although appreciating the superintendent's belief in him, he decided to continue with the subcontract while working to build support for the charter school he really wanted.

After two years of running his contract school, DeBoer reapplied for charter school status. By this time, there was a new entrepreneurial superintendent and a new school board. The district granted his request and approved the charter application, allowing him to work with as many families and students as selected his program. The New Visions School opened in September 1994. DeBoer says the charter status gives the school "real autonomy. That's what we need."

DeBoer sees the charter movement as just one more opportunity to "demonstrate what can be done." He often tells people that charter schools are a lot like automobiles. "There are lots of different kinds of cars. People get into the car and use it in a variety of ways. Each school seems to be an expression of the focus, vision, mission, and ideas of the founders. I think that's one of the more exciting ideas about the concept."

DeBoer also says it is important for charter proponents to know what they stand for, not just what they oppose: "It's easy to criticize; it's much more difficult to create something which works to help kids." DeBoer sees some charter school developers become almost paralyzed through their opposition to committees and any form of bureaucracy. Active in Minnesota's charter school movement, he meets regularly with other charter school directors and visiting legislators to help them understand what charter schools are trying to accomplish. He is also working to encourage the Minnesota State Department of Children, Families, and Learning to be more responsive and to provide more information to the state's charter schools.

Students

This inner-city K-8 school serves approximately 150 youngsters, many of whom have not succeeded in more conventional schools. Many of New Visions' students were classified as special education students in previous schools.

Educational Views

New Visions Charter School may represent one of the more dramatically different of the nation's charter public schools, and the best way to understand its curriculum is to see the way it developed through the experience of its founder. While teaching in the local high school, he was concerned to notice that some of the students who were graduating had only 6th-grade reading levels. When his daughter was born with disabilities, he began learning about teaching students with special needs, beginning with kindergarten students who had failed the Minneapolis test designed to determine whether they could enter 1st grade. About 10 percent of the districts' students failed the test. In one hour a day over the course of a summer, DeBoer and his wife were able to significantly increase the achievement of a group of these youngsters. They used visual perception games and physical exercises on the balance beam and monkey bars, along with crawling and creeping. These activities are designed to boost disabled students' ability to process information more effectively.

These students have "readiness deficits" that prevent them from achieving their potential. DeBoer believes it is critical to "stimulate students' brain processing capabilities and help their brains learn how to organize information more efficiently." After the first summer, he ran a three-hour-per-day, five-days-a-week program for seven weeks during subsequent summers to serve youngsters with special needs. Evaluators found that the students, on average, made a six- to eight-month gain in reading over that seven-week period.[12]

DeBoer's work came to the attention of several Minneapolis area foundations, including the General Mills Foundation, McKnight, Honeywell, Cargill and Bush Foundations, partly because of developments in the external society. DeBoer points, for example, to a Minneapolis business executive's push for children's "success by six." The local United Way adopted this theme, and many foundations made it a priority. DeBoer smiles as he says, "We had a dream to do this before it became hip. But the corporate support allowed us to carry out our plans."

These foundations helped him establish a program called A Chance to Learn in which he worked with hundreds of students over a four-year period. He developed a series of physical exercises to strengthen students' muscles and, in one of the most intriguing aspects of his work, created a computer program that provides biofeedback to students in ways that help them learn to focus their attention and master internal impulses. A number of these students spoke eloquently to Secretary Riley during his visit to the school, telling him that with the biofeedback practice they were now able to concentrate much more.

DeBoer's activities have been very controversial, and some university professors have questioned his work. DeBoer has listened to their criticisms, made some modifications, and continued his program. Meanwhile, evaluations show that students who have considerable problems in traditional schools are making substantial progress at New Visions.

DeBoer believes that the children he teaches have an enormous potential that can be realized. Kids who were struggling at other more traditional schools are becoming calmer and more focused and effective people as well as students. Although he praises the hard work and commitment of the New Visions teachers, he does not think the students' success is entirely due to teachers' hard work. He thinks the gains are also coming from the use of a carefully designed research-based curriculum and other strategies that can be replicated. In fact, as mentioned earlier, portions of his program are being replicated already.

Facilities

During its first year, the school shared space with a Catholic elementary school in a low-income section of Minneapolis. New Visions now has the whole building. The classrooms are old, but the ideas are state of the art.

PS1

PS1 founder and director Rexford Brown calls starting this Denver inner-city charter school "the hardest thing and probably most satisfying thing I've ever done."[13] Brown has been a teacher in public schools, a university professor, educational researcher, and author of articles and books. But as he puts it, "Nothing compares to getting a school up and running."

Students

PS1 has sixty students, ages ten to fifteen, and intends to double in size for the 1996–97 school year, enrolling about 120 students. Over the next few years, the school intends to enroll about 400 students, ages five to eighteen. One of the founders' commitments is that the school will reflect the racial and economic diversity of Denver. Walking around the school, a visitor sees plenty of diversity: Hispanic, Native American, African American, and white students talk and work together, in ways that would make most Americans proud. There is joking, yes, but also plenty of respect. In fact, that is one of the strongest impressions I had during my visit: respect among students, respect among faculty, and respect between students and faculty.

Educational Views

The school's mission is "to enrich life in the urban core of Denver—to add to its attractiveness, increase its economic viability, enliven its cultural life and bring out its hospitality. PS1 will make its

contributions to this mission by enabling young people to work together as a learning community on challenging projects that make
a difference in the quality of city life and in the process, draw students toward higher and higher standards of character, conduct,
work, academic achievement and community service." The school's
educational efforts begin with home visits to each of the students.
An individual education plan is then prepared for every youngster,
based on the school's expectations and the priorities of the student
and parent. Part of the school's curriculum includes carrying out
community service projects while learning academic subjects. In just
the school's first year, PS1 students planted vegetable and flower
gardens, helped stock food shelves, and assisted with a United Way
holiday program. A Denver downtown business group gave the
school an award for helping to stimulate community revitalization.

A second award came from the students' performance in a city-
wide Shakespearean festival. The teenagers researched and wrote
a skit entitled "10 Best Ways to Die in Shakespeare." The skit included death scenes from *Macbeth, Othello, Romeo and Juliet, A Mid-
summer Night's Dream,* and *Hamlet.* As part of the project, students
wrote reports on one of the characters and put together a costume
appropriate for the person being portrayed. Brown sees this kind
of project as central to what PS1 is trying to accomplish: "We want
to encourage and challenge every student. We promote rigorous
work."

Students are also expected to make periodic public presentations, both individually and in small groups. As Brown explains,
"We want to encourage them to think about what they're doing.
We don't want passive students." And that is not what the school is
producing. One Monday morning, as a group of visitors listened,
students described three-day field trips they had taken the previous week. Some students had gone to Estes Park, some farther west
in Colorado to Glenwood Springs, and one group of students had
gone to Los Angeles. One twelve-year-old told me, "The teachers
push us to do our best, and they give us lots of ways to demonstrate
what we've learned. It's a good kind of challenge."

At least one teacher, who has taught in different schools in the
United States and Europe and spent time managing a law office in
Chicago, was attracted to PS1 because she "wanted to work in a
school which promotes learning, which uses active approaches I

know will work." She likes PS1 "most days . . . but it is a lot of work." Brown agrees that staff "have plenty of work to do. But starting a charter school shouldn't be too easy. We're using public funds, and we're working with young people who depend on us." Would he do it again? Brown smiled as he replied, "Oh yes!"

Facilities

Like the program, the school's building is unusual. Youngsters have already decorated many walls in the former Veterans of Foreign Wars post that now houses the school. A group of plants sits in a window well of what was once the bar and now serves as cafeteria and science classroom. Next to the plants is a carefully lettered sign: "Please don't bother us. We are photosynthesizing." Across the street is a park that PS1 students have helped beautify.

The schools described in this chapter differ in important ways, in their structure, philosophy, governance, and appearance. But they are united on one central critical point. The faculty who work in them believe that these schools can make a difference in the lives of students. And these faculty are willing to put their jobs on the line in order to show that education can make a real, measurable difference in young people's lives.

Opportunities to do that do not just suddenly happen. The next chapter shows how the charter school idea was conceived and born. It was a complicated, difficult birth.

| The Birth of a Movement

The charter school movement is one part of a more than two-hundred-year push in the United States for expanded educational opportunity. It complements the efforts to expand voting rights, to earn a fair wage, to gain respect. As one insightful union official pointed out to me, "The people who start charter schools in the 1990s are the kind of people who started unions in the 1930s." Just as expansion of voting and workers rights was opposed by people who had power and did not want to share it, so the charter school movement has been opposed by a broad array of powerful education groups.

Ideas and people change history. The story of passing the first charter school legislation in the country includes advocates with a vision of a new way of educating our children, politicians who decided to give promising ideas a chance despite intense organized opposition, and teachers who believe in themselves and the power of education. Indeed, the dedication of charter school advocates across the country explains how, despite well-financed opposition from major educational groups, the idea has spread from a small group of Minnesotans to half the states in the country. This chapter chronicles the charter school movement through the birth of the first charter school legislation. It outlines how the charter movement built on the successes and frustrations of innovative public schools created in the 1960s and 1970s. Above all, it illustrates the importance of ongoing advocacy: educating the public and politicians about the functions, goals, and practical workings of charter schools and building a coalition of interests to support strong charter school legislation.

Early Actions

The charter school story begins in the late 1960s and early 1970s, at a time when parents and innovative public school educators all over the nation were joining together to design distinctive educational options, or *choices*. The first innovative schools, such forerunners of charter schools as Metro High School in Chicago, City as School in New York, Parkway in Philadelphia, Marcy Open School in Minneapolis, and St. Paul Open School in St. Paul, gave public school teachers the chance to create kinds of schools they thought made sense for a variety of students. These schools featured things like internships and apprenticeships in the community, site-based decision making, and extensive family involvement. By creating distinctive schools and giving families an opportunity to choose these schools, educators in these districts hoped to serve youngsters more effectively than they could with the prevailing one-size-fits-all model. New York City public school teacher and MacArthur "genius grant" winner Deborah Meier spoke for such teachers when she wrote that "[public school] choice is an essential tool" in the effort to create good public education, which needs schools "with a focus, with staffs brought together free to shape a whole set of school parameters . . . [for schools that are] small, largely self governing and pedagogically innovative."[1]

The efforts of educators and parents to create small distinctive public schools took a new direction as a result of congressional action that began in the mid-1970s. Courts and political leaders faced with massive public opposition in many communities to "forced busing," in which families were assigned to schools outside their neighborhoods, selected giving families options among public schools as one effective way to promote racial integration. Congress allocated millions of dollars to create magnet schools (see Introduction), optional schools with special, sometimes enhanced curricula designed to attract a racially diverse group of students.

There were several key differences between the small innovative schools created in the late 1960s and 1970s and magnet schools. First, the earlier schools generally were designed by groups of parents, community members, and teachers and principals. The magnet schools generally were designed by central office administrators, often with little parent, community, or teacher involvement. Second, the earlier, innovative schools had no admissions requirements and were open to a variety of students. The magnet schools, as noted earlier, often had admissions tests. Third, the earlier schools generally operated at the same per-pupil cost as other, more traditional schools. The magnet schools often cost more per pupil than neighborhood schools.

In the late 1970s and early 1980s, the distinctive school idea went through yet another metamorphosis. Public school districts began creating schools to which they assigned alienated, disruptive, and unsuccessful students. In many communities, the term *alternative school* was applied to these schools, and that term took on the connotation of a school or program for troubled students.

Meanwhile, the truly innovative public schools were finding that as time went on, they had less control over their budgets and faculty. Sometimes districts assigned administrators to these schools who questioned or even disagreed with a school's program philosophy. Moreover, district seniority arrangements often meant that faculty, too, were assigned to the innovative schools regardless of whether they agreed with a particular school's philosophy.

These events deeply concerned many of the original innovative school developers and interested parents and community members. The symptoms of loss of control were the subject of debates and conferences throughout the 1970s, 1980s, and early 1990s. However, the innovators found they could do relatively little to affect the way school boards and policy makers were altering the ideas the innovators had pioneered in their small distinctive schools offered as choices within the public school system.[2]

The situation led many innovative teachers and frustrated parents to consider new approaches. In the mid-1980s, the California public alternative school group Learning Alternatives Resource Network (LEARN) developed a proposed bill responding to many of these concerns. It stipulated that if thirty or more parents and/or pupils request a new school, teachers within the district choose to teach in it, and operating costs are no greater than those of programs of equivalent status for the same pupils, the district "shall establish a public school or program of choice responsive to this request."[3] The proposed bill was never introduced, much less adopted. But it signaled the frustration many parents and educators were feeling with the public education system.

School Choice in Minnesota

In Minnesota at about this same time, Governor Rudy Perpich introduced proposals for several public school choice programs. Perpich, a Democrat, felt it important to expand educational opportunities for families who could not afford to move from one community to another in order to change their children's school. He also felt that thoughtful, controlled competition could stimulate public school improvement. Perpich's 1985 proposals were strongly supported by an unusual coalition that included the Minnesota PTA; directors of the War on Poverty agencies in Minnesota; individual teachers, administrators, and parents; and the Minnesota Business Partnership (MBP). It was the first time that the MBP, representing the chief executive officers of the state's largest companies, had joined a grassroots coalition to promote school improvement.

By 1988, the Minnesota legislature had adopted three key parts of Perpich's proposals:

1. *Postsecondary options.* The Postsecondary Enrollment Options Program (1985) allows public high school juniors and seniors to take all or part of their coursework in colleges and universities, with their state funds following them and paying all tuition, book, and equipment fees. Opponents had predicted that this legislation would take many extremely successful students away from high schools and that these students would do badly in college. They were wrong on both counts. As of 1996, only about 10 percent of the state's students participated, and the vast majority were not straight-A students. Many youngsters who had compiled average or even below-average grades in high school blossomed in the collegiate environment, where they were given more freedom and treated more like adults. At the University of Minnesota, the high school students had a higher grade point average than the freshman class.[4]

2. *Options to attend other public schools.* The Area Learning Center Law and the High School Graduation Incentive Act (HSGI) (1987) allow teenagers and adults who have not previously succeeded in school to attend public schools outside their district. (Together, these two laws are known as the "second-chance law.") The

HSGI also allows students to attend private nonsectarian schools if a local district contracts with these schools. Many youngsters in the programs report they have higher aspirations due to going to a new school. Among youngsters attending public schools under the second-chance law, the percentage saying they planned to graduate and continue their education in a postsecondary institution increased from 19 percent to 39 percent. Among youngsters using the second-chance law to attend private nonsectarian schools, the percentage planning to graduate and go on to postsecondary education increased from 6 percent to 41 percent.[5]

3. *Open enrollment.* Open enrollment legislation (1988) allows K–12 students to apply to attend public schools outside their district, as long as the receiving district has room and their transfer does not increase racial segregation.

These proposals were extremely controversial when initially proposed. Most major Minnesota education groups, including teacher unions, school boards, and the superintendent association, opposed these public school choice proposals. The Minnesota Education Association (MEA) spent thousands of dollars on a videotape that was circulated around the state. Among other things, it claimed that if the cross-district public school choice law were adopted, school districts would "use . . . pretty cheerleaders to sell students on coming to their schools."[6] This didn't happen.

As people's experience with these choice programs grew, support increased. A 1985 poll by the *St. Paul Pioneer Press* found that only 33 percent of the general public supported cross-district public school choice.[7] Seven years later, a poll conducted by the major education groups in Minnesota found that 76 percent of the general public supported cross-district public school choice.[8] And a 1988 Minnesota Education Association poll of its members found that more than 60 percent supported the idea of cross-district public school choice.[9]

The full story of Minnesota's initial three-year battle for public school choice has been told by others.[10] Many of the same arguments used against postsecondary options and cross-district public school choice were to be used a few years later against the charter school idea. However, once the legislation had passed, support increased for public school choice around the state because thousands of youngsters were benefiting and because people were hearing about it, partly through newspaper and television stories. People heard, for example, about the two girls who had achieved a record for absences in their assigned school (missing eighty-nine days out of one hundred) but whose performance improved after they were transferred to a nontraditional program outside their district. The girls found that people at their new school "care more and they give you a chance, and don't just blow you off." They also "give you work that you actually want to do." These students were now planning on graduating from high school and perhaps even going on to postsecondary education.[11]

Susan (again, all student names are pseudonyms) was another student who benefited greatly from school choice.[12] She was in the bottom 25 percent of her high school class and undergoing therapy for depression that was at least in part related to her lack of academic accomplishment. Her special education teacher urged that she be allowed to enroll at the University of Minnesota. Her high school grade point average was 1.78 (C−/D+). Her university grade point average was 3.2 (B). And she wrote to the postsecondary options program director, "I owe a lot to you . . . a heartfelt thanks is going out to you."

Sam came to the University of Minnesota after having dropped out of high school a year earlier. He had never "fit in" at high school, where it was far "too rigid and stifling." His high school grades averaged D+/C−. He maintained a B+/A− average at the university.

Paul was in the 59th percentile of his high school class, and his high school counselor called the University of Minnesota twice to protest that he should not be allowed to attend the university. However, his University of Minnesota grade point average was 4.0, and his writing instructor found him "highly motivated" and his skills "outstanding . . . at a level beyond many juniors and seniors. His papers are a pleasure to read . . . he is a very good, highly motivated student. It is a pleasure to have him as a student."

Jon, a disruptive, hostile, highly argumentive inner-city high school student, failed seven of his eight classes his last term before he dropped out. Nine months later, he began college full time, earning an A average while taking courses in philosophy, English, and political science. During his second term, he was allowed to register in a graduate English course, a course in which he received an A. He has published several magazine articles and is attempting to market two of his completed novels. He wrote:

> If I hadn't had the opportunity [to enroll in the Postsecondary Enrollment Options Program], I would certainly not have become an honors students much less a college student. . . . High school was just holding me back. I was into trouble in grade school; my junior high and high school performance was poor. But when I found out about this program I decided to go for it. . . . Here at the U I have yet to get a C. All my grades are A's and B's. I never used to get an A or B. This program was a saving grace for me and changed my life around. . . .
>
> This program allowed me to get out of the nowhere world of high school and let me recognize my own potential. It allowed me to get away from bad influences literally and become my own person away from peer pressures, annoying administrative restrictions and the intellectual staleness that high school was for me.

Moreover, the choice programs were changing the lives of good students as well as those of students in trouble. Sara, for example, was successful in high school but opted for more challenge and enrolled in one course during the fall of her high school junior year to see how she would do in college. In what would have been her senior year in high school, she was admitted as a full-time student at the University of Minnesota's Institute of Technology. During that year, she began working as a research assistant under a NASA and National Science Foundation grant. She earned a bachelor's degree in physics, with honors, at the age of twenty.

Spreading the Idea of Charter Schools

As success stories grew and public support for choice programs increased, some Minnesotans felt that the existing laws gave families more choice, but not enough choices. Some Minnesota districts had turned down educators and parent and community groups who wanted to create new kinds of schools. State Senator Ember Reichgott (now Reichgott-Junge), who had authored the cross-district public school choice program in 1988 after Governor

Perpich proposed it, began looking for ways to expand the real choices for families and for educators.[13] Some answers came in 1988, when she and several other Minnesotans who had worked on open enrollment and postsecondary options were invited to a Minneapolis Foundation–sponsored conference about improving public schools. The foundation had scheduled two powerful speakers with impressive credentials to provide thought-provoking information and ideas to the invited audience.

The first speaker was Sy Fliegel, a warm, entertaining, and charismatic educator from East Harlem who had helped dozens of educators start new schools and schools within schools in his extremely low income section of New York City. Fliegel described how he and other district administrators had not used a master, strategic plan but had simply asked a few educators if they wanted to create some new schools. Soon, other teachers were also bringing in their ideas. Within a few years, there were many buildings in East Harlem with two, three, or even four innovative schools, and the results were encouraging. When the effort began, only about 15 percent of East Harlem students were reading at or above grade level. A decade later, more than 60 percent were "above average" readers, and educators from throughout the world were visiting East Harlem to see how the combination of choice and teacher empowerment worked.[14] The conference gave Senator Reichgott the opportunity not only to hear Fliegel but to spend several hours talking with him, asking him what a legislator could do to promote his ideas.

The second speaker was American Federation of Teachers (AFT) president Albert Shanker. Shanker's address was shaped by his recent reading of *Education by Charter: Restructuring School Districts,* by an educator named Ray Budde.[15] Budde recommended that school districts give innovative teachers the opportunity to create a new kind of program—perhaps a new kind of primary program at an elementary school or a humanities two- to three-hour block at a high school. He used the metaphor of the "charter" (as noted earlier, originally a document that forged an agreement, often between explorers and their usually royal sponsors). Budde recommended districts be reorganized and that innovative teachers be given explicit permission by the school board to create innovative new programs, and like the explorers hundreds of years earlier, report back about their discoveries. Budde had been writing about this concept for years. In fact, he first applied the term *charter* to innovative schools in a 1975 conference presentation.[16] In his book, he points out that the term goes back more than 1,000 years, citing the Magna Carta (Great Charter), the agreement guaranteeing rights and privileges that King John and the English barons signed at Runnymede in June 1215, and the charter that English explorer Henry Hudson signed with the East India Company authorizing him to seek a hoped-for shortcut from Europe to Asia.[17]

Shanker liked Budde's idea of giving teachers a chance to create innovative new programs—and extended it to include entire new schools. Shanker suggested that both the school board and the majority of teachers working in a school be required to approve these new schools. Shanker knew some AFT members were frustrated by district bureaucracy. So on March 31, 1988, Shanker made a speech at the National Press Club in Washington endorsing the idea and remarking,

> One of the things that discourages people from bringing about change in schools is the experience of having that effort stopped for no good reason. I hear this all over the country. Somebody says, "Oh, Mr. Shanker, we tried something like that 15 years ago. We worked around the clock, and we worked weekends. . . . I never worked so hard in my life. And then a new school board was elected or a new principal or superintendent came in and said, 'That's not my thing.'" And that's the end of the school or program. You'll never get people to make that kind of commitment if our educational world is just filled with people who went through the disappointment of having been engaged and involved and committed to building something only to have it cut out from under them.[18]

Shanker had then urged the AFT to endorse the charter school idea, which it did at its 1988 annual convention. Shanker's next column (a column that appears weekly as a paid advertisement in the Sunday *New York Times*) praised the charter idea, again citing the problems of teachers who tried to create new, innovative "schools within schools": "Many schools within schools were or are treated like traitors or outlaws for daring to move out of the lockstep and do something different. Their initiators had to move heaven and earth to get school officials to authorize them, and if they managed that, often they could look forward to insecurity, obscurity or outright hostility."[19]

(Ray Budde had no idea that Shanker would endorse the charter concept. He learned of Shanker's interest for the first time when his wife was reading the *New York Times* that Sunday. "Oh look, Ray," she said to him. "Al Shanker is writing about you and your book!"[20])

Shanker continued to write supportive articles. In one, he cited the East Harlem program as a good model and recommended that "administrators and teachers should welcome the advent of charter schools as an opportunity to break out of the lockstep and respond directly to those students for whom the general school program is not working."[21] Shanker's speech at the Minnesota conference repeated these themes.

After hearing Shanker and Fliegel speak about the two ideas of allowing more choices among schools and developing policies that give teachers a chance to create them, four of the conference attendees offered to help Reichgott develop these ideas for Minnesota. Barbara Zohn was a parent and former Minnesota PTA president who had strongly supported Governor Perpich's proposals. She was now responsible for answering the toll-free telephone number the state department of education had set up to field parent and student questions about public school choice. Elaine Salinas was a former public school teacher who had been hired as education program officer of the Urban Coalition of Minneapolis–St. Paul. She was an advocate for low-income students who had been pushing hard for more information to help families select among schools. Ted Kolderie had been executive director of a Twin Cities–based organization called the Citizens League, a nonpartisan public policy research group. He had also been involved with a project called Public Service Options, which studied ways to change bureaucratic systems. And I was the fourth person. I was a former public school teacher and administrator who had been hired by the National Governors' Association to coordinate a project recommending priorities for governors who wanted to improve education.

The four of us helped Reichgott refine the ideas we had all heard at this conference. The idea of options in public education was not new to any of us. We had worked together on the state's open enrollment legislation. But as Kolderie put it, that legislation had simply opened up opportunity on the demand side. Parents now had the legal right to choose among public schools. But in 1989, most families still had little real choice because very few districts offered different kinds of schools. It was time to open up the supply side, providing these different kinds of schools so the right of choice would be meaningful.

The charter concept also needed fleshing out, and the Citizens League created a committee to study the idea. The Citizens League had been the first Minnesota group to promote cross-district public school choice. Legislators often used its reports in areas from transportation to housing to education because of their carefully researched ideas and specific recommendations. The committee included the president of the Minneapolis Federation of Teachers and teachers, businesspeople, and others concerned about education. Its co-chairs were a public school teacher and John Rollwagen, CEO of the Minnesota-based computer company Cray Research. After several months, the Citizens League issued a report that all committee members signed, recommending the creation of charter public schools sponsored either by a local school board or the state board of education. It also suggested that the state board be allowed to sponsor charter schools on appeal if they had been turned down by their local boards.

Next, Citizens League members and some of the people who had attended the conference where Fliegel and Shanker spoke met with State Education Commissioner Tom Nelson. This group included Doug Wallace, a state school board member; and Peter Vandepoel, former director of the state planning agency, a former newspaper reporter, and later, a Citizens League member. A widely respected former public school educator and state legislator, Nelson was a strong supporter of public school choice who had worked closely with Senator Reichgott while in the Minnesota Senate and, as chair of a key school funding committee, had been an early proponent of Governor Perpich's ideas. He asked the group to form an ad hoc committee to develop a legislative proposal.

Developing and Passing a Proposal

The group members gradually developed a proposal for the 1990 legislature. The concepts they incorporated in this document came from ideas of the pioneering teachers and parents who had created alternatives and options within public education since the 1960s; they came from business and union groups who supported school site management; they came from legislators and members of the public who wanted to see more accountability for results in public education. Thus, the proposal included the concept of increasing student achievement, expanding choice for families, expanding opportunities for educators, and stimulating change in the larger public education system. It combined these ideas with new ones to produce a unique charter proposal that called for all the elements listed in the model charter strategy discussed in the Introduction.

Successful ideas have champions, individuals who make them real to large numbers of people. As mentioned earlier, Senator Ember Reichgott became the principal legislative champion of the charter school concept. She moved the charter idea through the Minnesota Senate in 1990, but the House rejected it. Then in the elections of November 1990, Governor Perpich was narrowly defeated and a new, Republican governor, Arne Carlson, took office, appointing the MEA's lobbyist as his commissioner of education. Neither the new commissioner nor the new governor supported the charter school proposal.

So Reichgott no longer had strong support from the governor's office. Within two years, Governor Carlson became a strong charter school proponent. But he was not promoting charter schools in 1991.

Reichgott was joined by Minnesota Representative Becky Kelso, also a suburban Democrat and a former school board member. She supported the charter idea because "public education needs a fair, thoughtful challenge. Not vouchers, but the stimulus of another kind of public school, competing for students."[22] Kelso tried to move the charter idea in the Minnesota House of Representatives, but the teachers unions were able to frustrate her efforts. Thus it was up to Senator Reichgott to move the idea ahead in the senate.

Reichgott smiled a little sadly at the end of the 1991 Minnesota legislative session: "Well, we gave it a really good try this year. Let's see what happens." Reichgott had spent the last two years trying to get the legislature to adopt the charter school notion. As mentioned, it passed the Minnesota Senate in 1990 but was rejected by a House-Senate conference committee. A year later, the senate endorsed the concept and again brought it to the conference committee.

The 1991 Senate bill reflected a number of changes suggested by teachers union officials. For example, the original bill permitted charter schools to hire people with special skills in such areas as art, music, and world languages whether or not they were certified teachers. This was changed in response to union officials' demands, as was language authorizing an unlimited number of charter schools. The proposal was changed to limit the number of charter schools to fifty, although the unions still considered this too many.

Along with the total number of schools to be permitted, the key controversies were over sponsorship and autonomy of the charter schools. Union officials wanted to restrict charter school sponsors to local school boards and to ensure that charter schools would follow local union-management agreement provisions unless both the local school board and the union agreed to waivers. This really bothered Terry Lydell, an innovative public school teacher who worked in Reichgott's district and helped her design the charter legislation. Lydell spent hours at the capitol, after school and on weekends, helping Reichgott explain why a strong charter law was important. He recalls being criticized by union officials for coming to the legislature. But Lydell, who had helped create alternative programs in both inner-city and suburban districts, had seen how district and union officials obstructed efforts of teachers to create distinctive schools. He once remarked, "Whether it's giving schools the power to select their own teachers, getting the materials we order to us in a timely manner, or rewarding schools which make progress with students, public school systems make it very, very difficult."[23]

Lydell participated in some of the negotiation sessions with Reichgott and union officials. He remembers being told by some union lobbyists that he "didn't belong" at the legislature. This amused him. "I deal daily with kids. I know what challenges teachers face. Legislators need to hear directly *more* from people like me, not less." Lydell and other innovative public school teachers pointed out that if school districts wanted to create innovative schools, they already had the power to do so. But most districts were not doing it, and the innovative schools (such as Lydell's) frequently encountered bureaucratic problems that made it difficult for them to succeed.

Peter Vanderpoel, who had helped develop the charter legislation, also spent hours at the capitol during the 1991 legislative session. He recalls, "Though I had not been an educator like some of the people supporting the charter concept, the idea made a lot of sense to me. It seemed like something which could stimulate a lot of positive change in a very large, complex and bureaucratic system."[24] Vanderpoel spent day after day, and plenty of nights, at the legislature in 1991, helping explain the charter concept to legislators and showing how it built on Minnesota's successful experience with other public school choice programs.

With encouragement from people like Lydell and Vanderpoel, Reichgott insisted that the Senate bill allow charter schools to be sponsored either by a local or the state board of education. This provision was in the bill that was agreed to by the Senate and then went to the House-Senate conference committee, of which Reichgott was a member.

There, three of the five House members on the committee had to support charter schools for the bill to be approved. The bill had only two of these votes initially. At that point, Reichgott and Kelso called the bill's supporters—a handful of innovative teachers, some advocates for low-income groups, some businesspeople, and a few people interested in education policy—to ask for their help in getting that third vote.

Among the public school teachers who began calling conference committee members was Launa Ellison, a veteran of inner-city schools who now taught at Barton Open School, a Minneapolis inner-city elementary school that had been named one of the finest in the nation by the U.S. Department of Education. Ellison, who was later to write an eloquent book about teaching called *Seeing with Magic Glasses*,[25] had seen the way school districts made her job and that of her colleagues difficult: "District officials often look down on those of us who work day to day with kids. It takes too long to get materials, and sometimes staff are put into our school because of their seniority, not their commitment to our school's philosophy."[26] One of the Minneapolis teachers involved in developing the charter concept, she understood teachers' needs and had suggested, among other things, that charter school teachers be allowed to continue their membership in state retirement programs. One spring evening, she called Ken Nelson, a conference committee member from the House who was wavering. He listened.

Teachers unions had supported him as he had risen to chair of the Minnesota House Education Finance Committee, which dealt with elementary and secondary school funding. Union members had been active in his election campaigns, both raising money and going door to door, urging people to vote for him. Nelson had himself introduced charter legislation in the House in 1989. It died for lack of support.

Now the MEA, the state's largest teacher union, was calling the charter school concept "insulting" and "a hoax,"[27] and the teachers unions were threatening not to support Nelson. This stunned Nelson, who felt he had not just supported but battled hard over a number of years for public schools funding. Nevertheless, Nelson respected Ellison as a veteran talented, committed Minneapolis teacher. She made sense. Despite intense union threats, Nelson had voted in 1985 for cross-district public school choice. He felt that was a good decision and that the unions had overreacted in their opposition. (As mentioned earlier, a poll conducted in 1988 by the Minnesota Education Association of its members showed that more than 60 percent of the teachers supported the cross-district public school choice idea.)

Nelson proposed modifications to the Senate charter provisions that charter proponents thought significantly weakened the bill. These amendments meant, for example, that in Minnesota

Charter schools have to get permission to operate from *both* a local school board and the state school board, rather than having the option of gaining sponsorship from a local school board *or* the state board of education.

Only eight charter schools were to be permitted.

A majority of a charter school's board members have to be teachers in the school. Nelson believed that good teachers like Ellison should be in charge of the learning enterprise. However, this meant that charter schools would not have a free hand in developing a board, teachers would have board duties added to their workload, and many people who were not teachers but would make desirable board members would not be able to serve.

With these changes made, Nelson provided the critical third vote. The charter school provisions then became part of a larger education bill. The unions were not satisfied. They pressured conference committee members to remove charter provisions from the omnibus bill. Failing at that, they tried to defeat the bill when it returned to the House. They came within a few votes of succeeding. But a slight majority of House members voted to support the bill, including its extremely modest charter provisions. The concept, even in a drastically watered-down form, would get a try.

Senator Reichgott had conflicting emotions at the end of the 1991 legislative session: "I was delighted and disappointed. Delighted that the charter concept had been accepted. Disappointed that the final provisions were so weak."

The 1991 charter law was a long way from what Reichgott and Kelso intended. Most charter school proponents were deeply disappointed by the 1991 compromises, but Senator Reichgott's view was: "Let's give this a try and see what happens. We can always come back next year and try to improve the law."

That is what happened over the following years. Gradually, the legislature increased the number of charter schools allowed to forty. After watching local board turndowns such as the ones described later in this book, the legislature also modified the approval process, permitting those proposing a charter school to appeal to the state board of education if two members of the local board had voted in support of the proposal. But charter groups often find it difficult to gain those two votes. In 1995, the Minnesota state legislature approved a modification of the state's charter law, allowing three charter schools to be sponsored by a public university. This step was proposed by Rep. Matt Entenza, a liberal inner-city Democrat who had run with teachers union support. Despite efforts to deter him from making this proposal, he convinced his colleagues to give the idea a try.

Other changes make it clear that charter schools *are* public schools, that their employees may be members of the state's public employees retirement association, and that charter schools may either run their own transportation systems for students or be a part of the transportation routes of districts in which they are located.

Because the way had been prepared by earlier more modest legislation; because advocates and politicians researched, discussed, and developed their ideas, wrote the proposed legislation, and committed themselves to passing it; because a coalition of individuals and groups supported the idea; and because many legislators, educators, parents, and business people were dissatisfied with the status quo and ready to try out the charter school concept, charter school legislation became law in Minnesota. Furthermore, people around the nation responded to Minnesota's action in far greater numbers than Reichgott or any of the other Minnesota proponents had imagined they would. People wanted more choices in public education. They wanted accountability for results.

So the charter school concept was planted in Minnesota. A Minnesota farmer once explained to me that "to be a successful farmer, you have to have good seeds—like good ideas in education. People disagree about the best kind of seeds, so you have to decide what makes sense to you . . . what's likely to work. But good seeds aren't enough. You need to prepare the soil, so that it's ready to accept and nourish the seeds. You can't just put seeds in the ground. You have to keep the weeds and insects away. You hope for rain and sun in the right amounts. You stay vigilant and work hard. If it comes together, you have a good crop."

In many states, the ground was ready. Many people want more effective, accountable public schools. The charter idea is a seed that is spreading, changing the schooling and lives of thousands and thousands of youngsters. ·

Part Two

How Charter Schools Are Changing the System

Chapter Three

Breaking the District Monopoly

Earlier, I pointed out that just as expansions of the right to vote and of workers' rights were opposed by people who already held power and did not want to share it, so the charter school movement has, on its own smaller scale, been opposed by an array of powerful educational groups. Despite the many committed, talented educators, our public education system often does not prize progress or reward risk takers. In fact, the system often frustrates innovative teachers and caring parents. There is too much bitterness as school boards, teachers unions, and district administrators blame each other for their frustrations. There are too few incentives for improvement in the current system. The charter school movement can help produce some critically needed changes.

This chapter explains why change often is slow and difficult. Then it illustrates how strong charter school laws have encouraged improvement.

Most changes in any field are controversial. And so it is in education: teachers, parents, administrators, and school board members who propose new approaches know that some people will resist because it generally is easier and less stressful for people to continue doing things in the same way. Ted Kolderie explains some of the resistance: "As they consider proposals for change, the superintendent, board, principal, union and teachers weigh the potential benefits to the kids against the risk of creating 'internal stress.' They want to help the kids. But upsetting people might create controversy. It might produce a grievance. It might lose an election. It might cause a strike. It might damage a career."[1] Ultimately, some changes are made because of the heroic efforts of certain educators, parents, and school boards. But the system does not encourage it.

In a study of almost 1,000 elementary, junior high, and senior high classrooms, one of the largest studies of U.S. classrooms ever undertaken, John Goodlad, then dean of the School of Education at the University of California, Los Angeles, reported he had identified some classes that used effective teaching techniques including "hands-on, active learning." But most classrooms did not use these techniques. There were many barriers. Among Goodlad's conclusions: "The cards are stacked against deviation and innovation."[2]

System defenders have argued that there is no crisis in the public education system. Marvelous teachers like Deborah Meier, Jaime Escalante, and Jessica Siegel know there is. Teachers of the Year know it. In one Northern state, three of the last twenty statewide Teachers of the Year have been laid off under "last hired, first fired" rules. Eighteen have reported that parent and community groups had invited them to discuss how to improve public education. Only two have been invited by their local school boards and superintendents to suggest ways to improve local public schools.[3] What kind of organization would survive by ignoring the skills of its finest employees, and when layoffs are necessary, terminating people who have been recognized throughout the industry as outstanding? Some of public education's troubles, clearly, come not from the problems students bring to school with them but from the educational system that unions, school boards, administrators, and legislators have created. Consider the following two examples.

A Suburban District Ignores Teachers

Why do many committed, talented teachers become bitter and cynical?[4] Why did the national Twentieth Century Task Force call many school boards "an obstacle to—rather than a force for—fundamental educational reform"?[5] A suburban school board helped answer those questions.

In 1993, prior to asking for a charter, award-winning teachers in this suburban district presented twenty-two new approaches they wanted to incorporate into their alternative school, which serves some of the areas' most challenging young people, students ages sixteen to twenty-one who have not succeeded in traditional high schools. The teachers' concepts included a longer school day and a longer school year, sharing space with a commercial facility to provide students with direct access to employment, and teachers' assuming greater responsibility for improving student achievement. Many of these proposals would not cost more money. Some *saved* money. Faced with this list, however, the school board chair told the teachers, "I heard nothing . . . that merited further consideration." The teachers were stunned.

The district superintendent also opposed change. After a December visit to the alternative school, he had written, "I give every member of the staff much praise and thanks." Staff reported that he had even suggested applying for charter school status. But then he wrote a six-page statement opposing that idea and saying, "any unmet needs now or in the future can be accomplished under the current structure." The teachers disagreed. The superintendent felt the charter would cost about $150,000. Staff pointed out that the district would keep local property taxes now allocated to the alternative school, so that more money, not less, would be available for the other students in the district.

The teachers reported that "at least three of our proposed program improvements had previously been denied by administration." For example, staff had wanted to share space with social service agencies, making better use of taxpayers' dollars. No. Because many of the staff work eleven or twelve months rather than the traditional nine and because the school serves young people with significant problems, the staff asked for a few more days of training to help them be more effective with students. No—it would set a bad precedent. In addition, the administration now wanted to remove the alternative school's principal, who had helped found the program and had enormous staff support.

The staff voted 32 to 2 to submit a proposal for a charter school, that is, for a contract in which they would take responsibility for student results in exchange for receiving the power to run the program as they wished. A state education department official described the teachers' charter proposal as "outstanding." The local teachers union was neutral toward the request. Moreover, three school board members supported the teachers. One explained that "it's just endless what we can learn from this." The second added, "If they've done such a wonderful job so far, think of what they could do if we knock down some walls."

But the superintendent recommended rejecting the teachers' proposal, and on a 3 to 4 vote, it was rejected. The local union president said of the board's action, "The whole thing is over power and authority." Yet after rejecting the teachers' request for accountability and authority, the school board, on a 7 to 0 vote, passed a resolution saying it was "proud" of the alternative school and that it supported the staff because of their "dedication and commitment." Neither vote impressed the teachers. The school counselor felt the board "discounted the professional judgment of thirty-two people whom they praised." Another staff member felt that "their praise is so hollow. It feels like we've been kicked in the teeth." A teacher asked, "If we're so great, why not let us take the risks we're willing to take?"

A Rural School District Squanders an Opportunity

A rural school district's handling of a charter proposal shows how distorted the incentives for outstanding teachers can become.[6] Several members of the local school board were intrigued when they were approached by a teacher I will call Ms. R about the possibility of a charter school. Ms. R, who lived in the district, had created a school-within-a-school option at an elementary school in another district, about twenty-five miles away. Her program was popular with parents, in part because she was extremely knowledgeable about computers and had written several successful grant proposals to bring computers into her multi-age classroom. Her students represented a cross-section of the community: "We have some youngsters who had lots of trouble in other classrooms, some who are handicapped, and some who are looking for additional challenge," she said. "What I try to do is find each youngster's strength, tap into that, and build on it."

The first student I met when I visited Ms. R's program was a nine-year-old who explained, "This class is different. My mom said it would be more of a challenge. I think it's more fun. People obey better and they're quieter. You get things done easier." Most of the nine-, ten-, and eleven-year-olds in the class agreed. A ten-year-old student said, "I like to work on independent projects and to write reports. I think this class teaches you to think and to do things that you could keep on doing for the rest of your life."

I was struck immediately by the vast array of activity going on at any one time. One day between 9:30 and 10:00 A.M., Several students were learning more about geography by playing a world traveler game. Three students were videotaping the sports news broadcast they had written, which would be played for other students later in the day. Other youngsters were using a computer program developed by National Geographic to create a map of the Middle East, including various landforms: mountains, plateaus, and plains. One group was cooking Navajo fry bread as part of their study of that culture. Several students were reading and answering and discussing questions on how they felt about and reacted to certain difficult situations (such as someone's telling them to do something they did not want to do). Another group of young people were writing directions to make a computer move various Lego objects they had created.

Ms. R was supervising all this with the help of a parent volunteer and remarked, "I have no trouble getting parents to help out. . . . Sure, family structures are changing. But if I offer different ways to be involved, most parents respond."

Various measures show that Ms. R's students accomplished the three objectives she set: "to create an environment that promotes rather than stifles creativity, adaptability, and most importantly, questioning; to develop knowledge and understanding of modern issues and their impact in our changing lives; and to develop mastery of communications skills, both verbal and written."

While Ms. R was heartened by her program's success, she preferred to teach in the district where she lived rather than make a daily fifty-mile round-trip. So she became one of the first teachers in her state to ask for information about charter schools once the state legislature adopted the idea.

She contacted a number of people in the district about her ideas, including parents, businesspeople, and college professors. A professor at the nearby college worked with her on the proposal and told school board members his college would be interested in placing student teachers with Ms. R. After she met with union members, the local teachers union decided to remain neutral about her proposal. However, the local superintendent did not support Ms. R's proposal. He prided himself on being an innovator, but unlike the parents and businesspeople, he did not see much benefit to the district from working with her.

The school board disagreed with the superintendent. Encouraged by some community members who supported Ms. R and thought she had a great deal to offer, the majority of board members thought it would be a good idea to offer her option in the district. After months of conversations between Ms. R, the superintendent, and the school board, a decision was reached. The school board would not sponsor a charter school but would ask the superintendent to work out an arrangement to bring Ms. R's school-within-a-school to the district.

Ms. R put together a proposal for a school within school, and because I had a positive relationship with both the superintendent and Ms. R, I was asked to join their conversation to help make the discussion constructive and successful. Two points were immediate problems. First, the superintendent insisted Ms. R conform to the existing "chain of command" in the district, which was that all teachers were supervised by a principal, even though Ms. R would be the one responsible for improved results and was staking her job on that kind of accountability. The principal would have the power to veto Ms. R's teaching strategies. Second, the superintendent intended to pay Ms. R under the district's existing salary structure, which meant she would be earning approximately $12,000 less than she was in her current district because she would not get credit for her fourteen years of teaching experience. The superintendent explained that teachers new to the district were given credit only for degrees earned, not for years of service in other places. Accepting considerably more responsibility than a conventional classroom teacher while taking a $12,000 pay cut was a problem for Ms. R, a big problem. When I asked about exceptions to the rule, the superintendent first said there were none, but then acknowledged that the two local high school principals had insisted on the right to hire whichever football coach they thought would do the best possible job for their school, and to attract the best coaches, incoming coaches were given credit for their years of teaching in other districts. But the superintendent was still unwilling to make such an exception in Ms. R's case. Imagine a business whose board of directors wants to hire a person who has done an outstanding job elsewhere but asks that person to take a $12,000 pay cut? How long would such an organization survive? How many excellent employees would it attract?

The superintendent's insistence that she take almost $12,000 less than her current salary deeply offended Ms. R. It ended the conversation. She felt insulted and deeply disheartened, and she has since left public school teaching.

Some Root Causes of Resistance to Educational Change

The current public education system promotes a great deal of finger pointing. A recent article in the national magazine for school administrators lists the "top 10 factors judged to be the most detrimental to the success of the public schools" by two hundred administrators around the country, 76 percent of whom are public school superintendents. Among the groups making the list as detrimental factors are school board members, educators, citizens, and families![7]

Today's educational problems are not going to be solved by parents' keeping quiet or by a new superintendent or a new school board. Instead, they are central to an educational system that holds a monopoly on public education and that in most states gives funds to school districts whether the graduation rate or student achievement improves or gets worse. In most states, not only does the system fail to react to schools whose students are not achieving, it also fails to reward schools where there is progress.

Public school apologists can and do write books insisting that most of education's problems are outside the system. They insist that the critics of our schools have produced a "manufactured crisis." They correctly argue that a major problem for education is the many troubled families in this country. They are right. These defenders insist that it is unjust and outrageous that some suburban districts spend $18,000 per pupil while inner-city districts just twenty to thirty minutes away spend about $6,000 per pupil. They are right about this, too. This is an evil, shameful disparity. It should be changed. Funding disparities are not all that is unfair in the current public education system. In most districts, only parents who can afford to pay tuition at a private or parochial school or to move to another district have real options. Affluent families have far more choices among schools than low- and moderate-income families.

These are all real problems. Charter school proponents, like many excellent educators frustrated by the current system, believe that public schools can have a significant, positive impact on children, including those who come from troubled families. They believe the barriers to educating these children include not just inequitable funding but a public education system that has little competition and can make excuses rather than be held accountable for progress with these young people.

School districts have been given an "exclusive franchise,"[8] a monopoly. U.S. Secretary of Education Richard Riley states, "Many parents feel that their right to be involved in school policy, to be full participants in the learning process, is ignored, frustrated and sometimes even denied. They do not feel valued."[9] You do not have to be a public school "basher" to see the parallels between the discredited rail, steel, and oil monopolies and the public education system. There are very few captive markets left in the United States. No one has a monopoly on gas stations, department stores, restaurants, computers, automobiles, or virtually any other consumer product or service. No one guarantees any corporation its customers. Moreover, no one guarantees that a corporation will continue to receive revenue regardless of what customers think of its products or services.

Yet most public schools receive their revenue regardless of their achievement. Some educators unquestionably try to improve their skills, but overall, are public school educators rewarded for seeking dramatically new, more effective approaches? Will teachers or principals earn more money if attendance or graduation rates increase or test scores rise? Conversely, do people in schools lose their jobs if attendance declines, dropout rates increase, and test scores go down? In most states and districts, the answer to these questions is no. The word *accountability* is used a great deal in public education, but generally it is meaningless at the school site. One group of researchers described the cynicism of many educators, "yawning wearily in the face of yet another promised reform."[10] This is not a system that rewards those who try to improve schools. Superintendents come and go. School boards are voted in and voted out. But how much accountability is there at the local school level? Not much.

Adults are well protected in the present public education system. Mature teachers and principals, regardless of their performance, are almost impossible to fire. It can cost a district several hundred thousand dollars to fire a tenured teacher because of the extended, extensive legal battle often required. So what incentive does the district have to try removing an incompetent or mediocre teacher? It receives funds regardless of how well students do. Unless the teacher has committed a clear and blatant crime against a youngster, the case for dismissal can (and such cases do) drag on for years, producing bad feelings and bitterness.

The crisis within public education frustrates and embitters educators and parents. It is time to try a different kind of system.

A more effective system will recognize and reward talent, expanding opportunities for committed educators and parents who want to create new kinds of public schools. This can unleash enormous energy, encourage talented educators eager to offer a new, potentially more effective approach to public education and test a new form of accountability. The Twentieth Century Fund report cited the charter approach as one of several that "in a spirit of innovative experimentation, the Task Force believes . . . should be welcomed and their results monitored closely for the lessons (both positive and negative) that they provide."[11]

Part of the path toward progress involves introducing more competition into public education, as charter schools and programs such as Minnesota's Post-Secondary Enrollment Options Program do. When school districts know they cannot take students and money for granted, they have turned to teachers to create new and more effective programs. The following examples look first at the effect on public schools of Minnesota's postsecondary options legislation, which preceded charter school legislation (see Chapter One), and then at three examples of the effects of charter school legislation, in Boston, Massachusetts, Jefferson County, Colorado, and Detroit, Michigan.

Effect of the Post-Secondary Enrollment Options Program in Minnesota

The effects of the Minnesota law that allows high school students to attend colleges and universities full- or part-time show how innovative approaches to public schooling can encourage the broader educational system to improve. When the Post-Secondary Enrollment Options Program was first proposed in Minnesota, many school districts criticized it as competition that would take away their money. But the state legislature decided that it allocated money for the education of students, not just for the maintenance of districts, and the proposal was passed.

After its passage, in 1985, many school districts began offering new classes such as Advanced Placement courses, which allowed high school students to earn college credits while still in high school. Over the first seven years of the postsecondary options program, the number of Advanced Placement courses available more than doubled.[12]

School districts all over the state also created new cooperative courses with colleges and universities. Pete Holden, a counselor at Highland Park High School, thinks that school's International Baccalaureate and College in the Schools courses attract many students who otherwise might simply leave high school to attend college. His experience with the program has been "generally positive." Most students who use the program are either "way ahead" academically and seeking more challenge or "somehow don't fit in" at the high school. "They're much more comfortable at college."[13]

Bob Vaadeland, superintendent of Yellow Medicine East School District, likes the postsecondary options program, which he believes has pushed his daughter to "work harder and learn more" while taking courses at Southwest State University. In response to the postsecondary options, Yellow Medicine has created cooperative courses with Southwest State University and Southwest Technical College that give students both high school and postsecondary credit. Vaadeland believes "this has been a real plus."[14]

Such experiences are not unique. A 1996 survey of Minnesota high school principals found that more than half (52 percent) reported that one impact of the postsecondary options had been to "increase cooperative efforts between high schools and post-secondary institutions."[15] It is not just the Minnesota high school students who attend colleges and universities who gain from the Post-Secondary Enrollment Options Program. People who gain from such laws include the students who remain in traditional public schools. That is what happened in Massachusetts.

Effect of Charter School Legislation in Boston

The 1993 Massachusetts charter school law gives local school districts no authorizing or supervisory power over charter schools. Noting school board resistance to charter schools in other states, the Massachusetts legislature decided to bypass local districts. Individuals and groups wishing to establish charter schools go directly to the Massachusetts Executive Office of Education, a state agency.

In Boston, it soon became clear that a number of local people and groups were eager to start charter schools under the new legislation. They included innovative teachers already employed by the district, local community groups, parents, and a few companies. Eighteen of the first sixty-four charter school proposals in Massachusetts came from Boston, and five of the first fifteen approved charter schools were located in Boston. This message was not lost on local school district and union officials. The Boston public schools and the Boston Teachers Union did not sit back passively during this initial period. Even as the legislature was considering the charter concept, the school district and local teachers union had been discussing the possibility of creating a within-district chartering policy.

Their disagreements about this policy had not been resolved when the charter law passed. However, within six months of the law's adoption, the Boston Teachers Union and school district had reached agreement about what they call *pilot schools*. The pilot school program allows local teachers to apply to the district and union for waivers of any or all provisions of district policies and the union master contract. In the fall of 1995, five pilot schools opened in Boston. Moreover, the Boston pilot school program has at least one feature that makes it even more attractive to prospective school founders than the state charter school law. The pilot school program includes start-up funds, which the state legislation did not offer to charter schools. One charter school has actually changed over to become a pilot school.

When the charter school law was passed, Boston public school administrators Larry Myatt and Linda Nathan saw a great opportunity to create the kind of school they had been seeking for more than a decade. In 1983, they had established Fenway Middle

College High School as a school within a school, designed to serve a true cross-section of the city's secondary students. In 1992, they were delighted that the state chose their school to be one of the fifteen original charter schools. As they wrote, "We saw the charter movement as an answer to the four kinds of autonomy we had always coveted: the power to create our own budget, based on teaching, learning and counseling needs; the freedom to teach our own curriculum and to grant diplomas by portfolio and exhibition; the ability to hire the best teachers regardless of union and central office restrictions; and the unhindered pursuit of a new brand of intimate, supportive governance to be provided by our own Board, independent of a rigid bureaucracy and a political school committee."[16]

However, Myatt and Nathan were also pleased when the pilot school program was created: "In a spring-time moment of enlightenment and opportunism, a host of former antagonists suddenly came together. . . . [T]hanks to the Charter initiative, Boston had 'seen the light' and we had been offered a wonderful opportunity to actually help push the system along."

Part of Fenway Middle College High School's goal was to produce improvement in other Boston schools, not just to create an individual innovative school. After considerable discussion, Myatt and Nathan applied to the school district for permission to be a pilot school. Recognizing the value of their ideas, along with their skill implementing those ideas, the Boston school committee named their school one of the first five pilot schools. In the summer of 1994, Fenway was wooed both by the state and the Boston public schools. What a nice situation for a school—to be able to select from a couple of potential sponsors and to ask important questions about which sponsor offered greater technical assistance, security, and responsiveness. Such an opportunity is available to educators only when two or more organizations have been authorized to sponsor charter schools. Believing that being a pilot school would allow them greater opportunities to work toward broader improvement in Boston, Myatt and Nathan chose pilot over charter school status.

As 1996 opened, they experienced some frustration with the Boston school officials: "Half way through our first Pilot Year, we are yet to find the going easy with the school department. Although in theory the central administration is supportive of the need to create more autonomous school units, changing past practice has proven to be difficult. Issues such as burdensome monitoring/compliance paperwork, purchasing procedures, arranging payment for teacher overtime and stipends, and the use of consultants"[17] still cause anxiety and frustration.

Regardless of their experience with the pilot school program, Myatt and Nathan cite it as a positive response to the charter school legislation. Give credit to the Boston School Committee and to the Boston Teachers Union. Faced with a challenge, the two groups created new opportunities. This is the kind of thing we may see much more of around the country, if states are willing to adopt strong charter school legislation giving charter proponents the opportunity to apply for sponsorship from some group other than a local board.

Effect of Charter School Legislation in Jefferson County, Colorado

The partly suburban, partly rural district of Jefferson County, Colorado, had been frustrating parents for years. More than one thousand students were on waiting lists for the district's alternative public schools. For seven years, parents had pleaded unsuccessfully for these award-winning programs to be replicated. Like most other public school districts, Jefferson County felt it did not have to respond to this customer demand. After all, it was the only place for people living in the district to get free public education.

The district's superintendent was a strong opponent of public school choice, as he had been in his previous position in Minnesota, and an outspoken critic of Colorado's charter public school law. According to M. A. Raywid's report in the national education magazine *Phi Delta Kappa*,[18] this superintendent recommended to the school board that "no district facilities be turned over to charter schools." A Denver newspaper criticized this proposal as a "most alarming misreading of the charter law and spirit," and a state legislator accused the superintendent of "a flagrant disregard for the law."[19]

The state Senate Education Committee endorsed a law that amended existing law to require districts to make empty schools available for charter schools. Meanwhile, Jefferson County parents were pleading with the local board to approve either new alternative schools or, in several cases, new charter schools. The superintendent wrote an editorial strongly criticizing public school choice and charter schools, and the school board turned down six of the eight proposals submitted to it.

The two charter schools that were approved represented significantly different approaches. One, Jefferson Academy, was an elementary program for about 190 students and featured a back-to-basics curriculum. The other was a K–12 school of about 450 students that used a highly innovative approach reflected in part by its name, the Community Involved Charter School (CICS).

Pressure continued to build on the local board to respond to parents, teachers, and community members who wanted different kinds of schools in the district, but the charter law also allowed advocates to appeal to the state board of education, which could direct the local school district to try to work out an agreement with charter proponents. This gave the district's frustrated parents additional clout. Finally, "following seven years of inaction, in the spring of 1994 when the first round of charter school proposals was being reviewed, the school board actively sought proposals for new alternative schools to function as options within the district. In fact, it invited both CICS and Jefferson Academy to become alternative schools within the district, rather than charter schools."[20]

By the end of the 1993–94 school year, Jefferson County had more than doubled the number of innovative schools it offered to families. Colorado's charter law had encouraged the local school board to listen to parents who had been ignored for years. As Raywid concludes, "It would appear that the district has become considerably more willing to heed the preferences of its constituents."[21]

Effect of Charter School Legislation in Detroit

Unlike many of the other school superintendents depicted in this chapter, the Detroit, Michigan, superintendent counts himself as a charter school supporter. David Snead has publicly recommended that Detroit sponsor charter schools. In a state that allows public universities as well as local school districts to sponsor charter schools, Snead believes that districts have three charter school options:[22]

Decide not to be involved in the charter opportunity. If you
make that decision, you simply decide to decline the
opportunity to grant charters.

Do what we did in Detroit and decide that you will become a
district that will grant charters.

Decide to sit on the sidelines and wait and see what happens
with those of us who decide to go for it.

Snead selected the second option because he did not want the
district to lose the opportunity to influence the kind of charters
started in the district and because he did not want the district to
lose students, along with revenues. Moreover, "just as important as
the loss of revenue is the potential loss of outstanding teachers, administrators, principals, and educational leaders who end up looking elsewhere for an opportunity to lead." Furthermore, Snead
looks forward to being a potential source of services for charter
schools, which have the right to purchase services where they
please. He says, "We welcome the opportunity because we can be
as competitive as anyone else. . . . When charter schools look
around to find those services, we know they will often turn to us."[23]

A year after making this statement, Snead was even more supportive of the charter concept. "We're finding the charter idea is
helping encourage other schools in our district to examine what
they are doing," he told me. "I don't agree with those who are de-
fensive. We are proud of many things about the Detroit schools.
But we can, and must do better. Charter schools are helping us
move in the right direction."[24]

Competition Produces Educational Benefits

Giving more than one organization the opportunity to offer public education can produce broader and wider educational improvements than seemed possible before. It is not just the students
who attend Boston, Jefferson County, or Detroit charter schools
who are benefiting from their state's laws. People who gain from
school choice laws include those students who remain in the traditional schools and are given new opportunities within those
schools.

Sometimes simply proposing a charter school produces a positive response. In Rochester, Minnesota, a private nonsectarian

Montessori school asked the local school board for a charter. The board then decided instead to create its own Montessori school. After the district's successful experience with that Montessori public school, the board responded again to dissatisfied parents, this time to those who wanted a more traditional elementary school option. According to veteran Rochester school board member Carol Carryer, "We learned that working with parents to help create the kind of distinctive schools they think make sense is much better than trying to satisfy everyone by offering the same kind of school for all students and families."[25]

The school system in Forest Lake, Minnesota, went through a similar reappraisal. For several years, it had rejected parents' request for a Montessori elementary school. When the parents began to discuss going to another district to get sponsorship for a Montessori charter school, the Forest Lake School Board changed its mind and agreed to create a Montessori school.

The superintendent of Northfield, Minnesota, public schools reported that a proposal in his district for a charter school "made it easier to change things. If we weren't progressive enough and didn't change, then somebody else would come along and do it for us." After the district turned down the charter proposal, it did create a Spanish-language immersion program option for first and second graders, introduce optional multi-age classrooms, and enrich the math program for middle schoolers.[26]

The Boston-based Pioneer Institute reports several "ripple effects" of that state's charter school law in addition to the effect described earlier. For example, the Nauset regional school district is opening a new school within a school to compete with the Cape Cod Lighthouse Charter School, and Marblehead's middle school site council is implementing reforms described in a Marblehead Charter School proposal.[27]

The Duluth, Minnesota, superintendent, Mark Myles, recently recommended that his board request proposals from groups interested in opening an elementary charter school in a vacant building. The Duluth School Board had turned down several charter proposals, but a local university was seriously considering sponsoring a charter. George Balach, Duluth school board member who had opposed earlier charter proposals, was quoted in the local paper as saying it was time to take action or be left behind: "We recognize that charter schools are here to stay, and we don't want to be in a situation where this is foisted on us. If we're viewed as standing in the way, somebody will eventually go around us. The pathway is there."[28]

Finally, it's worth reviewing Randy Quinn's reaction to the Colorado charter school legislation. Quinn is executive director of the Colorado Association of School Boards and a self-described initial opponent of the state's charter legislation, which allows an appeal to the state board of education for review if a local school board turns down a charter proposal. However, in a column that appeared shortly after the charter legislation passed, Quinn reflected on the possible impact of that legislation, noting, "Rather than serving as provider, the board has an opportunity to become the purchaser of education services on behalf of the citizens of the community served by the board. This is a role that opens up all kinds of possibilities for school boards." Quinn suggested that school boards might

Identify the kinds of schools a community wants through a broad strategic planning process and then "charter" some provider to deliver those programs.

Consider whether a business, an industry, or another form of government might be willing to cooperate in providing physical facilities to house a public school.

View charter schools as a way to respond to "competing philosophies" among parents.

Quinn concluded, in an open, thoughtful way, "Colorado school boards would be well advised to tap the depths of their creative insight to examine how this new concept best can serve their communities' children. . . . Moving away from the role of exclusive provider of education service may be a blessing in disguise."[29]

These examples illustrate how school districts respond to charter schools, whether existing or proposed, by reexamining and trying to improve what happens in the traditional public schools. Such ripple effects are exactly what charter school proponents hope will happen as legislation expands to allow more charter schools. But when states pass weak charter school laws, frustration mounts, as in the examples given earlier of school boards that could block proposals because there was no other organization that could sponsor charter schools.

The local school board monopoly should end. Lawyers and doctors are able to establish and operate professional partnerships accountable to the public. Public school educators should have this professional status and similar opportunities while being accountable to the public for results. They should not be restricted to obtaining permission from a local school board before they can create the kind of school they think makes sense. They should be able to go to a statewide authorizing agency with a charter school proposal that the agency can accept or reject. That is what is happening in states such as New Jersey, Massachusetts, Delaware, and Arizona (see Appendix A). Every teacher in every state should have the charter school option.

Many teachers have enormous talent and energy, but in addition to their frustrations with the kinds of education they are able to deliver in the public education system, they have also been frustrated by the way administrators and school boards have often treated them. They have sometimes complained of a "Father Knows Best" attitude from administrators. Discontented teachers have formed unions. The next chapter examines how teachers unions have reacted to the charter school concept.

Chapter Four

A New Role for Unions

In most states, teachers unions have tried to prevent the charter school concept from getting a real test. The idea threatens their power and their concept of how public education ought to operate. However, because some legislators of both parties have stood up to this opposition, and because some charter schools are having real, measurable success, some teachers union leaders and members are rethinking their opposition.

Unions have made important contributions to social progress in this country. It is important to recognize their significant, valuable role and to discuss how the charter movement can provide new opportunities not only for educators but also for their unions.

So this chapter looks back not just at the history of struggle over charter schools but at the kinds of conflicts unions have faced and the way unions have evolved. It tries to describe fairly the ways unions have challenged the charter concept and the ways unions might, and in some cases are, changing to create new roles for themselves and new opportunities for their members.

Many people in the charter school movement recognize the long central role unions have played in advancing justice and economic opportunity in this country. Unions developed in the 1800s and 1900s in response to powerful corporations that exploited workers. The organizing of autoworkers, coal and iron ore miners, textile and garment makers, farm- and steelworkers, and the like is a proud part of the nation's history. A few powerful corporate owners were making enormous fortunes at the expense of their employees. Those employees frequently were treated like little more than peasants or chattel. Let's be clear—unions have played a distinguished role in representing their members, winning them a healthier work environment and a more prosperous life.

Unions have been an important part of broader efforts to work for justice. Many unions made major financial contributions to the civil rights movement in the South. Owing to their financial contributions and their participation in demonstrations, unions were rightly viewed as allies by many people who devoted their lives to expanding people's economic, legal, and educational opportunities.

At one time, unions were weak and struggling. Their members were harassed, beaten, and gassed as they attempted to gain a living wage. Organizing workers was a dangerous, low-paying job. But many of today's unions are powerful and well funded. Union conferences are held in some of the nation's most beautiful and expensive hotels and resorts. Unions have hundreds of thousands, and in some cases millions of members, and play key roles in elections throughout the nation. They are no longer powerless, and many members of the public no longer view them as weak or struggling. Indeed, in some ways they have become part of the powerful establishment they were established to challenge and confront.

Ironically, some of the people most frustrated by the unions are excellent teachers, tired of being told by union organizers, "Don't stay around too long after school, you'll make the other teachers look bad." Or, as happened in the case of one community, "Don't give up your lunch period once a month." The latter became an issue when a group of elementary public school teachers created an innovative school within a school. The teachers wanted a closer working relationship with parents, so they started meeting with parents once a month at noon to review how things were going at the school and to discuss ways parents could help students at home. The parents were delighted, but the local union went to the local school board to protest that these teachers were violating the labor-management agreement by giving up their "duty-free lunch."

The innovative school teachers were stunned and hurt by this opposition. However, because these teachers had volunteered to meet with the parents, and because program parents and teachers spoke eloquently about the value of the monthly meetings, the school board decided not to ban the meetings, which was what the local teachers union was asking. The union then sent a regional union organizer to try to convince the teachers to stop meeting with parents at lunch. The teachers listened politely, thanked him for his compliments about their dedication, and told him that they would continue meeting with parents.

But the story does not end there. An outside consultant's evaluation found that students' achievement was improving steadily. Nevertheless, the school board did not responded to parent requests to expand the program, in part because none of the other local elementary school teachers volunteered to teach in the innovative school, despite requests from administrators. Moreover, two teachers have left the program for personal reasons, and neither has been replaced. In this case, the school district is not responding to parents or to evidence of improved achievement. The parents are asking for expansion of a successful program that costs no more money than the traditional program. But with union opposition, the program is controversial, and the board is trying to keep the peace. So family preferences are ignored.

This kind of mentality frustrates teachers like Jaime Escalante, who inspired the movie *Stand and Deliver*. Escalante reports that one reason he left Los Angeles was that union leaders criticized him for having too many students in his calculus class. In a letter to his union president, Escalante wrote, "If you looked into what is going on in this school in the name of the union, I think you . . . would be appalled."[1]

Many union officials privately acknowledge these problems. They think schools have to change and sometimes are frustrated by resistance from some of their members. Some have pointed out that supporting school reform can get them in trouble with many union members, who in various polls say their highest priorities for the unions are that they work for higher wages and better working conditions for teachers.

So far, most unions have fought the charter school concept, seeing it as a direct threat to their power. Much of a union's work is to bargain on behalf of teachers, taking the teachers' point of view against administrators and school board members. This arrangement assumes that teachers have relatively little power beyond what happens in the individual classroom. The charter school breaks apart this notion. Suddenly, teachers can, and often are, running schools. The teachers decide whether the school needs a principal, and if so, who it will be. The teachers decide the school's budget. Teachers and other members of a charter school board select the faculty, not on the basis of seniority but by determining who will do the best job with students. The board and the teachers set salaries and working conditions. They may decide to work longer hours or more days than teachers at nearby public schools. Teachers develop the evaluation process (which in most charter schools involves yearly assessment and feedback).

Giving this kind of power to individual schools threatens many unions. They have helped construct an adversary system in which decision making is often "us against them." Using the factory model of production and management, many teachers unions have promoted the idea that seniority should decides who gets a job and, when layoffs occur, who loses a job. Unions have also helped create a situation in which it is difficult to fire a teacher.

As part of their opposition, unions have tried to depict charter school legislation as just as bad an idea as vouchers. But now that President Clinton and many state legislators who oppose vouchers support charter schools, unions have had to do some rethinking. In many states, this has meant that they have tried to weaken rather than to oppose charter legislation.

However, some union officials have realized that charter schools provide important new opportunities for their members and can lead to important new roles for the unions themselves. Despite all the opposition, there are grounds for hope.

This remainder of this chapter looks at some specific examples of union opposition in several different states, at attempts to weaken legislation and to intimidate potential sponsors, and finally, at the ways unions have already changed, the ways they seem to be changing in relation to charter schools, and the reasons they should change more.

Opposition to Charter School Legislation

In many states, teachers unions fought charter school legislation. A federally funded study of the first eleven states that adopted charter legislation found that "none of the charter school bills passed the state legislature without controversy, and much of the opposition came from teacher unions. Unions generally opposed charter schools because the laws shift power, particularly in the areas of funding and personnel, away from the district and the master contract to the individual schools."[2]

Former public school teacher and chair of the California Senate Education Committee Gary Hart reports, "The California Teachers Association (CTA) brought its immense power against efforts to create a charter law which give teachers freedom to create the kind of school they thought made sense. The CTA would only support a law which retained union authority over charter schools."[3] Hart, a Democrat, had hoped to have teachers union support for his charter school bill. He had a good working relationship with the union as chair of the California Senate Education Committee. But he found that the union "intensely opposed" the bill. He added a provision requiring a certain number of teacher signatures for any charter school proposal, but that did not satisfy the union. What it really wanted, he concluded, was veto authority over charter schools. It did not want schools to be able to depart from the master contract without the union's permission.

Colorado charter school advocate and former alternative school teacher Mary Ellen Sweeney tells a similar story. She reports that the Colorado Education Association (CEA) "lobbied actively to kill the [charter school] bill, and at the last minute when it was apparent that the bill would pass they supported the bill."[4] She also notes that the union's opposition to the charter bill was inconsistent with its other actions: "The irony of this situation is that they [the CEA] have stated that they want teachers to be empowered to create new programs and schools." Representative Peggy Kerns, a Colorado Democrat who coauthored that state's charter law, says that individual teachers have joined the charter movement more quickly than their teacher organizations. This may be changing, she says, as the Colorado Education Association is helping Colorado Springs teachers create a new charter school. This school will serve students who have not done well in conventional public schools. On the other hand, Kerns notes that in 1996 the CEA opposed her efforts to lift the cap on the number of charter schools and to obtain the same per-pupil funding for charter schools as other schools receive.

Massachusetts and Michigan legislators tell parallel stories. Massachusetts charter advocates described "strong opposition and hostility" from teacher unions.[5] The unions opposed the original Massachusetts charter legislation, according to former governor's special assistant, Steve Wilson. "When we first proposed the charter legislation, the Massachusetts Teachers Association [MTA] openly attacked the idea. They said it would 'destroy public education.'"[6] Despite this, Massachusetts charter school proponents succeeded in passing a law that allowed interested groups to apply directly to the state. In the original round of applications, sixty-four groups applied to the Massachusetts State Executive Office of Education for its sponsorship. But the legislation also reflected pressure from the MTA; it allowed the state office of education to sponsor only twenty-five charter schools.

After the legislation passed, the MTA simply shifted its sights to oppose expanding the law to allow more charter schools, despite the fact that almost one hundred groups have now applied for charters through three rounds of applications and that the existing charters are attracting many students and, according to Wilson, "winning praise from both newspaper editors on both the left and right." Wilson describes the MTA's new strategy as continued opposition to expanding the bill and as trying to find ways to weaken what exists. The MTA has strongly, and to date successfully, resisted efforts to permit more than twenty-five charter schools in the state, despite the number of applications.

Michigan charter school advocates encountered similar vigorous, continuing union opposition. A federally funded study of charter legislation noted that "the Michigan Education Association spent 2 million dollars in advertisements against the charter school bill and its chief sponsor, Governor Engler."[7] A Michigan Education Association (MEA) publication entitled *Michigan—The Far Right's New Frontier* defines the far right as "one of a number of terms used to describe individuals/organizations who seek to impose their religious, political and personal beliefs and opinions on others, usually through deceptive practices, personal attacks, political connivery or stealth activities."[8] The publication then lists far right activities in Michigan, asserting "It's All Part of the Same Plot." Included in the list are demonstrations against outcome-based education, requests to teach abstinence, and the "academy schools [charter schools] statute passed by the Michigan legislature."[9] Calling charter schools a far right activity would come as a surprise to President Clinton, who as noted earlier endorsed the idea in a number of speeches around the nation. Nevertheless, Michigan charter advocates note that the MEA vigorously opposed the charter school concept and the state's governor, John Engler, who proposed it.

Union opposition to Minnesota's charter school legislation has been partly described in Chapter One. The Minnesota Education Association (MEA) called the proposed charter school legislation "a costly hoax" and sent a letter to Minnesota state senators stating that "the Minnesota Education Association is opposed to chartered schools."[10] The MEA president predicted that charter schools "may turn out to be the biggest boondoggle since New Coke" and concluded that "charter schools are just plain bad public policy."[11]

The Minnesota Federation of Teachers (MFT) was just as opposed to charter schools. It laid out clearly what it wanted: a non-charter-school charter school law. The MFT unanimously passed a resolution stating it would support only

> legislative initiates [*sic*] for alternative schools including chartered schools that require
>
> 1. that all teachers staffing the school hold a valid license under the provisions of the Board of Teaching;
> 2. that all staff be a part of the bargaining unit in the district that authorize [*sic*] the school;
> 3. that the school be required to comply with the master agreement of employee groups in the authorizing district; and
>
> be it further resolved that only local districts be authorized to establish any style of alternative or chartered schools.[12]

In 1993, MFT president Sandra Peterson reiterated her opposition to the 1991 charter school legislation that had been passed, alleging, among other things, that charter school teachers have no bargaining rights. (In fact, charter school teachers in Minnesota have much more power than teachers in conventional schools. Minnesota charter school teachers must, by law, make up a majority of the board running the charter school. This board makes critical decisions about the charter school, such as wages and working conditions, and it develops evaluation and other personnel policies.)

In many states, teachers unions successfully resisted charter school legislation. As of early 1996, the unions had helped prevent such legislation from being adopted in Washington, Vermont, Virginia, Indiana, and Nevada. The Nevada case illustrates how some state teachers unions fought the concept. Ricci Elkins, a parent who worked hard on the charter school program, recalls that "Nevada Education Association [NEA] staff called charter school people 'elitists' who were out to destroy public education. They said we were just interested in getting public funds for private schools. Neither of these charges was true, but the NEA repeated them again and again."[13]

The elitism charge is particularly ironic because, in most states, unions have not opposed creation of magnet schools, which have admissions tests and are allowed to spend more money per pupil than other schools in the district. Which is more elite, a charter public school that cannot screen out students and receives the state's average per-pupil funding or a magnet public school that screens out students on the basis of an admission test and that spends a thousand dollars per pupil more than another public school a few blocks away?

Elkins recalls that some legislators encouraged the charter school advocates and the Nevada Education Association lobbyists to sit down and try to resolve some differences. The proponents were willing to do this, but as Elkins recalls, "Nevada Education Association staff refused to meet with us to discuss the legislation, even after some legislators encouraged them to talk things over and try to find common ground. It was attack, attack, attack. And many legislators told us privately that the NEA played key roles in campaigns, so a lot of legislators were reluctant to cross the union."

It was a somewhat similar story in Vermont. The state senate passed a modest charter school bill in 1994 and 1995. But with strong opposition from the Vermont Education Association (VEA) along with other state education groups, the Vermont house has refused to pass any form of charter school law.

These dual efforts—block expansion and weaken the concept—are being used throughout the country. State NEA affiliates in most states are vigorously opposing strong charter school legislation. In some states, they are trying to stop any legislation in this area from being adopted. In other states, they are helping to weaken proposed legislation or to find legislative sponsors who will introduce weak charter bills.

Efforts to Weaken Charter School Legislation

Within two years of the first charter school legislation in 1991, state teachers union strategy changed in many states. In some places, teachers unions continued to fight hard and successfully against any kind of charter school. However, it had become obvious to unions all over the country that the charter school notion appealed to many legislators, including those who had and in many cases continued to oppose education vouchers. Indeed, support for charter schools from President Clinton and Secretary Riley, both of whom opposed vouchers, showed just how high the level of support had become.

By 1993, with strong leadership from Democrats, charter school legislation had passed in two more states: California and Colorado. In each case, the chief advocates were Democrats whom the teachers unions had regarded as allies. None of them supported vouchers for private or parochial schools. Colorado governor Roy Romer, state senator Gary Hart of California, and state senator Ember Reichgott-Junge of Minnesota all had been endorsed by teachers unions and had worked for many of the things teachers unions wanted. These people could not be dismissed as "anti–public education." Reichgott-Junge wrote an eloquent column for Minnesota's largest newspaper, titled, "Charter Schools Will Work Better Than Private School Vouchers."[14] She pointed out that charter schools will do a better job of innovation, provide fair competition, and be more inclusive than many private or parochial schools. She addressed Governor Arne Carlson's recent letter to legislators, in which he had praised charter schools while arguing that "vouchers are the next step in school choice." Reichgott-Junge responded, "I say, Wrong."

With charter school proponents, many with long records of supporting public education and criticizing vouchers, it has become harder for unions to criticize charter schools as just another form of a voucher system. When unions have argued that charter schools are elitist, charter school proponents have pointed out that charter schools cannot pick and choose among students. When unions have argued that charter schools benefit primarily white, wealthy students, charter school proponents have pointed out that many of the nation's charter schools are serving predominantly students from low-income, racially diverse families.

So state teachers unions switched tactics. They began to say they were in favor of charter school laws as long as those laws were of the right kind (that is, posed no threat to the power of school boards and teachers unions).

In Louisiana, when teachers union officials met with state senator Cecil Picard and other legislators to tell them of union support for charter school legislation and the union's desire to work with legislators on this concept, it became clear that union officials wanted legislation that gave local public school boards the exclusive right to establish charter schools. When asked why they wanted such a restrictive law, union officials replied that they thought it was important to "give local districts a chance to try this idea."[15] But of course, local Louisiana districts already had the option of creating innovative schools and had done so only in a few cases, primarily as a way to promote integration (via magnet schools) or to create schools for disruptive students (via alternative schools). Ultimately, Senator Picard felt he did not have wide enough support to overcome union opposition to a stronger bill, so Louisiana's charter school legislation allows only a small number of charter schools to be established and gives only local school boards the power to sponsor them.

Washington State charter school proponents encountered a similar strategy to weaken legislation. "We do support charter schools," asserted Teresa Moore, assistant executive director of the Washington Education Association (WEA).[16] But the charter school bill WEA "supported" allows only local school boards to sponsor charter schools. The WEA opposed other legislation that permitted appeals to the state superintendent of schools. And the WEA-endorsed bill allowed a total of only twenty-seven charter schools around the state, while a stronger bill allowed an unlimited number of charters.

Editorials in state newspapers early in March challenged the Washington Education Association. The lead editorial in the *Tacoma Times,* a newspaper in the state's second largest city, criticized the state's largest teachers union because "the Washington

Education Association and other parts of the public school establishment wish the whole charter schools movement would go away." In praising the charter school approach, the editorial insisted that "parents . . . deserve a wider range of public school choices for their children."[17]

The *Aberdeen Daily World* urged that "the Senate this week should shirk off its jitters about the consequences of making the Washington Education Association unhappy and follow the House's lead by backing a strong charter school plan."[18]

Another newspaper also urged support for charter schools: "A charter schools law, such as the one outlined in HB 2910 (which the Washington House passed), would give parents and educators the ability to work outside the established education bureaucracy and apply new approaches to teaching. This is a proposition that alarms many within that bureaucracy. Understandably. But it's just the sort of flexibility that motivated teachers and an increasing number of parents have been seeking."[19]

Finally, a column by a *Seattle Times* editorial writer who endorsed the charter school concept described a Washington Education Association (WEA) meeting for teachers, who went expecting to learn ways to improve their schools, "but . . . instead they found themselves in a campaign strategy session. According to one teacher who attended, a WEA leader depicted charter school as "partisan," "anti government and racist, a ploy promoted by 'arch conservatives' and the 'religious right.' " The columnist concluded, "This is nonsense. Arch-conservatives generally don't support charter schools, they want vouchers. Liberals are cowed by the union. So charter schools are supported by moderate Democrats and Republicans and have been set up primarily in progressive states."[20] Washington has yet to pass charter school legislation.

Arkansas Education Association (AEA) officials adopted a different strategy. They helped develop the charter school legislation, including two key provisions: first, only local school boards would be allowed to sponsor charter schools; and second, the local teachers union would have to approve each charter school proposal before it could be approved by the local school board. Almost a year has passed since the law was enacted, and the state department of education reports it has received "a total of one inquiry from a school district that wants to establish a charter school."[21] (As a later chapter explains, stronger laws produce much greater responses.)

New Jersey Education Association (NJEA) officials were able to delay adoption of a strong charter school bill for several years. Several New Jersey legislators reported that "early on, the toughest opposition to the charter schools idea came from the New Jersey Education Association."[22] But legislators in that state persevered, made some concessions, and finally succeeded in adopting one of the nation's strongest charter school laws, allowing up to 135 charter schools. The New Jersey legislation also stipulates that all charters will be awarded by the state. However, A *New York Times* story noted that the NJEA, representing 149,000 educators, had an impact on many of the law's details.[23] For example, any existing public school whose faculty want to convert to charter school status will be bound by the local labor-management agreement. The NJEA may regret this provision because it makes conversion (and close ties between a charter school and the district) less likely. The union also succeeded in convincing the legislature that all charter school teachers must be certified and in preventing existing private nonsectarian schools, even those that have no admissions test, from converting to charter schools.

Policy makers in Delaware and Louisiana report a similar pattern: state union officials tried and, because of their political power, succeeded in weakening both states' bills. The Delaware law allows only five charters per year over the next three years, though both local boards and the state board can sponsor charter schools. The Louisiana bill allows a total of only eight charters, and permits only local school boards to sponsor them.

Unions have also tried to intervene at the level of individual charter school proposals. For example, Dennis Michael Mah, principal of the Bowling Green Elementary, a charter school in Sacramento, reports that the local teachers union opposed that school's conversion to a charter school when the school decided it did not want to follow the local labor-management agreement. Ironically, before it became a charter school, Bowling Green was identified as one of the lowest-achieving schools in the Sacramento City Unified District. The amount of state money it lost because of poor attendance was the highest among the approximately sixty elementary schools in the district. During Bowling Green's first year as a charter school, student attendance was the highest it had been in five years. The union's intense opposition has continued until recently when, as Bowling Green students showed improved individual achievement and attendance, the union wrote a letter to the school board supporting an extension of Bowling Green's contract.

However, despite the increased performance and attendance from this charter school's students, the union has pushed hard on the district to restrict the freedom it gives to charter schools. In the most recent local union–school board negotiations, Mah reports, the district agreed that from now on, it will insist that any new charter schools follow the same contractual procedures as are outlined for other schools in the district.[24]

Eric Premack, who has helped teachers in California develop charter school proposals, points to many instances of the California Teachers Association threatening and intimidating teachers who had signed petitions supportive of charter schools in their districts.[25]

Intimidation

In some states, teachers union officials have attempted to stop creation of charter schools by intimidating organizations that are considering sponsoring them. University officials in Michigan and Minnesota report direct threats made by union officials when the universities considered sponsoring a charter school. One of the first threats was made against Saginaw Valley State University (SVSU) in Michigan. The executive director of the Michigan Education Association's Regional 12-D Uni-Serve Office, wrote a letter to the president of Saginaw State, stating the criteria the MEA and others had developed that the MEA wanted the university to follow: "SVSU cannot operate any charter schools on its campus"; "charter schools must adhere to collective bargaining agreements and maintain collaborative relations with the local MEA"; "the local school district in which the charter school would exist must authorize the institution along with SVSU"; and "home school districts can include students in charter schools in their state count which determines the amount of financial aid paid annually."[26]

Adherence to these conditions would dramatically restrict the freedom of charter schools to establish independent arrangements for teachers, eliminate the possibility of housing a school in unused or underused space on campus, give local districts the right to veto a charter school operating in "their" district, and send the money allocated by the state for the students attending the charter school to the district. Following such criteria would effectively eliminate the possibility of independent charter schools.

Moreover, the MEA letter threatened the university, stating that

if your university establishes charter schools exclusive of adopting the recommended criteria from our work group, the MEA will

1. Strongly encourage the teachers we represent to discontinue accepting the placement of SVSU student teachers;
2. Encourage professional staff to decline any involvement with the University relative to professional development or graduate course studies, etc.;
3. Encourage our members to refrain from any monetary contributions as alumni or University supporters;
4. Encourage local school Superintendents and Boards of Education to discontinue their support and participation in University programs.[27]

Saginaw Valley State University president Gilbertson responded to the letter by calling it a "naked threat against our students. . . . [T]here's no way the university can tolerate an attempt to intimidate it from exercising any of its lawful options. That sort of intimidation—the threat to take action against our students because someone might not like what the university does as a matter of policy—seems to me to be possibly illegal, and most certainly unacceptable in any other way as well."[28] Those were strong, thoughtful words. But as of March 1996, Saginaw State University has sponsored only one charter school.

Saginaw State University is not the only Michigan postsecondary institution to be threatened by union officials. Jim Goenner, senior associate director of the charter school office at Central Michigan University (CMU), reports similar direct and indirect threats against his university. Goenner regrets the intimidation, observing, "We think sponsoring charter schools is an important, valuable role for the University. We believe these charter schools offer an important, valuable option for students, educators, and families."[29]

Recently, according to a local newspaper report, a Michigan Education Association (MEA) local president wrote to Grand Valley State University (GVSU) School of Education criticizing that institution for sponsoring a charter school and commenting that "there is no justification for charter schools."[30] In his letter, the local president said that in the future he might not accept student teachers from the university because of its sponsorship of charter schools. He also sent copies of his letter to all teachers in his area.

Jim Goenner believes the kind of intimidation these three Michigan universities received is having an impact. Although CMU has sponsored of number of charter schools, "most of the Michigan public universities which are eligible to sponsor charter schools are not doing so. I've talked with officials from other universities who have made it clear that they are hesitant to undertake the political battles associated with chartering schools."[31]

Central Michigan University has also felt heat from the MEA in another way. Recently, plans were developed for the university, the Michigan Partnership for New Education, and the Traverse City Public Schools to apply for a $300,000 teacher training grant. The three partners would have set up a professional development school designed to train teachers and help improve teacher preparation by giving prospective teachers more experience in working with elementary and secondary students. The Michigan Partnership for New Education already operates nineteen professional practice schools around the state. However, early in 1996, "the Traverse City district put plans on hold after the teachers union's newsletter asked members not to support the grant because of the involvement of CMU and the Michigan Partnership," even though the Traverse City superintendent would have liked to submit the grant and carry out the proposal and felt that failing to do so "deprived our staff of a learning opportunity and deprived our school district and our region of much needed dollars."[32]

Threats also have been made against a Minnesota university campus after it began developing plans to sponsor a charter school. A university official reports that a local union official called to say that if the university sponsored the charter school, he would make sure that none of the students had an opportunity to student teach in the community. Ultimately, the university decided not to sponsor the charter school.

Other university officials in Minnesota report similar threats. They come at a time of competition for funding, when university officials do not want to alienate potential financial supporters, and a time of competition for students, when universities do not wish to anger secondary teachers who may suggest that students not go to a particular university.

The threats in Minnesota are having an effect. A year after the legislature authorized public universities to sponsor charter schools, not a single one has done so. There have been conversations between charter school proponents and university officials. But to date, not one has led to sponsorship.

Union Change in the Past

Teachers unions have evolved. In most states, they have the right to bargain with the school district, but they did not always have this power, and at one time, the National Education Association (NEA) did not support collective bargaining. The NEA represented teachers and administrators at first, but gradually it came to represent teachers only and to push for the right to bargain on behalf of teachers. In many states, it won that right. It also won the power, in many states, to take money for the bargaining it does on teachers' behalf even from teachers who are not union members. The American Federation of Teachers (AFT) also has changed over time. At one time, the AFT focused primarily on organizing teachers, and it never welcomed administrative members, as the NEA did. But the AFT has now expanded its membership, working hard in some communities to organize teachers aides and other paraprofessionals.

At one time, the NEA and AFT saw each other as intense rivals. But this also is changing. In communities from San Francisco to New York City, the two unions have merged on the local level. In some states, they have signed formal agreements pledging they will no longer compete against each other for the right to represent teachers in a district. Nationally, after years of criticizing each other intensely, the two national unions are talking about forming one organization.

The point is that teachers unions have often rethought the ways they operate, to their benefit.

Recent Union Change

Rethinking the way it operates is exactly what an organization must do if it wishes simply to maintain, much less expand, its power and effectiveness. The charter school movement offers teachers unions a chance to rethink themselves again, and it has been fascinating to watch the different directions the NEA and the AFT have taken in reacting to the charter school concept.

As we saw in Chapter Two, AFT president Albert Shanker, a principal proponent of charter schools in the 1980s, has more recently written vigorously against them. In 1993, for example, he insisted that "vouchers, charter schools and for profit management schemes are all quick fixes that won't fix anything."[33] Some youngsters attending charter schools and their families would dispute the idea that these schools "won't fix anything." Shanker has also questioned the charter school idea because "our education system has not even decided the business of schools."[34]

Shanker argued that we need national standards, curricula, and assessments. When we have such a system, then "it makes sense to give people in the schools the freedom to decide on how to meet the standards—on things like how the school day should be structured and how best to teach their particular students to read, write and count."[35] Note there is no suggestion that teachers have the right to decide their salaries and working conditions or whether they will be members of a union.

It is ironic that Shanker would make such arguments, given that he is one of the people most responsible for introducing the charter school concept to policy makers. But that concept has shifted in an important way since Shanker first wrote about it. Charter schools in states with strong charter school laws are no longer under the control of unions. And while Shanker has changed his mind about a variety of things in the many years he has been president of the American Federation of Teachers, he has been very consistent in this area. He wants more power for teachers, but *not* at the expense of unions. If the unions are willing to grant waivers, that is fine. But union power has been, and remains, critical.

Shanker's attacks and questionable assertions on charter schools continue. In a 1996 column titled "Risky Business," he wrote that charter schools "are set up under state law to be independent of state and local control though they are funded by public money."[36] But charter school laws give school districts or the state the power to *close* charter schools that do not fulfill their contracts. Does that sound as though the schools are independent of state and local control? In the same column, Shanker cited the case of a Los Angeles charter school that was closed because funds were misappropriated. But charter advocates have applauded this decision as an example of accountability—the kind so often lacking in other public schools.

At its annual meeting in August, 1996, the American Federation of Teachers released a report, *Charter School Laws: Do They Measure Up?* The report calls charter schools "a useful vehicle for school reform, provided that they can demonstrate improved student achievement."[37] But the report illustrates the union's resistance to the laws which challenge the status quo and its confusion about accountability.

First, the report illustrated the AFT's opposition to the kind of charter legislation that will have a real impact. AFT included the full text of only one charter law, Rhode Island's, which the AFT calls "an example of good charter legislation."[38] Louisana State University analyst Louanne Bierlein has described Rhode Island's charter law as one of the nation's weakest.[39] Unlike many other states that adopt strong charter legislation, not a single charter school was authorized in Rhode Island in the year following adoption of the law. The State Department of Education received only three applications, none of which were approved.

It is easy to understand why Rhode Island charter legislation produced so little activity. For example, Rhode Island teachers working with charter schools must remain members of their local union, earning the same salary and fringe benefits as other union teachers, unless the local union approved a waiver. Nationally, some charter schools pay teachers more and some less than other teachers. But Rhode Island is one of the few states giving a local union the power to approve, or deny, differences between a charter school salary and benefits and that of other public school teachers.

The Rhode Island legislation is weak in other ways. It permits only ten charter schools per year in the first two years, it does not permit any noncertified teachers to work at a charter school, and it does not grant an automatic waiver of most rules and regulations. States with similar laws such as Georgia, Kansas, and New Mexico have the same results as Rhode Island: no charter schools or just a handful of charter schools, even three years after the law has been approved. Weak laws like these don't provide competition to the existing system. Apparently, according to the AFT, a "good" charter law produces few charters.

Second, the AFT report also says that accountability provisions in some charter laws are inadequate. The union criticizes several laws, for example, because the AFT asserts that laws don't require comparisons between charter and other public schools, insisting that "without this basic information, it will be impossible to hold charter schools accountable."[40]

Most states with statewide tests of academic standards require charter schools to use them, allowing the comparisons that AFT recommends. But comparisons don't produce much improvement unless there are rewards for progress and consequences for failure.

As the AFT suggests, more work is needed to develop assessment methods, in charter and other public schools. But some states don't have a statewide testing program or state academic standards, so comparisons are difficult. Every charter law requires that charter public schools reach academic goals specified in their contract or go out of business. That's real accountability.

Conversely, the NEA initially was opposed to the charter school concept, writing to U.S. senators on January 16, 1992, that the "NEA is unalterably opposed to any legislative initiative that would provide federal funds" to any of several kinds of schools including charter schools.[41] Recently, however, the NEA national office has established a Charter School Initiative (CSI), described as a "five year exploration into charter schools."[42]

The initiative has several parts. First, the NEA has established a technical assistance team that will help teachers trying to create charter schools. Initially, the NEA will focus its assistance in six states: Arizona, California, Colorado, Connecticut, Georgia, and Hawaii, helping school founders in areas such as assessment, facilities, philosophy, fiscal practices, and other areas as requested by the teachers. The second part of the initiative is to assess the impact of the charter schools. An academic team headed by a professor at the University of California, Los Angeles, will document what is being accomplished in each of six schools. According to the NEA, "the CSI project is taking NEA into some uncharted territory. We expect that the learnings about new ways that the Association may need to operate and organize itself to service members in charter schools will be as powerful for us as it is for members working in them."[43]

The NEA's project is worth watching. First, it shows that the NEA is recognizing the charter school movement as an important concept that it would be unwise to continue simply opposing. That is a recognition of both the idea's power and the NEA's political sensitivity. When a number of long-time powerful political allies end up supporting something an organization opposes vigorously, the wise organization does some rethinking. NEA is an enormously powerful organization. Many of its staff are very bright and deeply committed to youngsters. There is no question that its officials also are very committed to maintaining union authority. So the shift at the NEA indicates that the organization no longer believes that outright opposition to the charter school concept is in its best interests.

Second, however, the professor selected to head the charter school evaluation raises questions about the kind of assessment that will be done. That professor is well known among public school choice and charter school supporters as a vigorous critic of these ideas.

Third, the NEA actions indicate that at least some officials are beginning to consider a new role for unions. In an interview, a union official reiterated that the NEA "does not see charters as the only way to improve education. But we know that we [teachers unions] are going to have to change our role. We do not yet know what the role of a union will be when we do not do traditional bargaining." The charter school movement puts teachers unions in what this official accurately calls "a tricky situation." But give her and her NEA colleagues credit for recognizing that "there may be an important role for unions."[44]

At its 1995 annual national conference held in Minneapolis, the NEA presented a film featuring a handful of teachers who are making a difference in students' lives. Milo Cutter and the City Academy (discussed in Chapter One) were among the people and places depicted. Cutter is also now on the advisory committee of the NEA project that assists union members who are starting charter schools. Moreover, the NEA Representative Assembly "has adopted a resolution favoring charter schools, as long as teachers are licensed . . . and school employees are involved in [the schools'] design and implementation."[45] Despite the resolution, state NEA affiliates often oppose strong charter bills.

Although many union officials perceive a number of their members to be resistant to the idea of charter schools, there are also public school teachers who are urging unions to recognize the potential of the charter school movement. One such teacher wrote, "just once, I would like to see our union get in front of an issue like charter schools that have much to offer. . . . Wake up! Get on board now. Otherwise watch as teachers who are already disillusioned with the process for education as it exists also begin to feel that the union does not represent a forum for positive charge in education but a superfluous adjunct to progress."[46]

Unions could have an important role in the charter school movement. For example, unions could contract with charter schools to provide services the schools need. As happened in Boston, the charter school movement also can encourage school districts to give other public school teachers opportunities to create new programs and revise existing ones. This kind of teacher empowerment is precisely what many unions say is one of their key goals. Thus, although many unions strongly oppose charter schools, some union officials are beginning to understand that the charter school concept offers a great deal to students, teachers, and the unions themselves.

Gayle Fallon, president of the Houston Federation of Teachers counts herself as a supporter of charter schools that do not have to be sponsored by local districts: "If we don't at least give this idea a chance, we're going to be back dealing with vouchers."[47] The

Texas charter school law allows both local school boards and the state to sponsor charter schools. The Houston Federation of Teachers is helping to create both a charter school sponsored by the local district and a charter school sponsored by the state. Fallon thinks the charter school run by the Houston educational system is "having trouble because the district is having real difficulty delegating responsibility to the school." And she says that is often the case: "School boards and central office administrators talk about delegating authority, but they are pretty reluctant to do it."

Fallon thinks the charter school that is independent of the district and that the union is helping to plan in conjunction with the Tejano Center for Community Concerns, a community organization, is much more likely to succeed. This school will serve about two hundred 7th- and 8th-grade students at high risk and in danger of dropping out. Each child will be assessed at the beginning of the year, and teachers will develop an individual education plan for each student. The school day will be extended by two hours—to 5:30 P.M.—so that children will have the opportunity to hear various speakers, attend tutorials, and be involved in leadership development with mentors. The after-school program also will offer boxing, martial arts, and art. The school planners hope to have a junior ROTC along with Boy Scouts and Girl Scouts. Parents will pledge to be involved in their children's education and to allow their youngsters to participate in the extended school day.

The Houston Federation of Teachers has agreed to help publicize and staff this new charter school and to assist it in developing policies and contracts. Fallon will hold one seat on the board of directors. Most of the remaining board members will be local businesspeople or residents of the Southeast Houston neighborhood the school will serve.

The Houston Federation of Teachers is not the only union cooperating with the charter school. Fallon has requested and obtained a commitment from the local AFL that some union members who have volunteered time to bring the charter school's building up to code will have the union's approval. Teachers at this external charter school may be paid more than teachers in the traditional system, but Fallon thinks that is all right: "They are going to work longer hours, and they are taking a risk. The charter school has a real responsibility for results." Also, these teachers will be forced to resign from the district to take a position with the charter school.

Richard Farias, president and chief executive officer of the Tejano Center, is the key person developing the charter school that has been approved by the state. Farias feels that the Houston Federation of Teachers, besides wanting to protect the rights of its members, has a sincere interest in students in the community. "They are doing more than just protecting teachers' rights. They are helping us a great deal with the charter school proposal. We welcome their help, because we know that setting up the school is an enormous task and must have community involvement."[48]

Fallon knows a number of teachers union officials around the country have opposed charter school legislation and the development of such schools in their districts, but that is not the approach she is taking: "We can rant and rave about charters, and distance ourselves from them. Or we can help make them work. I'm interested in helping them work." She praised the Texas law that "clearly made charter schools public schools."

At least one AFT staff member admires what Fallon is doing (in fact, she suggested that she be contacted for this book).

Hope for the Future

Federal administration support, adoption of charter school laws in twenty-five states, and the success of many existing charter schools may stimulate union thinking and rethinking. Some union leaders are beginning to see that the charter school movement can offer important new opportunities to teachers and to the teacher organizations themselves. Unions have changed their positions before. They can do so again, although there will be many issues to resolve.

For example, the teachers unions generally have stuck to a salary structure in which there is no relationship whatever between the quality of a teacher's work and her or his pay. Evaluating and comparing teachers is harder than evaluating and comparing the outputs of salespersons. This does not mean, however, that it is impossible to reward a teacher for outstanding achievement.

Another facet of teacher salary that unions will have to face relates to the difficulty many school districts have in finding teachers with certain skills—such as the ability to teach advanced mathematics or science or to speak a certain language. For example, many districts are trying hard, and generally without success, to find teachers who speak Hmong, Cambodian, or Vietnamese, in order to better teach the large numbers of Southeast Asian students whose families recently have immigrated to the United States. A corporation needing to hire a professional with a certain skill would generally set the salary of the position high enough to attract someone. However, teachers unions generally still insist on use of the master teacher contract across all positions.

This is yet another instance of how the current system does not put the needs of students first. If school funding depended on improvements in student achievement, school districts would make sure they found skilled teachers who spoke Asian languages. Teachers unions are correct in assuming that charter schools are a direct threat to the status quo. Charter schools must put the needs of students first, before the needs of adults. If, and only if, students learn more, will charter school teachers retain their jobs.

Another issue unions must resolve is that charter school teachers in states with strong charter laws have the right to form their own bargaining units and affiliate with a state teachers' union. Some charter teachers have decided to retain their union membership because of the insurance, legal, or group purchasing benefits the union offers. It may be that unions' concerns about their own futures are one of the major reasons union officials have fought so hard against the charter school concept.

What might change attitudes of unions toward charter schools? One thing might be the possibility of something unions want even less than charter schools: school vouchers. In many states, charter schools have been adopted as an acceptable alternative to vouchers, yet the voucher threat remains a potent one in many states. It probably is one of the reasons the National Education Association has decided to adopt a more open mind about charter schools.

Another thing that might pressure union officials to change is the widespread organized public dissatisfaction with public schools. Throughout the 1980s, educators noted that in a series of polls, adults ranked the schools in their local communities as more effective than those around the nation. At a variety of national meetings, called by organizations such as *Fortune* magazine or the

Committee for Economic Development, union and business officials cited these findings as evidence that the public was reasonably
satisfied with the schools they knew best.

But of course, one reason parents and other community members often felt positively about their local schools is that local
school board members, teachers, and administrators were regularly announcing that the schools were doing the best job possible.
At local, state, and national levels, many key union officials have
devoted enormous time and energy to convincing the public and
the business community that schools are achieving as much as they
can with the available resources.

However, a report from the Public Agenda Foundation in 1994
questioned whether the public is as satisfied as some had suggested.
This report cited a study of 1,100 adults that showed that "the public's trust is wavering."[49] Among the study's findings were that 61 percent of the general public and 70 percent of African American
parents believe that "academic standards are too low and kids are
not expected to learn enough." Furthermore, the public does not
see money as the central need of schools. When asked, "What is the
most important thing public schools need in order to help kids
learn?" the top five responses were good teachers (42 percent), dis-
cipline/respect (25 percent), to teach values (15 percent), involved
parents (11 percent), and enough money (8 percent).[50]

Some union leaders responded to this study by increasing efforts to remove disruptive students from schools, and the Public
Agenda report did show that substantial numbers of Americans are
concerned about drugs and violence in the schools. But the report
also showed that 92 percent of the general public believe that
"schools should place much greater emphasis on making learning
enjoyable and interesting to elementary school students," and 86
percent of the public believe schools should do the same for secondary school students.[51] A policy that emphasizes "getting tough"
with students rather than improving instruction appears to misread
what the public is suggesting.

It would be very disturbing to many union officials if schools
showed that without controls and restrictions from a school district
and without a labor-management agreement, they could do a better job with students, especially students from low-income or limited English-speaking backgrounds. It would be very threatening

to have schools and successful teachers who decided that they did not need to be represented by unions.

At this point, a majority of union leaders are fighting the charter school concept, either directly or by attempting to weaken it so that it does not give charter schools a true test. These strategies may be successful but also shortsighted. Meanwhile, a few union leaders recognize that people in the charter school movement are some of the most talented and committed educators in the nation. These union leaders are trying to strengthen public education and their own organizations. Union leaders like Gayle Fallon and Andrea DiLorenzo may be the pioneers of modern teachers unions. It will be fascinating to review the situation in five years.

Part Three

Creating
Charter Schools

| Getting Started

Several years ago, a wonderful veteran teacher was describing his classroom to a group of people. When they expressed admiration for what he had accomplished, he smiled and responded, "The problem with good ideas is that they inevitably degenerate into hard work." That is true of a fine classroom and true of a fine charter school.

This chapter describes how some of the best charter schools began (see sidebar on p. 122). The following two chapters discuss promoting the school to the community and the operation of the school once it is up and running. Charter schools do not all face the same challenges or the same opportunities. Charter schools that are conversions of existing schools, for example, will have a somewhat different set of issues from those that must be addressed by brand-new schools. But there are also some things, like business operations and evaluation systems, with which all charter schools must deal.

Existing charter schools have found there is no set formula, no one best way to do things. But some steps are critical. Moreover, charter school operators stress that dozens of details are critical. Reliance on theory is not nearly enough to get a school up and running. But having said that, 110 charter school directors interviewed in the 1995 national survey of the Center for School Change and the Education Commission of the States urged people with the commitment and the energy to "go for it."[1] The central message from these directors is that although starting and operating a charter school is extremely hard work, it is also very gratifying and fulfilling. The following pages are intended to provide helpful advice. Although the tasks may be daunting, remember that many other

Advice from Those Who Have Done It.

The 1995 survey that contacted 110 charter schools to gather information about them and to seek their advice produced nine key recommendations for those planning to start a charter school:

- Establish a clear vision, mission, and philosophy to which all involved in the school are committed.
- Give yourselves plenty of time to plan.
- Be prepared to work hard.
- Visit other charter schools.
- Look for partners with special expertise; do not try to do everything yourself.
- Spend as much time as possible communicating with parents.
- Hire experienced teachers and administrators.
- Develop support as broad as possible within the community.
- Start small and get the operation going well before you expand.

The charter school operators also had advice for state legislators:

- Allow charter schools real autonomy by making them their own districts; do not require charter schools to follow local district work rules.
- Allow charters to get funds directly from the state.
- Allow more than one organization to grant charters.
- Make the law clear and provide someone at state level who has the power to cut through bureaucracy.
- Provide start-up funds.
- Provide legal and other technical assistance to new charter school organizers.

Source: A. Medler and J. Nathan, *Charter Schools: What Are They Up To?* (Denver: Education Commission of the States, and Minneapolis: Center for School Change, University of Minnesota Humphrey Institute, 1995).

people have done it before and that people starting charter schools now have the advantage of learning from the mistakes and the successes of others.

Understand State and Local District Processes for Sponsoring a Charter School

As the examples in this book have shown, state charter school laws vary enormously (see also Appendix A). In Massachusetts, a state agency is the only authorized sponsor, and the local district has no direct role in charter school selection. In other states—for example,

Alaska, Georgia, Kansas, and Wisconsin—the reverse is true, and only local school districts have the power to sponsor a charter school. Yet other states—for example, Arizona, Michigan, Minnesota, New Jersey, and North Carolina—allow more than one kind of organization to sponsor charter schools.

Moreover, state laws can change. Minnesota and Michigan legislators have made major changes to their charter school legislation since it originally was adopted. Do not assume that the legislative information presented here is up to date. Many state legislatures are considering the charter school idea. New laws will almost certainly be adopted and existing laws modified after this book is published.

The place to start learning about charter school sponsors is at the state level. Contact your state superintendent or commissioner of education or one of the agencies listed as contacts in Appendix A. Ask for anything and everything the state has available about its charter process.

You will want at least the following items:

- A description of the process used to analyze and approve charter school proposals
- A list of existing charter schools, including descriptions, addresses, and telephone numbers
- Information about any funds the state legislature has allocated or the state has received from the federal government to help people plan and or start charter schools
- Sample contracts between charter schools and sponsoring agencies
- Names of accountants, attorneys, and other professionals who have indicated an interest in working with charter schools
- Copies of evaluations of existing charter schools
- Names of foundations that have provided grants to help start charter schools

You should be able to get the first three items from every state that has charter school legislation, and many states are now gathering the other items on the list (see Appendix B for other resources).

Be sure you understand the approval process in your state. In some states—Massachusetts, for example—there is a competitive application. Massachusetts state law presently allows only twenty-five charter schools. For the last three years, the state has accepted applications once a year and selected a certain number of them. In Minnesota, charter school organizers can apply at any time to a local school board or public university and then go on to the state level if necessary in an appeals process. In Delaware, state officials set a date by which applications for the first five charter schools had to be submitted. The process of gaining approval varies enormously from state to state, so your first step must be to understand how your state operates.

Also ask the state official in charge of charter schools if there are groups available to help people establish charter schools. Support organizations are developing in many states, such as the Colorado League of Charter Schools and CANEC (California Network of Educational Charters). Some states are contracting with organizations to provide assistance to charter school organizers. Massachusetts has an arrangement with the Pioneer Institute; Michigan has contracted with the Michigan Partnership for New Education.

Ask the state official if these technical assistance organizations sponsor meetings open to the public. CANEC, for example, sponsors an annual conference that has grown in size every year, now attracting hundreds of people. The Minnesota charter school group has periodic informal meetings. The Colorado League of Charter Schools has periodic conferences. The Pioneer Institute in Massachusetts sponsors workshops for people considering establishing charter schools. A great deal of experience, both positive and negative, is shared at such meetings.

Five years ago, very little information was available to charter school organizers. So take advantage of the progress made. There is absolutely no reason to start at ground zero. You will still have plenty of work to do, but gathering the information described here will let you learn from other people's efforts and work more effectively.

Develop Your Three-Month Work Plan

Next, it is important to develop a work plan for the next three months, either by yourself or with a small group of fellow organizers or support people. After getting the information described earlier and reading through this book, especially Part Three, you will have a good sense of the work that needs to be done. The plan should include general tasks, such as writing a mission statement, listing your beliefs about learning, writing a preliminary proposal, finding potential building sites, looking for faculty, applying for start-up grants, visiting existing charter schools, and attending charter school conferences. Decide your highest priorities for the next few months, the individuals who will be responsible for making sure they are carried out, and what the timeline is. Do not let the fact that much must be done discourage you. All progress is made step by step. Once in a while, you will take a giant step, such as getting your charter application approved. But getting to that point will require many smaller steps.

Make Your Organization Tax Exempt

Apply as early as possible to the federal government and your state for tax-exempt status for your charter school. You need this tax-exempt status for many reasons. Foundations and other groups that you will approach for donations find it much easier to give to tax-exempt organizations. You probably will need an attorney or an accountant to help you so that you will not waste a lot of time redoing the application until it is right. If your group does not include an attorney, contact the local legal aid society, or if you are near a university with a law school, call that school. Some charter schools have been able to get valuable legal assistance at no or low cost early in their school's development from legal aid attorneys or law students.

Visit Charter Schools

Visit charter schools, especially ones nearby. There is no substitute for talking directly with people who have created one of these schools. Make an appointment for your visit and also ask the school to send you some descriptive information ahead of time, so you will know as much as possible before you arrive. Offer to pay for this material; most charter schools have very tight budgets and are committed to spending their funds to promote learning for youngsters, not to inform visitors.

Read the school's material and come prepared with a list of questions. Also, be sensitive to the amount of time you are taking up. Some charter school operators have talked about the enormous demands interested people make on them. Most charter school educators want to help others start similar programs, but at the same time, charter schools generally do not have much administrative structure or people who are free to conduct tours. That is why you will find that some charter schools, deluged with inquiries, have decided to limit visitors to one day a week or month.

Develop a Mission Statement

Developing a brief mission statement should be one of your first steps. The statement should be clear and informative. To determine what to include, you might start by asking these questions: What ages will your students be? What is your school trying to accomplish? What will make it distinctive from other schools?

Here are some examples. The O'Farrell Community School in San Diego says the school wants to "promote excellence by providing all middle level students a single, academically enriched curriculum within a multi-ethnic, student-centered environment. The mission of the school is to attend to the social, intellectual, psychological and physical needs of middle level youth so they will become responsible, literate, thinking and contributing citizens."[2]

The Options for Youth charter school (OFYCS) in LaCrescenta, California, says its "primary purpose is to offer students who are not attending traditional schools an additional, alternative educational program. Enrollment in OFYCS is voluntary. The program provides students with the opportunity to (a) complete or make up credits so that they can return to their regular school, (b) prepare for the GED or CHSPE if that is their choice, or (c) remain at OFYCS until they are ready to graduate."[3]

The Community Involved Charter School, in Colorado, has a mission statement that explains, "We believe in the giftedness of each individual. We will provide a nurturing and challenging educational environment to develop the whole person. We will promote and advocate choice, self-direction, experiential learning, shared responsibility, lifelong learning skills and a joy and happiness for learning."[4]

Academy Charter School, in Colorado, says the school's mission is to "provide a challenging academic program based on the Core Knowledge curriculum that promotes Academic Excellence, Character Development and Educational Enthusiasm for its students."[5]

We know a number of important things after reading these statements. O'Farrell will focus on middle-level students, the school will have a single curriculum rather than offer different tracks, and staff will not be content to work only on students' academic needs. The Community Involved Charter School also is concerned to develop the "whole person." This Colorado school also mentions its interest in experiential learning, an interest carried out in its program and activities. Another Colorado institution, Academy Charter School, uses its mission statement to inform people that the curriculum is based on the Core Knowledge model. Academy's mission statement also shows that the school intends to promote character development and enthusiasm for learning as well as academic learning. Options for Youth focuses on young people who are out of school and have not succeeded in traditional schools. Unlike many other charter schools, OFYCS is geared toward helping students make up credits or gain the credits needed to graduate, and these specific goals are stated in the school's mission.

Most strong charter schools have mission statements like these. Writing a mission statement is an important place to begin the formation of a new school. In addition, effective charter schools, like other wise organizations, periodically review their mission statements and sometimes revise them if the school has new directions and priorities. Changing a mission statement is fine, as long as the contents have real meaning.

List Your Beliefs About How Children Learn

It is important to list your beliefs about how children learn. This list will probably be a page or two long. Again, there is no best approach, but these clear statements of belief will be very helpful for people who may wish to work at your school and for families who are deciding whether to enroll their children. Here are a few examples of possible statements. You will see important differences among them:

- Students learn best in classrooms directed by responsible, well-trained adults.
- Students learn best when they are out in the community on trips and activities that they and responsible adults planned.
- Students learn best when they spend much of their time gathering information, writing reports, and producing projects with the help of the computer.
- Students learn best when they have a strong grounding in traditional academic subjects such as reading, writing, and mathematics.
- Students learn best when they are carrying out interdisciplinary, theme-based projects.
- Students learn best when they are working with children approximately their same age.
- Students learn best when they have the opportunity to move at their own pace, which probably means they will be working on projects with students who are not only the same age but are also younger or older.
- Students learn best when graduation is based on demonstration of skills and knowledge.
- Students learn to read best when phonics is a central part of instruction.
- Students learn to read best when they have extensive opportunities to write about their own experiences and to produce books about those experiences.
- Students learn to read best using several approaches, including phonics, whole language, and other ideas.

As you compile your own list, remember that the idea is not to come up with a definitive list of possible learning methods. Even the most thoughtful educational researchers often disagree with each other about the views just listed. Your goal is to be clear about *what you and others with whom you are working believe.*

The group developing the list of beliefs about how children learn should include parents, educators, and at the secondary level in many cases, students. In developing the list, group members may want to visit some unusually effective schools and teachers and ask for suggestions. Group members may also want to read recent books about school reform, again recognizing that authorities disagree dramatically and often vigorously. Ultimately, you will have to decide for yourself what you believe and what you will practice.

Discuss What Students Should Know

Begin to discuss what you want students to know and be able to do by a certain point in time. *This discussion must include decisions about how you will measure progress.* Some states and districts leave evaluation of learning entirely up to the charter school. In other states, state-mandated assessments of certain skills are given to all public school students, including those attending charter public schools. For example, Minnesota is developing mathematics, reading, and writing tests that all students must pass before graduating from high school. The Center for School Change recently surveyed more than twenty secondary schools around the nation that had decided graduation would be based on demonstration of certain skills and knowledge. To assess students, some of these schools have retained a system of credit hours and grades; others have created an entirely new system based more directly on demonstration of knowledge.[6]

Charter schools serving students of any age, not just high school youngsters, must think fairly early about this question of goals and outcomes. Because one of the central features of the charter school movement is that the schools are responsible for improved achievement, educators and parents need to think carefully about what it is they are trying to achieve and where the school will be held accountable.

Gain Support for Your Proposal

Gaining public support for your charter school is discussed more fully in the next chapter; however, even in the early stages of planning, as you talk with individuals and organizations in the community about your school, ask if they would be willing to support your proposal. At some point, you must convince some group to sponsor your school. It might be a local or state board of education. It might be a college or university. But any charter school proposal looks more impressive when it is supported by local business groups, advocacy organizations, service groups, the city council, the mayor, and the like. Wide support gives your proposal more credibility. It suggests to the potential sponsor that others have looked at your ideas and plans and that they think the proposal has merit. This makes it easier for the sponsor to agree to work with you.

Lessons from the Early Stage of Planning

A member of a charter school group in the discussion stage offers these suggestions to people getting started:

- It is important to keep going. If things look bad one day, get up the following day determined to make progress.
- An enormous amount of energy is waiting to be tapped. Parents, teachers, and community members in the area will come together to help plan and organize the new school.
- The charter school discussion group on America Online is a great resource.
- Educators who tell parents, "You're the only one with these concerns" are inaccurate. Many other people want a different kind of school for their children.
- The charter school concept is key for moving innovative school supporters ahead. It is no longer necessary to convince all or most of the teachers in a school or district to change. Now there is another way to get options.

Chapter Six

Building Support

It is one thing to have an idea in your head about how a school could operate. It is quite another to transform that dream into reality. This chapter is for practical visionaries who are not satisfied to read or think about charter schools, who actually want to do one.

As potential founders plan their school, they must also inform the local community about the proposed school, be prepared to answer questions from interested and critical people, and begin to look for likely students. They must also present their proposal to the hoped-for sponsor. This chapter suggests methods of building local support for the school and recruiting students, offers answers to common questions about charter schools, and suggests ways to prepare a presentation to a potential charter school sponsor.

Build Support in the Local Community

As you develop your charter school ideas, you must find local allies. One way to do this is to interest the local media in your proposed school. Charter advocates in a number of states have sent letters to the editors of area newspapers, describing their intention to start a new public school and inviting others interested in the concept to contact them. Charter advocates have also found it useful to contact local talk radio programs. An appearance on one or more of these programs helps get the word out and may generate additional interest in the proposal.

Charter school advocates have found that speaking to local business and service clubs is extremely valuable. People in the community will talk about what you are trying to do. The question is how much accurate information they will have. If you or others in your group speak to local organizations, it gives people a chance to hear directly about what you are trying to do and to get accurate information. These presentations also may bring you people with influence or skills that can help your school.

In your presentations, it is vital to stress the value of *options*. Some students are served well by existing programs. Acknowledging this will help reduce opposition from those who are satisfied with existing public schools. However, other students will thrive in a new kind of school. It is valuable to adopt an attitude of humility. Describe how you are doing certain things differently and explain how your school builds on educational research, but do not overpromise. After all, your school has not even started yet.

Recognize that reporters love controversy. They often will try to tempt you to attack existing schools. Resist that temptation! You are asking for the opportunity to provide an educational option, not to instantly change everything going on in other schools in the community.

Many charter proponents have found it valuable to prepare a clear concise brochure about the proposed school. These brochures can be given to interested people and distributed at public presentations. A brochure should state your mission, core beliefs about learning, the ages of students you intend to serve, and academic goals and methods of evaluation along with sample school activities. Have several noneducators read the brochure before you print it, to make sure it sounds reasonable and clear and does not contain too much educational jargon. The brochure should be polished and professional looking, but not slick. Your brochure gives people an impression of the school. You want that impression to be a positive one. In some places, charter school advocates have found that local businesspeople will contribute their time and design abilities to help charter school supporters create an effective brochure.

Respond to Criticism and Concerns

Although the charter school movement is growing rapidly, people continue to raise important questions about the concept. It is important to listen to these concerns, consider them, and respond appropriately. Here are some of the major challenges typically offered to charter schools.

Aren't Charter Schools Really Elitist Private Schools?

Charter schools are not elitist private schools. In most states, charter schools may not have any kind of admission tests. This means they cannot screen out students on the basis of achievement or behavior. It is worth noting, however, as pointed out earlier, that magnet public schools in many of the nation's largest cities do have admissions tests. Indeed, the federal government probably made a huge mistake when it allowed federal funds to be used to establish magnet schools with admissions tests. As I testified in a congressional hearing on the subject, "by supporting creation of schools which are allowed to pick and choose among students, the federal government is promoting great inequities. The magnet schools are allowed to take their pick of students, leaving the rest of the students to the neighborhood schools."

Do Charter Schools Serve Primarily White Middle-Class Easy-to-Educate Students?

Research is showing that many charter schools are being established to serve students who have not succeeded in traditional schools. More than half of the charter schools surveyed in 1995 reported that they focused on such students.[1] Louann Bierlein's 1996 research showed that "in most states, charter schools are attracting an overproportion of such [minority] students relative to state averages."[2] Another 1996 analysis also shows this tendency. As of March 1996, about 40 percent of the students in Minnesota's charter schools were from minority groups, while only about 13 percent of the state's total K–12 population represents minority communities.[3]

Moreover, charter schools are not allowed to spend more than the average per-pupil cost in their district or state. Once again, compare this to the magnet schools that frequently spend more than the average cost.

Mary Anne Raywid, a professor at Hofstra University, challenges those who argue that charter school programs are inequitable with an important question: "Choice is inequitable compared to what?" If the government does not step in to provide educational choices to low- and moderate-income families, then who will have such choices?[4] Only the affluent. Only those who can

afford to move to a different district or to pay tuition at a private
or parochial school.

What would happen if we applied the critics' argument to voting? On average, the more affluent people are, the more likely they
are to vote. So should we eliminate the right to vote because it is
not used in equal numbers by low-income and affluent people?
Does it not make more sense to encourage low-income people to
be more active politically, as people such as Martin Luther King, Jr.,
have done?

Are charter schools inequitable? Compared to what? If they are
compared to magnet schools, clearly they are more equitable because they are not allowed to pick and choose among students as
magnet schools do.

Yet another study, this one of Michigan's first six charter
schools, found that five of the six had larger percentages of low-
income students when compared to the neighboring districts.[5] And
Bierlein notes that, although, "unfortunately, concrete student profile data do not exist. Early information . . . reveals that charter
schools are not 'creaming off' the best and brightest students as
critics often challenge."[6]

The best available information seems to show that minority students are overrepresented in charter schools and that more than
half of all charter schools focus on students who have not succeeded in traditional schools. This information suggests that charter schools are expanding opportunity for low-income and
minority students, rather than serving as elitist academies.

Don't Charter Schools Hurt Existing
Schools by Taking Money Away from Them?

One of the central rationales for the charter approach is encouraging the existing public school system to respond with innovative
changes of its own. Opponents insist that public schools do not
have enough money to respond to competition. But the evidence
is growing that public schools can and will react to competition.

Recall the Boston public schools' response to the Massachusetts charter school legislation. The Boston public schools established a way to create new, potentially more effective programs
called pilot schools. Remember what 52 percent of Minnesota pub-

lic school administrators said had been one of the results of the state's law allowing high school juniors and seniors to take all or a portion of their coursework in college: the administrators said the law had encouraged greater cooperation between high schools and colleges. In fact, the number of Advanced Placement courses at high schools more than doubled in the six years after the law was established, and dozens of high schools established cooperative courses with colleges and universities so that students could earn postsecondary credit while still in high school. Jefferson County, Colorado, more than doubled the number of alternative schools it offered after the state's charter school law went into effect, finally responding to parents who for seven years had been urging expansion of the innovative schools that had substantial waiting lists.

Some argue that allowing public funds to go to private or parochial schools would also stimulate this kind of improvement. Perhaps. But many private and parochial schools want to be allowed to pick and choose among students as well, which most public schools cannot do, and they want the freedom to charge whatever seems appropriate, which, again, public schools cannot do. This is unfair competition.

Finally, charter schools usually do receive some waiver of state regulations, but public school districts in most states can apply for the same waivers. So there is a "level playing field" in this area also.

Controlled competition can stimulate educational improvement. Of course, it is not a panacea. But public educators do respond when they no longer have that exclusive franchise.

What About Charter Schools Run for Profit or as Home Schools?

Should for-profit companies should be allowed to establish charter schools? And is there a place in the charter school concept for an alliance with home schoolers? Each of these issues is intensely controversial.

Most state laws stipulate that charter schools may not be started by for-profit companies and that charter schools will not be a guise under which home schools may operate. A few states are experimenting with either or both concepts; however, so far, the results are not clear.

Policy makers need to understand that including either or both of these ideas in a charter school bill will increase the opposition to it. However, some charter school advocates in California argue that including home schoolers in that state's charter school law made great sense because California was providing some financial assistance to home schoolers before it passed the charter law.

Thoughtful people disagree about both home schooling and for-profit companies in public education. I myself am ambivalent on these issues and do not know that there is a right or wrong answer regarding them. These ideas must be publicly discussed, debated, and resolved before any legislation can be finalized.

Prepare a Sponsor Presentation

Your presentation to the potential sponsor of your charter school should be carefully prepared. The details will depend in part on which state you are in and what questions the sponsor wants answered. My talks with state department of education officials and local school board members suggest that the strongest charter proposals have much in common. Here are suggestions for such presentations, gathered from around the country.

- Be clear about what you want to accomplish. Write your list of academic and other goals in language people can understand.
- Be specific about the ways student achievement and progress will be measured and the variety of tests and other measures that will be used. Using the standardized test employed by the local district or the state will build confidence in the proposal.
- Show that you have built support in the community. As noted earlier, allies can be extremely valuable. Ask supporters to attend the meeting at which your proposal will be reviewed or, if that is not possible, to contact decision makers ahead of time. Ask them for letters of support that can accompany your written proposal. You want the people reviewing your proposal to see that it is an idea with broad support.
- Be ready to explain how you will recruit a cross-section of students. Be prepared to explain how you will get information out to and attract interest from communities that traditionally have not been much involved with schools and whose students

do not achieve well in existing schools. Most charter school laws prohibit admissions tests, and most legislators who support charter school legislation are eager to see at least some charter schools help youngsters who are not succeeding. Showing that you will help such youngsters will increase the receptivity of most chartering authorities to your proposal.

• Practice your presentation ahead of time. Look for ways to be clear and specific. Have members of your group role-play the board members who will be reviewing your proposal and asking questions about it. Some charter proponents videotape the practice presentation and critique their own performances.

What happens if your proposal is rejected? Recognize that this has happened to some of the nation's most successful charter schools, as shown in the previous chapters. Bob DeBoer at New Visions Charter School was turned down by the Minneapolis School Board on his first effort to gain a charter. The same thing happened to the teachers who worked on and ultimately gained approval for the New Country School in LeSueur, Minnesota. Robert Stein of the O'Farrell Community School reports that he and his colleagues had to meet with the local school board several times before gaining approval.

Some states provide an appeal process. If that option is available, strongly consider using it. Several Colorado charter schools were authorized only after they appealed to the state board of education after being turned down by the local school board. Parents in Emily, Minnesota, offer an example of the persistence that may be necessary to reach your goals. When the local public elementary school was to be closed, and five- to eight-year-olds were faced with a journey of twenty-five to thirty-five miles to the nearest elementary school, these parents wanted a school for their elementary youngsters that would make extensive use of senior citizens and local businesses in the community and that did not require the students to travel so far. But first, they went to the school board and asked that the elementary school be kept open. The board refused to do this, insisting it would save money by busing Emily students to another town. Parents offered to do various tasks in the local school to help it stay open. The school board refused. The parents then applied to the local school board to start a charter school. The school board turned them down. The parents then applied to the Minnesota State Board of Education, which granted their charter. In the meantime, the school district removed much of the equipment from the Emily public school building and tore the blackboards off the walls (equipment that the local taxpayers had, of course, helped pay for). Nevertheless, the Emily Charter School is now operating in that building, much to the delight of the families in the community and of the local citizens who had made the school a focus for community events. The stronger charter school laws provide for more than one potential sponsor or for appeal to another group if a local school board turns down a proposal. If necessary, use these options.

One of the most valuable qualities in starting a charter school is persistence. Decision makers may not see the value of your program the first time it is presented. If your proposal is turned down, ask for feedback. How could the proposal have been strengthened? What items need clarification? Analyze the proposal and hearing yourself: What questions did the school board or other potential sponsor ask that your group did not answer well? It is vital to avoid defensiveness and bitterness at this stage. You will make more progress if you retain your determination to get your school approved and operating.

Recruit Students

When recruiting students, setting up a subgroup to focus just on that task probably makes the most sense. Recruiting students can take a great deal of time. If at all possible, one member of this subgroup should be someone whom prospective parents can call to get additional information. Because you do not yet have a school people can look at and visit, you need to have someone people can talk with.

Many charter school groups have set up evening meetings at various places in the community they intend to serve to answer the questions of families who are considering sending their children to the school. Check with churches, synagogues, family or community centers, libraries, and local businesses to see if they have a room you can use, preferably without cost.

Charter schools have used a variety of ways to get the word out that a new option exists. The news media should be an important part of the strategy. As noted earlier, you probably received some publicity before your school was authorized, but you also need a new, active campaign to work with the news media after your school is approved. Think of every conceivable news medium within an hour's drive of your school (radio stations, television stations, and newspapers), and try to get each one to do a story about the school. In some communities, there are newspapers written in various languages. Make sure to contact all of them. Use the same strategy for radio stations—contact every station heard within an hour's drive of your school. News media publicity is free and immensely valuable.

Ask local businesses if you can put a flyer in their window or on the community bulletin board some of them have near the front door. Convenience stores, gas stations, drugstores, fast-food franchises, grocery stores, barbershops, and hairdressers—the list is endless. You want to reach as many people as you possibly can.

Contact people who work with low- and moderate-income families to tell them about your school. These contacts will include social workers, probation officers, welfare officials, and people in similar occupations. Give them copies of a one-page summary of the school program or copies of the school brochure that they can give to families with whom they work.

Call the local offices of advocacy groups such as the National Association for the Advancement of Colored People (NAACP), Urban Coalition, American Indian Movement, Hispanic Alliance, Lao Family Center, and so forth. Offer to meet with their staff to answer questions and to give the staff flyers about the school. The members of one charter school group met with the staff at a Hmong center and impressed the staff with their strong interest in and knowledge of Hmong culture. The charter school was willing to hire a person from the Hmong community who would serve as a translator and parent involvement specialist, and the school asked the Hmong staff for help in identifying possible candidates for the job. Within a month, the school had more than seventy-five applications from the local Hmong community.

Meet with ministers, rabbis, priests, and other religious leaders in the area your school will serve. Tell them about your plans, and once again, give them information they can share with their congregation. Offer to attend a meeting at the church, synagogue, or mosque with interested people, to share information and answer questions.

Make sure you contact real estate agents. They are constantly talking with people who are considering moving into your area, and they will appreciate having information they can share with prospective home owners. Real estate agents always are looking for something special they can tell prospective buyers. Your school qualifies as something special.

Local libraries are another place to distribute information. Most libraries have a place where people can either post a flyer or leave some flyers for others to pick up (or both). Libraries are a great place to get school information to families.

Some charter schools have placed advertisements in local newspapers. In addition to describing the school, these ads should tell people whom to call for further information and list the dates and places of any parent information meetings. Advertisements generally are not cheap. Check to see if the local newspaper(s) will give you a discounted rate. Some papers have lower rates for nonprofit organizations than for businesses.

If you have been able to work with the local news media to tell the community about your charter school, some families will contact you before the charter is approved to ask about enrolling their children. You need to be clear that you welcome these families' interest and support but that you do not yet have the charter.

It is also important that all interested parents understand that enrollment in most charters, by state law, is on the basis of a lottery when there are more applicants than the school can hold.

Finally, parents who help establish charter schools face a tough issue—will their own children be guaranteed admission? It is entirely possible that a charter school will not be able to serve all the young people whose families want them to attend. Many Michigan charter schools, for example, have encountered two to four applicants for every available space.[7] In most cases, however, the children of the people who help start a school are admitted. Some charter schools insist that no children, including those of the founding families, have preference, but other schools, with permission from the sponsor, have reserved a handful of spots (five to ten) for youngsters from "founding families."

Continue to Look for
Opportunities to Share Your Story

Once a charter school is running, it should not wait for additional supporters to come to it. Part of students' work should be to write to local groups to describe what the charter school is doing and to ask if the group would like a presentation about the school. Students can and should contact service clubs, city and county commissions, senior citizen homes, religious congregations, chambers of commerce, and any other local group.

Adult groups like to hear from young people. They are interested in what youngsters are doing, learning, and thinking. Today, we are deluged with negative stories about children, but people want to hear the good news. They want to hear how young people are rehabilitating empty but usable buildings. They want to hear about youngsters who discovered that something is wrong with the water in the local river and are trying to do something about it. They enjoy students' dramatic and musical presentations.

Moreover, people and organizations are looking for ways they can help. They want to feel needed. They want to feel that they are making a contribution. Charter schools can tap these wants.

Charter school proponents should continue to work hard to get information about their work in local newspapers and on local television and radio programs. One of the important lessons of the women's suffrage movement was that proponents constantly wrote for important mass market magazines. Through this forum, they reached the general public and brought them to understand the reasons for eliminating the male monopoly on voting.

In a similar vein, part of students' class assignments could be writing letters to local newspaper editors to comment on education stories and to explain what is happening at the charter school. Or part of their assignments might be to write to national education publications in reaction to stories about charter schools. This will serve the dual purpose of strengthening students' communications skills and getting the word out to more people about what charter schools really are, what they do, and how they function.

| **Staying in Business**

This chapter continues the discussion of the practical issues involved in starting and running a charter school. It describes such key activities as selecting faculty, evaluating students and faculty, determining school governance, and managing the business side of the school.

Selection of Faculty

Many sponsors and supporters will want to know who at least some of the faculty members will be. Other sponsors will not require that prospective faculty be identified before the sponsor considers granting a charter. However, all the strong charter schools I have visited had some of their faculty involved in developing the original proposal, and this is a key point.

There is nothing wrong with a group of parents and community advocates developing a charter proposal. In fact, parent and community participation produces a proposal with valuable outside support. However, the people who will do the majority of day-to-day work in the school are teachers. Having at least some of the teachers who want to work at the charter school participate from the earliest discussions on allows the parents and community members to get to know these educators well. It is extremely difficult to judge a teacher effectively during a job interview. But if you have worked with the person for months and know her or his strengths and weaknesses, you can make a much more informed decision about whether she or he is appropriate for the school. The teachers who participate in the founding are also likely to have a special commitment to the school and to its educational philosophy and particular expertise in its teaching methods.

Sometimes community activists and parents develop charter proposals, going through all the steps listed in this section of the book, without involving teachers. These charter advocates think they can look for teachers later, but this is a serious mistake. Again, every strong charter school I have seen was created in part by the teachers who ended up working in the school.

Here is another important warning, based on the experience of a number of charter schools. The skills required in creating a charter school proposal, winning community support, and convincing an organization to sponsor your school are not necessarily the same as the skills required to operate effectively as a charter school faculty member or administrator. Several charter schools have discovered to their dismay that the person who had done much of the work up to the opening of the school and who had been named the school's director had little interest in administrative detail and little skill at handling it. These schools had to make a quick staffing shift shortly after opening. They had depended on people with great vision whose essential interest lay in starting new institutions and who had very little interest in actually working in a charter school.

Other charter schools have discovered that founding teachers lacked critical instructional skills. Although having strong political skills and great persistence and playing a central role in winning approval for the school, these people were not especially effective teachers. Staff and parents were saddened to discover this fact, but within the first year these teachers were asked to leave. Such decisions were difficult because many people in the schools felt great appreciation for these particular educators. However, in a small school, even a single weak teacher can be devastating.

Another charter school had to make a major adjustment after its first year because a number of parents complained about one of the founding teachers who knew a great deal about using computers and was an extremely valuable resource to other faculty and to students but who could also be abrasive and was not especially good at monitoring students' work or organizing their projects. To resolve the problem, the rest of the faculty rearranged assignments to give this teacher a different role in the school, one that would use the teacher's strong technology skills but not require the teacher's major participation in organizing classes or serving as a student adviser.

What should you look for in faculty members for your charter school? The answer will depend in part on the school's philosophy, the age and other characteristics of the students you intend to serve, and the kind of curriculum and instruction you will use. However, a few recommendations can be made, drawn from observation of charter schools and other innovative public schools.

Hire mostly, if not entirely, veteran teachers with successful experience in other schools. Some charter schools have made the mistake of assuming that this is a good place for the beginning teacher, who is young, enthusiastic, energetic, and eager. You may want to hire a few first- or second-year teachers. But these people, no matter how committed, are just learning what it means to teach, and the first year or two of teaching is incredibly difficult. Beginning teachers require a great deal of mentoring from older experienced teachers, but in the first few years of your charter school, helping students must be the central priority. There will be so much to do for the children that helping a young inexperienced teacher probably cannot be a high priority. Teaching in a charter school is intense work, and at least initially, it is generally better to hire people who have already developed and demonstrated strong abilities to work with students.

Look for people who can tell you about projects they have worked on with others. Most charter schools require a great deal of cooperative work from faculty and parents. You want someone who is not only good with students but also can work cooperatively and comfortably with other adults. There are some teachers who are great inside the classroom but who are not team players. Generally, charter schools need faculty members who are skilled at both teamwork and teaching. Ask each prospective teacher what she or he has done to get families more involved in the past. Look for people who have concrete ideas and a positive attitude about families. One of the central characteristics of most successful charter schools is that they work closely with students' families and encourage their involvement. You want educators who view parents not just as customers but as allies and partners.

Look for people who can tell you about exciting things they have done with students. You do not want to hire teachers who can tell you what is wrong with traditional schools or who are familiar with the literature of school reform but who have few concrete ideas about what to do with real students. There is nothing wrong with having read widely in the field of school reform and reorganization, but faculty who have this background must, like all the other faculty, also know how to motivate students and organize a classroom or projects or a cross-country field trip. You want teachers who have clear, specific ideas about how to help youngsters learn, not those who simply talk about the importance of hands-on learning, field trips, high standards, whole language, or community internships. So look for people who have examples of their involvement with hands-on active learning or other kinds of projects and instruction that you want to see used with students in your school.

Look for educators who really seem to like working with young people. Look for passion and enthusiasm. Look for people for whom teaching is not just a job but a calling. Charter school teaching is going to be hard work. Look for people who appear to see working in your school as an opportunity to make a big, important difference in the lives of young people.

Selection of an Administrator

Most, although not all, charter schools decide they need someone who can coordinate and supervise what the school is doing, even if that administrative position is only part time. Some charter schools, especially relatively small ones, have created an administrative team consisting of several faculty members along with one or two members of the charter school board. This seems to have worked well in several schools, but it puts an enormous amount of additional work and stress on people who already have a great deal to do. In most cases, people who work full time with youngsters will not be able to fill the administrative supervisor or coordinator role. In many instances, then, charter schools hire someone specific to fill the position of principal, "team leader," "team coordinator," or "lead teacher."

This administrator spends at least part of her or his time checking that decisions the school's faculty and board have made are being implemented. Another reason to hire a principal is to have someone who will be in charge of evaluating the performance of faculty. Having a single person in charge of evaluation brings some uniformity and consistency to the process. Also, in some schools, it is extremely difficult for faculty members to be completely honest with each other even though such openness is an important goal. Having an administrator in charge of the evaluation process can resolve this problem and be extremely important to process accuracy and effectiveness.

Conversely, the wrong person in a leadership position can create enormous problems for a charter school. A number of teachers who have helped start charter schools say one of the reasons they want to work in an innovative school is to get away from a dictatorial administrator. Charter schools must be careful that administrators do not re-create the bureaucracy the charter school faculty wanted to leave behind.

Creating a System of Governance

Charter school governance should receive careful attention from school planners as the school is forming and when it is actually running. Indeed, the *Charter School Bulletin,* published by the Colorado State Department of Education, observes that "if there is one issue that can bog down the efficient operation of a charter school, it is governance!"[1] In creating a system of governance for your charter school, as in so many other areas, there is no one best approach. However, charter school operators have learned, sometimes the hard way, that certain general principles ought to be followed.

It is important to consider the kind of legal entity the school wants to create. In some cases, charter schools have established themselves as nonprofit corporations, controlled by a self-perpetuating board of directors. In these schools, the teachers work "for" the board. In other cases, the teacher-founders have formed a professional partnership. This gives them much more control over the school's policies and procedures.

Determine what your state law says, if anything, about charter school governance. Most states leave the composition of the board of directors entirely up to the people creating the school. However, some states, such as Minnesota, insist that a majority of the members of the board of directors must be teachers in the school. In some states, nonprofit associations run workshops for people setting up charter schools, teaching them how to develop a board of directors. These workshops may also provide training directly to the members of a newly created board.

Bill Windler of the Colorado State Department of Education urges charter schools to study boards of successful nonprofit organizations. He recommends, among other things, that well-functioning boards make sure they keep full and accurate minutes, maintain a policy book, conduct a written annual evaluation of the school's director and of the board itself, create a rotation system for board membership, and develop a method of sharing information about the school with parents, the sponsor, and others interested in the school.[2]

Remember that the goal of the school is to help young people learn, not to spend a great deal of time on decision making. Some innovative schools have floundered because educators and parents exhausted themselves with meetings, committees, and internal disagreements. The purpose of the governance system should be to help the school achieve its overall goal—helping young people learn more. This simple point needs to be carefully and continuously considered. Otherwise, despite doing everything else right, your school may implode as people can become exhausted from too many meetings and too much decision making.

Early on, develop a list of the key kinds of decisions that will need to be made about policies and procedures. You may want to contact a nearby school board or the state school board association for a sample list or manual of policies and procedures. Your list will probably not be as detailed as the list for a large school district, but the sample list can give you an idea of the range of issues you will face. At a minimum, the key decisions will deal with school goals, curriculum choices, personnel choices, the budget, faculty evaluation processes, student evaluation processes, selection of an attorney and an accountant, insurance, fundraising, public relations, and methods of involving families.

Decide which of the necessary decisions will be made by your board of directors and which by the faculty. This is a critical decision. Being clear about who is responsible for what will simplify your work and make it much more likely that the school will function well. Conversely, a murky decision-making process produces frustration and wastes everyone's time and energy.

Setting Priorities

Set priorities periodically and focus on them. I was once present when the U.S. secretary of education and a U.S. senator visited an inner-city charter school. The hallway was jammed with reporters and camera as the two visitors talked with students, camera crews had taken over one teacher's classroom for a press conference, and the classroom teacher looked at the commotion and said, "Well, the kids are having an interesting, memorable day, and we'll talk about this for a long time. Tomorrow, we'll read the newspaper article about this visit and maybe write some letters to the politicians thanking them for the visit. Hoopla is nice, but we need to remember why we're here. It's the students."

This teacher understood her mission. If charter school advocates do that, the charter movement will grow, and youngsters will gain. Charter schools around the nation are being researched by graduate students, questioned by journalists, and challenged by opponents. There are also many day-to-day issues to resolve about all the peripheral elements that support the teaching and the running of the school. Under these circumstances, it can be terribly difficult to remain focused on the teaching mission. True progress requires setting priorities and paying attention to them. The contract for results that each charter school agrees to should remind everyone why the charter school was created: to help youngsters learn more.

Developing Relationships with Colleges and Universities

Postsecondary institutions have a great deal of potentially valuable expertise, and charter schools can benefit when they develop working relationships with colleges and universities. Moreover, these relationships can extend beyond teacher and administrator programs. Some charter schools have received invaluable help from professors of law, business, accounting, computer science, and architecture. Professors with a strong interest in innovative public education may volunteer time to help a charter school develop its bylaws, redo a building, set up accounting procedures, or carry out an evaluation.

Some charter schools are working closely with colleges of education by providing internships for prospective teachers. As the number of charter schools around the nation grows, many universities will recognize that charter schools offer job opportunities for their students. Some professional schools are always looking for places where their students can get internships. For example, Augsburg College music students and computer science students are working closely with students and faculty at the Cedar Riverside Community School located just a few blocks from their Minneapolis campus.

Teacher and administrator preparation courses often do not offer university students opportunities to have conversations with students or faculty from innovative schools. Charter school educators ought to contact teacher education departments and ask if they can bring charter school students to talk with students in teacher education courses. The current generation of people who are going into education ought to know firsthand, from charter school students and faculty, what the opportunities, challenges, and values of charter schools really are.

A charter school may also want to encourage college and university students to visit the school because a positive experience with charter schools can have a long-term influence on these people, who may become businesspeople or legislators and who will in many cases become parents. Although too many visitors can be a burden, the right visitors can offer a great learning experience for students. Each youngster at O'Farrell Community School in San Diego learns to feel more comfortable talking with adults by taking a turn at guiding adult visitors around the school. The use of student guides not only helps young people grow, it allows the O'Farrell faculty who would otherwise be conducting these tours themselves to continue to concentrate on their teaching.

In a few states, colleges and universities can sponsor charter schools. However, the majority of postsecondary institutions in these states have not sponsored charter schools because they do not want to anger public school officials and teachers unions (see Chapter Four).

Professional education journals often publish articles by college professors critical of public school choice and charter school legislation, and charter school proponents ought to recognize that much of what they stand for challenges what is taught by some education professors. Some professors argue that the public schools cannot be held responsible for improved achievement of students when students have so many problems outside the schools. Others argue that spending more money and equalizing expenditures among districts serving low-income and wealthy families is the primary solution to public education's problems. Some professors insist that there is a "manufactured crisis" in U.S. education. The subtitle of one such book, written by two university professors, reveals the tone: "Myths, Fraud and the Attack on America's Public Schools."[3] Finally, a recent report on public school choice released by a Harvard professor simply ignores much of the experience of alternative public schools over the last twenty years.[4]

Charter school proponents generally are not opposed to spending more money on public education. (Although, ironically, in most states, charter schools get *less* money than other public schools.) But they think it is also vital to offer new opportunities for people to establish innovative schools and to develop new incentives to encourage public school systems to be more responsive, innovative, and effective. Many college professors disagree. Therefore, as charter school proponents and those who work in charter schools try to interest postsecondary institutions in their work, they must be prepared to be ignored by some professors and attacked by others.

The charter school movement represents a gigantic challenge to the existing public education system. Teacher and administrator preparation programs are a major part of that system, and charter school proponents should recognize that reality. Charter schools can gain a great deal by working closely with colleges and universities. Higher education students and professors have a great deal of knowledge and skill that charter schools can use. At the same time, establishing working relationships with certain professors or departments may not be possible at present.

Focusing on Families as Well as Students

One of the wisest things many charter schools are doing is to begin the school year by developing agreements with students and their parents. So often, the first time a parent hears from a traditional school is when her or his youngster has done something wrong.

Charter schools avoid that situation with these agreements that build a strong, positive working relationship between the school and family before the academic year begins.

A conference with the teacher, parents, and student is generally held in August, runs for about fifteen minutes, and gives the young person and her or his parents a chance to discuss priorities for the coming year. The conference reduces anxieties on both sides and gives the teacher valuable information about the student and the family that might otherwise take months to learn. Here is an outline of the basic steps in a typical conference:

1. The teacher asks the student, "What do you really enjoy doing?" After hearing from the student, it is a good idea for the teacher to ask the parent to say more about the youngster's strengths, talents, and interests. A wise teacher can and will build on the interests and strengths of each student.

2. The teacher asks both the parent and the student, "What are your priorities for the coming year?" This question gives both parent and student a chance to tell the teacher what is really important for them to accomplish. It builds a feeling of partnership and ownership in the learning process. People who have helped to develop goals are much more likely to feel it is important to accomplish them than are people who are simply told, "Here are the goals we have set for you." Asking this question also helps the teacher determine whether the parent has any special concerns.

3. The teacher gives the parent a list of different ways that the parent could help out the school and asks which of them the parent would be willing to do. This allows the school to tap parent strengths and helps parents understand what they can do to promote learning. (A list of fifty ways parents can help charter schools is available from the Center for School Change, Humphrey Institute, University of Minnesota, 301 19th Ave. S., Minneapolis, MN 55455; please include a stamped self-addressed envelope with your request.)

4. The teacher reviews how the school will report the student's progress to the parents.

5. The teacher asks the parent and student if they have any questions or issues they would like to discuss. Depending on their

age, youngsters usually have a variety of questions, ranging from "Where will I sit?" and "Where do I put my coat?" to "Will this school help me figure out what I want to do next in life?"

The school should also arrange meetings with teachers, parents, and students at other times. Meeting three to four times a year with families is vital. Families need and want to know what is happening with their children. They will have important questions. They deserve good, accurate information about what their children are learning. In some cases, they will need reassurance. In other cases, they will need advice and assistance.

Charter schools appear to be doing much more than other public schools to promote parent involvement. For example, one study found that in 75 percent of charter schools "teachers regularly discuss strategies for involving hard to reach parents," while this practice occurs in only 58 percent of comparison schools. In 54 percent of charter schools, "all teachers send information home to parents explaining school lessons," while only 24 percent of comparison schools do so. In 46 percent of charter schools, "all teachers provide suggestions for activities parents can do at home with their children," while only 16 percent of comparison schools do so. And in 61 percent of charter schools, "¾ or more of the teachers create homework assignments requiring parental involvement," while only 37 percent of comparison schools do so.[5]

In other words, a much higher percentage of charter school teachers report that they are doing exactly what nationally recognized authorities on parent and family involvement recommend.[6] Indeed, a variety of polls show that educators say that increasing family involvement is the single best way to increase student achievement.[7]

In addition, some charter schools are requiring parents to sign contracts stating that they will be involved in their children's education. This practice, however, has been challenged by researchers who found that requiring such contracts kept certain families from enrolling their children.[8] The authors of the study also pointed out that 71 percent of the twenty-eight California charter schools they studied had some form of contract that parents were asked to sign, compared to just 8 percent of the comparison schools. Some of these contracts asked parents to volunteer a certain number of hours per week or month or make some other kind of contribution to the school. Others asked the parents to help their children in certain ways. But are some parents, especially nonwhite and low-income parents, intimidated by such contracts? The answer may be yes.

The question of parent involvement has been debated extensively in the America Online charter school forum. The general conclusion seems to be that it makes a great deal of sense to have a parent-educator-student conference in August, before school starts, so that all parties can learn about each other and develop a positive working relationship. It makes a great deal of sense to develop an overall plan for the student's year and to discuss ways the school and family can work together. It makes a great deal of sense for the family to be asked to help out the school in some way.

However, it probably is not a good idea to *demand* that the family help out the school *as a condition of the student's attending the school.* It may intimidate certain families who have already had bad experiences with schools to be told they must give a certain number of hours of volunteer time if their youngsters are to be allowed in the charter school.

Most educators talk about the value of parent and family involvement. But it is encouraging to see so many charter schools actually reaching out to parents and making them not customers but partners and allies. Sometimes families will challenge what goes on in the school. But virtually all parents want to help their children succeed. If the school builds on parents' hopes and energies, the results will be much more learning for youngsters. This is more important than fancy computers or beautiful carpeted hallways. Family support is critical for student learning and for charter school success.

Parents also are an incredible source not only of talent—helping charter schools find buildings and equipment, paint walls, lay carpet, write grants, and carry out many other tasks—but also of advocacy. Charter school parents' talk about the wonderful computer program at New Country School encouraged the local district to have its own teachers attend workshops at the school to learn what charter school students were gaining from the Internet. Parents have convinced local reporters that a school deserves a story in the local newspaper. When given the chance, parents will open up important new opportunities for charter schools and students.

Working closely with families should be one of charter schools' highest priorities. The students will gain. The school will improve.

Evaluating

Evaluation has many facets. This section focuses on types of evaluation, timing of evaluation, faculty evaluation, and using outside evaluators. As you make decisions about student and faculty assessment, it is important to remember that evaluation is not only a list of results that can justify a school's existence but a tool that can help the school improve.

Types of Evaluation

It is vital to determine early the expectations and requirements your state and, where applicable, your local district have about student outcomes and tests. In one case, a charter school waited more than two years after opening to discuss with its sponsor, the local school board, the tests to be used in measuring growth. Not surprisingly, this school is facing a real challenge in getting its charter renewed.

Although there are problems with standardized tests, many members of the public will ask how your students are doing on them. Joe McDonald, Bethany Rogers, and Ted Sizer at the Coalition of Essential Schools suggest using "the best standardized tests available in computational mathematics, reading, and expository prose—whether developed by commercial publishers or the states."[9] Of course, you may want to add to the list of outcomes and tests required by your sponsoring group.

The 1995 survey of 110 charter schools found they were using a variety of measures to assess student progress.[10] The most frequently cited were standardized tests and student portfolios, followed by such indicators as attendance, parent surveys, student demonstrations of mastery, and participation in state assessment programs. But other measures are used, too. These include reductions in the number of students involved with the criminal justice system and the observations of people who employ youngsters who are students at the charter school. The New Country School has several hundred required competencies. O'Farrell Community School has a list of "challenge areas."

McDonald, Rogers, and Sizer urge that standardized tests be viewed as supplementary to exhibitions, saying, "The point is to maintain a trendline of achievement in basic empowering skills, and so preserve political confidence while experimenting with richer accountability mechanisms."[11]

Timing

Some charter schools have made a serious mistake by waiting too long to administer standardized tests. In states where charter schools have a three-year contract and are required to ask for a renewal late in their third year, the timing of the testing program can make a crucial difference. If schools test early in the fall of students' first year, they will be able to test two more times (fall of the second and fall of the third year) before going back to the sponsor and asking for a renewal. Schools that test in the spring are finding that they will not have third-year test results in hand when they are asking for a renewal. Moreover, they will not get credit for the growth they produced between September and March or April of the first year. In other words, your baseline measurement should be what students' know around the time they enter the school. It is a big mistake to wait until March, April, or May of the students' first year to use assessment tests because your baseline will then be the students' knowledge in the spring of their first year, and their growth during that first year, which may be substantial, will not be measured.

It is true that the schools the students come from will have tested students the spring before they transfer to the charter school, but this does not necessarily resolve the difficulty. First, the students' original school may have used different tests than you are using, and making valid comparisons between different tests can be very difficult. Second, charter school students probably will not all come from the same school or even from the same school system, which means that you will be trying to compare your results to not one but several different tests, thus compounding the difficulty of getting a valid picture of student progress. It seems to me that the easiest and wisest thing to do is to test all the charter school students every fall, beginning the first year they enter the school (McDonald, Rogers, and Sizer agree with this advice).

Outside Evaluators

Many charter schools arrange for an outside evaluator to work with them. New Heights Schools in Stillwater, Minnesota, for example, hired a former school superintendent with considerable evaluation expertise. Toviola-Meadowlands Charter School, in northeastern Minnesota, and New Visions School both hired professors. Minnesota New Country School is working with a former public school teacher who has established her own evaluation consulting business and has done a great deal of evaluation work for foundations.

Sometimes the outside evaluator will contribute her or his services: this evaluator might be a graduate student looking for a subject for a master's or doctor's thesis or a professor who wants to write an article or a book about charter schools. For example, undergraduate students from Carleton College in Northfield, Minnesota, carried out several short-term research projects for an innovative elementary school, surveying former students who were now in a middle school. They also helped another innovative public school examine the impact of students' environmental community service projects. This was a win-win arrangement. The college students helped the school faculty, saw the practical applications of the research techniques they were learning in their courses, and gained a sense that they were contributing to public schools that were making sincere efforts to improve.

Students at the Options for Youth charter school have been assessed by a professor who asked the students shortly after they entered the school to write brief essays on one of two subjects—"a dream they had for their future or an adult they might emulate."[12] A year later, students were asked to write on the same topic, and the quality of their writing was compared. Using a variety of criteria, the professor found important gains among many of the students. Other methods used to assess the growth of students at Options for Youth were pre- and postscores on standardized tests, interviews with students, surveys of students, and interviews with teachers.

There are at least three good reasons to work with an outside evaluator: expertise, perspective, and credibility. First, relatively few people know a good deal about the best ways to measure gains in student knowledge and achievement. Some people who teach at universities and some people in school systems are experts. Wise charter schools tap their expertise.

Second, an outside evaluator can add another important perspective on your school to your existing perspectives. A good evaluator will encourage you to question your assumptions. A good evaluator will help you see what is really happening in your school with and to your students, not just what you would like to have happen. For example, an outside evaluator encouraged an innovative public school in which I worked to survey its graduates. From this survey, we learned that even though graduates were generally very pleased with the school, they had several suggestions, including the recommendation that we increase the amount of writing assigned. A number of the graduates felt they had not received enough writing assignments and that this had made their lives more difficult when they went on to college. After seeing this new perspective, the teachers did give more writing assignments and made writing a more integral part of the school's graduation requirements. Without the evaluator's advice, we might not have surveyed graduates and might not have strengthened the school.

The third reason to hire an outside evaluator is to increase the credibility of your assessment. At some point, the organization sponsoring your school will want evidence of your effectiveness. A highly regarded evaluation expert can help you convince the sponsor that important gains are being made. It is one thing for a group of parents and teachers to go to a school board or a state department of education hearing and explain test score gains and another thing for a well-regarded evaluation expert to contribute advice and assistance and to make the information you have gathered more convincing.

None of this means that a charter school should rely entirely on an outside person. It is also vital that you contact many charter schools and other innovative schools to determine how they are measuring progress. You will get many good ideas and may also get suggestions about outside evaluators who do a thoughtful job of evaluation. But it can take years for a school to develop its own expertise, perspective, and credibility in this area, and evaluation is one of the many things that many charter schools sometimes decide is worth purchasing, rather than doing it entirely by themselves.

Evaluation and Community Support

Evaluation efforts can help you build support in your community before you go to the sponsoring authority that will decide whether to renew your contract. The Minnesota New Country School (MNCS), for example, has its students participate in a "performance night" once every two months. At the performance nights, students display one project they are working on. The atmosphere is a little like a science fair: people go from project to project displayed in a large room while students explain what they are doing and what they have learned. A number of curious community members have attended one or more performance nights, and MNCS faculty believe that this bimonthly event definitely has helped the school broaden community understanding and acceptance of its program.

McDonald, Rogers, and Sizer at the Coalition of Essential Schools strongly recommend events like this, suggesting that exhibitions should be "a central feature of the school's assessment system." They believe that such assessment events will "show the school's stakeholders what the schools' students have achieved, help the school take stock of whether its systems are working to ensure high achievement of all students, and push learning deeper while they assess it."[13]

Faculty Evaluation

Most charter schools have found they want to give each faculty person yearly feedback. Because charter schools are usually small and are responsible for improved student performance, they cannot afford to have any weak teachers. A weak teacher literally could cost the rest of the staff their jobs. So there is a strong incentive to look carefully at the work of each faculty member.

Moreover, most charter schools have concluded that the job of evaluating a faculty member's performance should not be left to just one person. A number of charter schools evaluate faculty by asking each teacher to develop a list of yearly goals. Then fellow teachers, and sometimes parents and students, along with the principal or team leader give the faculty member feedback in relation to these goals. What is the person doing well? What might the person do the following year to improve?

Answering Everyone's Questions and Communicating Results

Evaluations typically must answer a variety of potential questions about charter schools. City Academy founder Milo Cutter learned in talking with St. Paul school administrators that they were interested in more than students' test scores. City Academy was working with young people who had been out of school before enrolling at the charter school, and the administrators wanted to know if these youngsters were going to graduate and what would happen to them after graduation. City Academy demonstrated that most of its students graduated, and a high percentage continued their education by attending a postsecondary institution. This information helped convince the local school board to vote unanimously to renew the school's charter.

Standardized tests are important. The public understands, or thinks it understands, that higher standardized test scores represent more learning. What many people do not understand is that standardized tests do not measure everything that schools should be teaching. Charter schools should be aggressive in explaining all the different ways to measure student progress. Another of McDonald, Rogers, and Sizer's suggestions is to publish an annual school report that contains evaluation data along with other information.[14] The report to the public by Sacramento's Bowling Green Charter School is an excellent example of such an explanation.[15] It looks like a tabloid newspaper and includes pictures of students' work, descriptions of various activities, charts of test results, and explanations of those charts. The school uses standardized tests and performance assessments in reading, writing, and mathematics. The report also shows that over the last five years, student attendance is up and suspensions are down. Many charter schools, including New Visions and Options for Youth, are producing such reports. It probably makes sense to share your report with the local news media and to place copies in the local library. You may want to give a report summary to each family. Students can contribute to such reports in a number of ways: for example, by writing a history of the school and a description of a typical day at the school.

The School as a Business

Determine how you will handle the business side of the charter school. A charter school is not just an educational institution, it is a small business. All charter schools that are successful find ways to handle their business and legal affairs competently.

Charter schools must start with a conservative budget. If a school attracts more students than it anticipates and has the room for such students, this is a real plus (and preliminary research shows that many charter schools have waiting lists of students who would like to enter).[16] But one way for a charter school to get itself in enormous trouble is to project more income than it really has and to set up a budget on the basis of overly optimistic projections. Several charter schools have encountered this problem, and some may be forced to close because they did not anticipate all their expenses.[17]

Several Minnesota charter schools have hired a retired accountant, Don Jacobson, who is very familiar with school finance, having been controller of a large Minnesota suburban public school budget for ten years. He does the accounting, the payroll, and the reporting of student data to the state of Minnesota on which state aid to schools is based. Many teachers have a simplistic view of the financial record-keeping systems required of public schools. Some teachers, says Jacobson, seem to think this aspect of administration is just a matter of "keeping a glorified checkbook, but there's much more involved."[18] He urges charter schools to hire someone with the "big picture," who understands budgeting, governmental accounting, how the state funds schools, and "how it all fits together." He also urges charter schools not to "underestimate this part—it's a lot of work and getting it right is critical!"

It is also important for your charter school to have a strong relationship with a banker. The charter may wish to borrow money and will certainly have a number of bank accounts. Charter school advocates in several states have discussed the possibility that banks may provide loans to help charter schools with start-up expenses. In most states, there typically is a substantial delay, between three to twelve months, in state payments to schools. But charter schools must have some money immediately to purchase chairs, tables, computers, paper, pencils, and the like—the essentials for a school, whatever its philosophy.

Charter schools also will need someone with extensive legal expertise, especially in the area of school law. Some charter schools obtain these services from a parent. Others have found interested professors at nearby law schools. Some charter schools have approached large local legal firms, asked for, and received pro bono (free) legal services. Legal expertise is critical from the relatively early days of a charter school. The school will be making many contracts—the most important of which involves the school's survival. In many cases, charter schools will also have to negotiate leases and to develop their own policies in virtually every imaginable area. A skillful attorney is critical. Most charter schools, however, do not try to hire a full-time person with business or legal expertise.

Some schools contract for business services with the school district that granted them the charter; however, many charter schools feel they can get better service and save money by subcontracting with someone else. After all, part of the reason for charter schools' existence is to demonstrate that schools with more autonomy than traditional public schools can improve services for students and increase achievement. Vaughn Next Century Learning Center, in Los Angeles, reports it was able to save more than $1 million, among other things, by arranging its own business services rather than going through the district. Using these savings, Vaughn purchased additional space and a number of computers for its students.[19]

Some charter schools have checked to see whether the local or state teachers union is interested in subcontracting with the school to provide business and legal services. Unions certainly have attorneys, accountants, and other people necessary for the operation of an effective organization. Why not obtain services from unions? Several union officials who have heard this idea are intrigued. At the same time, their unions overall were not especially excited about appearing to promote or work closely with charter schools. But within the next few years, we will probably see subcontracts with some unions for these critical services. Many charter advocates see this as an important potential evolution in unions' role.

The 1995 national survey of 110 charter schools found that 91 of the schools subcontracted for at least one kind of service:

50 contracted for accounting or other business-related services; 36 contracted for legal services; 34 contracted for meals; and 33 contracted for janitorial services.[20]

Another part of the business side of running a charter school that you will have to deal with is insurance. Your school probably wants some form of liability insurance for both the faculty and the board of directors. This is one of the items you must discuss with the state, because some charter school legislation explains how liability insurance is to be managed. Your school may be eligible to participate in state-operated liability insurance programs, or it may be able to join state school board associations, which sometimes offer liability insurance. Some charter schools have contacted teachers unions because teachers who are union members while working at charter schools generally are eligible to participate in union insurance programs, though the school may wish to pay all or a portion of the costs. Some charter schools have purchased liability insurance on their own, without going through another group. The same groups mentioned here also offer medical and dental plans that may interest charter school employees.

In a few states, charter schools are examining the possibility of joining together to reduce costs by collectively buying insurance and other items.

Finding a Facility

When asked about the challenges of creating a charter school, directors rated finding a facility one of the toughest. Charter schools have used a great deal of ingenuity in dealing with this issue. Here are a few suggestions they make.

Make sure you understand what your state law says about the facilities you may use. Some states allow charter schools to purchase buildings; others allow only leasing. From 1991 to 1993, Minnesota's law did not allow charter schools to lease space from a parochial school. The law was changed, and several charter schools are now leasing such space. So you need to know what your state will allow and what guidelines you must follow.

Many states provide funds to help local school districts deal with asbestos removal, handicapped access, and other facilities needs. Check whether your state provides such funds to charter schools. If it does, find out whether you get these funds automatically or whether you must apply for them.

A recent report from the Hudson Institute noted that charter schools in many states were frustrated by building codes.[21] Some charter school advocates have asked their legislatures to give waivers in this area, as they have in the education code. For example, some states require all five- and six-year-olds to be housed on the first floor of a building. Several elementary charter schools have been unable to use otherwise excellent space because it was on the second floor of a building.

The list of places that charter schools use is extensive. It includes unused or underused public and parochial school buildings; vacant space in a housing project, college, or university; and vacant space in office buildings and social service agencies (like a YMCA or YWCA). Some charter schools have been able to share space with city, state, or even federal government offices. Some charter schools have leased vacant storefronts in the community they serve.

A variety of people can help you search for an appropriate building. Some charter schools have asked real estate agents to help them. Others have talked with bankers, community service agents, and attorneys. In a few cases, a local person has donated a building for the charter school to use. (A little luck never hurts!)

Whatever building you use, have it checked by a local building inspector and by someone knowledgeable about asbestos hazards, access for people with disabilities, and other health and safety issues before you sign an agreement to buy or lease. Get a realistic estimate of how much a building will have to be modified and what it will cost to do this work. You might want to get two estimates and compare them. Also, check the status of the heating, cooling, and sprinkler systems and the age and quality of the roof. These things do not have much to do with student learning (until they go wrong in ways that make everyone uncomfortable), but they can have an enormous impact on your budget. Some charter schools have found, to their dismay, that the building they thought was in excellent shape required thousands of dollars in changes to be acceptable as a school.

Many charter schools have put sweat equity into fixing up buildings. As long as you have skilled people working with you, this is fine. As mentioned before, parents of students at Academy Charter School laid carpet, built walls, and put in some of the plumbing to modify the former grocery store their school is using. Parents and teachers from Minnesota's New Country School built ramps to provide access for people with disabilities, constructed tables, and painted the inside of the storefronts that school is using. Students at City Academy built some of the walls that helped make the city recreation building that school uses more appropriate for the school's operation.

Celebrating Accomplishments

Finally, take time to celebrate accomplishments. Putting together a proposal and then opening and operating a school are very challenging tasks. Periodically, put together a potluck dinner or take a walk in the woods or do something else to relax and give yourself credit for what has been accomplished. There always will be more to do, and you do not need to minimize the tasks still to be completed. But periodically acknowledging progress and taking time to laugh and smile are critical if you are going to keep going.

Many schools find it appropriate to review accomplishments and celebrate every two to three months. They then create a work plan for the next three to six months. The details depend on what has already been accomplished and what things now appear to be priorities. Everything cannot be accomplished at the same time.

Part Four

Where To, What Next

Chapter Eight

Key Early Lessons

The charter school movement has spread faster and farther than many people thought possible. That is in part because parents and educators came forward immediately to use the idea and because many of the youngsters who have gained from charter schools over the last five years have been those who did not do well in their previous public schools. The charter school concept also grew because in some places it encouraged broader improvements across the school district. (See the sidebar on p. 168 for legislators' views of charter school benefits.)

With an idea as new as the charter school concept, it is impossible to make definitive statements about its results. Think of the charter school movement as a five-year-old child. What will the youngster be like as an adult? It is difficult to say. We can make educated guesses, but so much is yet to happen that we cannot say much for sure. However, we can describe the five-year-old. The youngster already has skills and a personality. In that spirit of description, this chapter reviews seven important things we know about the charter school movement:

1. Charter schools can have a positive effect on student achievement, attendance, and attitude.
2. Charter schools are serving many youngsters who have not succeeded in traditional public schools.
3. Thousands of educators are coming forward who want to work with youngsters and are willing to accept the responsibility for improved student achievement.
4. The charter school concept will reach its potential only if the details of charter legislation are right.

Legislators' Reasons for Introducing Charter School Legislation.

Why are state legislators introducing charter school legislation? What advice do legislators who have introduced charter school legislation have for other states? A 1996 survey of fifty legislators and others who helped promote the charter school concept asked these questions. Policy makers answering these questions came from Arizona, California, Colorado, Delaware, Louisiana, Massachusetts, and Minnesota.

Legislators listed several major reasons for introducing charter school bills. The most frequent reasons given were

- To help youngsters who have not succeeded in existing schools
- To provide opportunity for educational entrepreneurs
- To expand the range of public schools available
- To increase overall student achievement
- To encourage the existing public education system to improve
- To provide an alternative, rather than a prelude, to vouchers

Legislators also were asked what advice they would give to strengthen charter school laws. The most frequent recommendations given were

- Give charter public schools the same per-pupil allocations as other public schools
- Permit more than one organization to sponsor charter schools
- Eliminate the cap on the number of charter schools
- Give charter schools a great deal of independence from local districts
- Provide some start-up funds

Source: J. Nathan and J. Power, *Policy-Makers' Views on the Charter School Movement* (Minneapolis: University of Minnesota Hubert H. Humphrey Institute for Public Affairs Center for School Change, Apr. 1996), pp. 11–12.

5. Charter schools must learn how to obtain start-up funds.
6. Charter schools demonstrate how to avoid putting up costly new buildings to house students.
7. Charter schools can build on the experience of successful inner-city innovative public schools.

Charter Schools Can Have a Positive Effect on Student Achievement, Attendance, and Attitude

Probably the single most frequent question from parents, legislators, journalists, and educators is about student achievement: Are there any examples of charter schools that have improved student achievement as measured by both standardized tests and other assessments? Yes, there are. But the oldest charter school in the country was just in its fourth year during the 1995–96 school year. Charter schools are still young, so this research, while encouraging, is, in all fairness, preliminary. Here are a few encouraging examples:

• During its first year as a charter school serving 1,200 inner-city Los Angeles students, the Vaughn Next Century Learning Center reported that students' average standardized test language arts scores improved from the 9th percentile to the 39th, while their math scores increased from the 14th percentile to the 57th. In the 1993–94 and 1994–95 school years, the school also used the Aprenda, a test employed at many California schools where students have limited English proficiency. Students' scores on the Aprenda gained an average of 6 percent in reading, 9 percent in math, and 10 percent in language.[1]

• Students at Bowling Green Elementary, an inner-city K–6 charter school in Sacramento, California, have shown improvements in reading and math on the Comprehensive Test of Basic Skills. Attendance and behavior also improved. These are noteworthy gains for a school that five years ago was one of the three lowest-achieving schools in the Sacramento City Unified District and that had lost the most money from the state due to its large number of unexcused absences.[2] The Sacramento school board recently extended Bowling Green's contract for an additional two years.

• Washington Charter School, an elementary school in Palm Desert, California, reported that California Test of Basic Skills scores were up in reading and math in all grades except 5th-grade reading. Students in 2nd grade in 1992 averaged 54th percentile in reading and 68th percentile in math. By 1995, those same students were scoring in the 76th percentile in reading and in the 90th percentile in math. The number of students on the school's academic honor roll has increased from thirty-seven to ninety-three in the past two years. Parent participation and involvement also are up at Washington. The school reports that the number of parents attending parent conferences increased from 483 in 1993–94 to 952 in 1994–95. The number of volunteer hours contributed by parents increased from 7,789 to 14,000.[3]

• In its first-year evaluation, the New Visions School in Minneapolis, a K–8 school working predominantly with inner-city students who have not succeeded in other schools, showed a 1.5-year average gain on the Slosson Oral Reading Test among its students of color and a 1.4-year average gain on the same test among its white students. New Visions also reported that 64 percent of the students made an average gain of nine months or more on the Gates-MacGinitie Silent Reading Test, 28 percent maintained their previous level, and 8 percent declined in achievement.[4]

• In February 1996, the Bluffview Montessori charter school in Winona, Minnesota, became the second charter school in the nation to have its contract renewed. Its students had improved achievement in standardized tests.

• The Charter School of San Diego serves about 485 students in grades 6 through 12 who are not succeeding in traditional schools. Using the Abbreviated Stanford Achievement Test, the percentage of 8th graders who scored at or above the 50th percentile in reading increased 5.5 percent, the percentage of 10th graders increased 9.6 percent, and the percentage of 12th graders increased 10.9 percent. In math, the percentage of students scoring at or above the 50th percentile increased 4.7 percent in the 8th grade, 12.4 percent in the 10th grade, and 28.4 percent in the 12th grade. The school's dropout rate is "significantly lower" than that in the sponsoring school district.[5]

• At Options for Youth, a California charter school, an outside evaluator found that student performance in writing mechanics "showed significant increases" after six months, student performance in reading and writing skills based on standardized tests showed small increases over a six-month period, and percentages of students scoring above the top of a writing grade-level scale increased from 6.5 percent on pretests to 19.4 percent on posttests. The percentages of students scoring below the minimum on the writing grade-level scale decreased from 41.9 percent to 29 percent. These figures indicate that the school was improving the skills of those who started with medium as well as those who started with poor writing skills. Student levels of "intrinsic motivation" (the degree to which students pursue their studies because of their interest in the work) showed "significant increases" between fall 1994 and spring 1995. Finally, student levels of academic self-concept "increased substantially and significantly."[6]

- Student achievement at Academy Charter School in Castle Rock, Colorado, has increased in several areas. After the first year, increases were noted on standardized tests in both writing and mathematics. The first year's progress report, based on the Iowa Test of Basic Skills, showed a 9 percent overall increase in math skills, a 4 percent increase in language skills, and a 3 percent gain in average reading scores.[7] Student achievement has continued to improve. In the spring of 1996, the Castle Rock School District extended the school's charter for another two years.

- Achievement is also up at City Academy, which serves youngsters who have left traditional public schools. Student achievement on standardized tests has increased, and during the school's first three years, seventy-eight of its eighty-nine students graduated (87 percent), and most continued their education in some form of postsecondary education program. The school has been accredited by the North Central Regional Association, perhaps the first charter school in the nation to win accreditation.[8]

Charter Schools Are Serving Many Youngsters Who Have Not Succeeded in Traditional Public Schools

Many charter school proposals focus on minority and low-income students along with students who have not done well in traditional schools. Charter school opponents feared that most of these schools would serve affluent, successful students, becoming "taxpayer-supported elitist academies."[9] This simply has not been the case. The 1995 survey of 110 charter schools in seven states found that most charter schools were designed at least in part to serve at-risk students.[10] A review of six states with the most charter schools found that "minority youngsters comprise 40 percent of charter school enrollments although the same minorities make up just 31 percent of pupils in the regular public schools in those states."[11]

A spring 1996 survey of almost five hundred parents of students attending Massachusetts charter schools found that 51 percent rated their children as average or below average achievers at their previous school. The study also found that more than 70 percent of the parents said their children were more interested in learning since transferring to the charter school, and almost 80 percent gave the charter school a better overall evaluation than their children's previous school.[12]

It is encouraging to see many charter schools open in inner-city and low-income rural areas. It is heartening to talk, as I have, with African American and Hispanic parents who find that charter school educators respond to their ideas and suggestions, in part because the schools need these parents' help to improve achievement and thus to stay open. As one inner-city parent told me, "I went to meetings for years. They ran me all around the mulberry bush. But our charter school, the teachers make me feel like they really want me involved, and not just in fundraising."

Moreover, many strong proposals for charter schools to serve youngsters who are not succeeding in traditional public schools have been made but have not been approved, largely for two reasons. First, most states limit the number of charter schools that can be authorized. For example, as we have seen, Massachusetts legislation allows only twenty-five charter schools, yet the state already has received almost one hundred proposals for these twenty-five slots. Second, at least some of the strongest charter school proposals have been rejected by school districts. A 1996 survey of state officials, who readily acknowledge they do not know of all the charter proposals that have been rejected, indicates that more than one hundred charter proposals have been rejected by local school boards. In Minnesota alone, which currently has eighteen charter schools operating, more than twenty proposals have been turned down by local school boards.

No one is arguing that every proposal should be accepted. But thoughtful, committed, talented energetic people are coming forward in many states with proposals for educating the very students educators and the public are most concerned about.

Thousands of Educators Are Coming Forward Who Want to Work with Youngsters and Are Willing to Accept the Responsibility for Improved Student Achievement

All across the country, educators are stepping forward who are willing to be held responsible for improving student achievement. Hundreds of charter school proposals have been made in the last five years, more than 260 charter schools are open and serving students, and the number grows almost every month.

Delaware's experience is typical. Shortly after the legislature adopted a charter school law, the state department of education convened a Saturday morning meeting to discuss the law and to answer questions from people who were considering developing a charter school proposal. As the state's largest newspaper reported the following day, "Enthusiasm for charter schools is growing not only among businesses and community agencies but among frustrated teachers," and many of the seventy-five people who came to the meeting were public school teachers.[13]

Colorado officials report the same widespread educator interest in creating charter schools. Arthur Ellis, assistant commissioner of the Colorado State Department of Education, finds it "encouraging . . . that there are numerous teachers and administrators in Colorado who recognize that charter schools are not simply a fad but an indicator of the future"[14]

Five years ago, opponents questioned whether educators would be willing to put their jobs at risk, basing them on whether student achievement improved. Five years later, we know the answer. Yes, teachers all over the country are coming forward. In fact, this may be a source of opposition to charter schools. When plenty of people are willing to accept the opportunity charter public schools provide, the charter schools that succeed will raise troubling questions among the public: If charter public schools can improve achievement, why can't other public schools?

The Charter School Concept Will Reach Its Potential Only If the Details of Charter Legislation Are Right

Giving the charter school concept a chance means allowing more organizations than local school districts to sponsor schools. It means giving educators the chance to be free of local labor-management agreements. It means permitting more than a handful of charter schools to be created. As long as educators can say, "Oh well, we can only have twenty of those schools in the whole state," most districts—or existing public schools—will not feel they are facing real, significant competition. It is a bit like permitting only twenty stores in a state to sell clothing. Those few stores will not feel much pressure from competitors.

The debate in many states is no longer about whether there will be charter school legislation. The conflict is over the form of that legislation. In most places, educational groups now say they are in favor of charter school legislation. But the kind of legislation they generally favor is the kind that will produce few, if any, charter schools and little, if any, pressure on existing schools and systems to change. One national teachers union spokesperson acknowledged in March 1996 that her organization recommended legislation allowing only local districts to sponsor charter schools, or as I heard her tell a national PTA audience, "the kind of legislation we favor is what charter proponents call 'weak.'" The dramatic difference in the number of charter schools started in various states illustrates the impact of the details of charter school legislation. In December 1995, 222 charter schools were operating in the five states with the strongest charter school laws and only 14 charter schools were operating in five states with weak laws.[15]

Charter activity in Arkansas and New Jersey helps illustrate the importance of legislative details. Arkansas' law requires both local school board and local teachers union approval. There is no appeal permitted if either the local board or union opposes the charter proposal. However, the New Jersey charter school law permits proponents to go directly to the state superintendent rather than having to apply to a local school board.

The difference in response to these two laws is significant. An official of the Arkansas State Department of Education notes that in the year following adoption of the legislation, while rules and regulations to implement the law were being developed, there was a total of one serious inquiry from an Arkansas school district about creating such a program.[16]

Meanwhile, hundreds of people contacted the New Jersey Department of Education within the first two months of its charter school law adoption in January 1996, before guidelines had been developed. These people were eager to get started on a charter proposal. When the department held a conference during the spring of 1996 to discuss charter procedures, almost four hundred people showed up.[17]

Central to the charter school concept is the idea that more than one kind of organization should have the opportunity to sponsor charter schools. Strong charter school laws allow some group other than a local school board to approve and sponsor charter schools. This feature is vital for producing the kind of ripple effect found in Boston, where the district and local teachers union decided to establish the pilot schools program once strong state charter legislation had been adopted, and in Minnesota, where the state's Post-Secondary Enrollment Options Program encouraged widespread changes. More than half of the 401 school administrators surveyed by Minnesota's legislative auditor said that one result of the postsecondary options program was to promote cooperative efforts between high schools and colleges.[18]

People who really believe in giving entrepreneurial teachers, parents, and community leaders a chance to create the kinds of schools that they think make sense need to recognize the critical differences between weak and strong charter school legislation. People who want to see widespread improvements in public education need to be clear about what they are promoting and why. It is not enough to say, "Oh yes, I'm in favor of charter schools." Real charter school advocates know that without strong legislation, not much will happen.

Once again, the strongest state charter school laws, such as those in New Jersey, Massachusetts, Delaware, and Arizona, allow charter school developers to request sponsorship from some group other than a local board. The most frequently offered advice to state policy makers from charter school developers in a 1995 survey was that state law permit them to go to a group other than a local school board for permission to establish the charter school.[19] Minnesota's original, heavily compromised legislation authorized only local school boards to sponsor charter schools. After watching local board turndowns such as the ones described in this book, the legislature modified the approval process, permitting those proposing a charter school to appeal to the state board of education if at least two members of the local board had voted in support of the proposal. But charter groups often find it difficult to gain those two votes.

Legislation in Massachusetts, Arizona, Delaware, Michigan, New Jersey, and North Carolina is much fairer to innovators, giving them a chance to go directly to the state for sponsorship, or in some states a public university.

Another key feature is that charter schools must be free to create their own working conditions, rather than bound by local district contracts. Schools like City Academy, Bowling Green, New Visions, New Country School, Academy Charter, and PS1 say they must be free, for example, to establish a longer working day and year and to create their own salary structure, which may include paying teachers more than the average in the surrounding district.

This independence from local labor-management agreements is another of the key recommendations made by people who have established charter schools around the country.

Without strong laws, the charter school concept cannot get a real test.

Charter Schools Must Learn How to Obtain Start-Up Funds

Most school districts can go to local voters, and sometimes to the state legislature, for money to construct a new building or alter an existing one. Most states do not give this opportunity to charter schools. The 1995 survey of 110 charter schools identified obtaining start-up funds for buildings and equipment as one of the biggest problems facing these schools.[20] They may have to spend "operating money to renovate and maintain buildings rather than pay teachers or buy books."[21] A 1996 study agrees: "Without doubt, the absence of capital funding, access to conventional school facilities, and start-up money to cover initial equipment, planning, etc. is the heaviest cross charter schools bear today."[22] Many charter schools are using buildings that previously housed other organizations. These buildings will not last forever, and at some point, major expenditures will be necessary.

Charter schools have received modest start-up funds from various places. Some foundations and corporations have awarded grants to charter schools. The Arizona legislature allocated $1.6 million to help charter schools with initial expenses.[23] Several states have allocated a portion of their federal Goals 2000 dollars to charter schools.

As this book was being written, the first federal funds allocated specifically to help establish charter schools were being awarded. Former U.S. Senator David Durenberger of Minnesota had been one of the first people to recognize the problem of funding charter school start-ups. Shortly after Minnesota passed the nation's first charter school legislation, Durenberger introduced the Public School Redefinition Act in the U.S. Senate. Durenberger and one of his key aides, Jon Schroeder, worked for three years to build bipartisan support for the notion that federal financial assistance should be given to start-up charter schools.

Congress first allocated charter school start-up money in 1994 in the amount of $5 million. The following year, President Clinton recommended increasing the allotment to $20 million, and for the year following that, $40 million. In mid-1996, Congress allocated $18 million, which will flow through state departments of education.

Charter Schools Demonstrate How to Avoid Putting Up Costly New Buildings to House Students

Although the fact that a number of charter schools are using space in buildings that previously did not house schools means that they face renovation expenses, it also can be a way to save construction or rental costs. One charter school meets in unused rooms in the local housing project where about 30 percent of its students live. Another meets in a building that formerly housed a VFW hall, and another rents space in a downtown YWCA, giving students access to excellent physical fitness facilities and enabling them to help in a day care center housed in the same building. Another charter school shares space with a city youth recreation building, giving students access to a high-quality gym that otherwise would be almost completely unused during the school day. Some charter schools are located in unused space in local parochial schools. A suburban Colorado charter school leases space in a former grocery store. Another school leases space in a downtown commercial building. Being in the center of a city gives students access to a vast array of business and community learning sites. Yet another school meets in an old elementary school that the local district decided it did not need. Without this charter school, five- to eight-year-olds in this community would have to go twenty-five to thirty-five miles to school. With the charter school, they can attend an innovative elementary school five to ten minutes from their homes.

The 1995 survey of 110 charter schools around the nation showed that twenty-two were leasing commercial space, twenty-one were leasing space in a nonprofit facility, eighteen were using space in a vacant school, eight operated as a school within a school in an existing public school building, four used donated space, and six had purchased their own buildings.[24]

Charter Schools Can Build on the Experience of Successful Inner-City Innovative Public Schools

Gerald Bracey, an educator and author who has observed school reform efforts for more than twenty years, urges that charter school advocates recognize that "you can't substitute enthusiasm for expertise. Both are necessary."[25]

Moreover, the public innovative schools that lasted followed seven precepts (all of which have been addressed in these pages):

1. They had clear, measurable goals.
2. They assessed student achievement in a variety of ways.
3. They kept in close touch with parents.
4. They periodically reviewed their programs and made needed changes.
5. They clarified who in the school and in its governance system was responsible for which decision.
6. They did not become overwhelmed by meetings and efforts to make decisions.
7. They established priorities and focused on them.

The charter movement also ought to take a careful look at the successes and problems of Great Britain's "grant maintained schools." These are schools allowed to "opt out" of local school districts, in order to have more control over the budget, curriculum, and personnel. Many of these schools soon learned they would benefit from training and assistance in a number of areas, including governance, curriculum, and evaluation. Many of these schools wisely wanted independence while welcoming advice.[26]

States wishing to see charter schools achieve their potential will help arrange opportunities for charter schools to work with and learn from each other and from other people with successful experiences in specific areas. Fortunately, several states already are working hard to provide just this kind of assistance by arranging workshops, putting information on the Internet, publishing information, and sometimes subcontracting with organizations to work with charter schools.

Education advocates who have been important allies for innovative inner-city public school teachers for many years are also proving to be vital allies in the new struggle to adopt charter school legislation and to create new kinds of schools. They include African Americans such as Rose Bottom, a former Chicago public school educator and national director of education issues for the low-income advocacy group ACORN, San Diego Urban League president John Johnson, and former Milwaukee superintendent of schools Howard Fuller. These people know that not all school choice programs are equally effective. They like the charter approach, which does not allow schools to use admissions tests, as many magnet schools have done.

Critics insist that many low-income families and families with limited English do not know how to select among schools. This is not the first time that those in opposition to new policies have argued that certain groups do not know how to make good decisions. The same argument was used against women's suffrage and against civil rights.

Unfortunately, even though many successful inner-city innovative schools have operated for twenty years or more, they are widely ignored by many university-based researchers. A widely circulated 1995 report from Harvard is the latest to ignore the record of these schools. The report's summary asserts that "actual choice experiments remain young and modest . . . very little is known about school choice programs."[27] Having their work ignored reminds some alternative school educators of African American author Ralph Ellison's observation in *Invisible Man:* "I am invisible, understand, because people refuse to see me."[28]

These academic critics simply ignore twenty years of research. They ignore scholars such as Hofstra University's Mary Anne Raywid who have written about the success that alternative innovative public schools are having with students.[29] She points out that public school choice is not just about competition; it tries to empower educators and acts on the recognition that there is no one best kind of school for educating all students.

We have much to learn in the future about the best way to provide public school choice, but there are also many lessons we can learn from the past. Although five years' experience is not exhaustive, it is encouraging. Individual charter schools are enrolling and helping a wide variety of youngsters. Strong charter laws are helping stimulate broader system improvements. Much has been accomplished. What comes next? That is the subject of the final chapter.

Chapter Nine

Charting the Future

Twenty years from now, will the charter movement be a chapter or a footnote in school reform? The charter movement's first five years have been a time of remarkable growth, fierce political struggle, and intense media interest. Yet it is impossible to know for sure what lies ahead.

Charter schools are no panacea. Just setting up a school like City Academy, PS1 Charter School, or O'Farrell Community School is not nearly enough. It must then carry out its mission and goals, day to day. As one Colorado charter school teacher told me, "This is the most exciting job I've ever had, and I love it. It's also the hardest." But those hard jobs are producing results. This chapter contains some final observations about what those in the charter school movement could do to help not just the thousands of students that charter schools presently serve but also the millions of American students who need a better education than they are getting.

Recognize That the Charter School Movement Is Part of a 200-Year Effort to Expand Opportunity

It is important for everyone to understand that the charter school concept has deep roots. It is an outgrowth of the 200-year effort in this country to expand educational opportunity, especially for those who are not wealthy and powerful. Those who have power almost always insist that major changes proposed are unnecessary and probably would lead to greater harm for the people they are intended to help. They distort the goals of new movements. They use their power to block, delay, restrict, and obstruct. This lesson is one charter school advocates have been learning as they attempt to expand people's access to an effective education.

Sadly, it took more than 150 years to win voting rights for women in most states. The civil rights and farmworkers' struggles made important progress, but people were beaten and even killed in those efforts. Opponents initially denied that any of these movements were necessary. Then they distorted the goals of these movements and defamed their leaders. They used their influence and power to discredit those who were trying to expand opportunity. People with power almost always insist that the changes proposed are unnecessary and probably would lead to greater harm for the people they are intended to help.

The charter school movement has faced similar attacks. Schools boards, administrators, and unions collectively have fought the charter school concept, in some states blocking any form of charter school legislation. In others, the educational establishment has been able to force adoption of extremely weak legislation. The motives of charter school advocates have been challenged, charter school proponents have been intimidated, and legislators who supported strong charter school legislation have been threatened. National articles have appeared that point to the closing of a California charter school that misallocated funds as an illustration that the charter school movement will harm youngsters. But wouldn't it be good if *more* schools that misspent money were closed?

Let me be clear. Allowing more than one organization to sponsor a public school threatens many powerful groups in public education. It is time to put away the notion that for every educational group the first priority is kids. Please. For some educational groups, the highest priorities are job security for their members, higher salaries, and fewer hours of work. The highest priority for other groups is maintenance of the existing power relationships among teachers, administrators, and school board members.

Frederick Douglass, the eloquent spokesperson for the antislavery movement, understood this phenomenon well. He said, "The whole history of the progress of human liberty shows that all concessions yet made to her august claims have been born of earnest struggle. . . . If there is no struggle, there is no progress. Those who profess to favor freedom, and yet deprecate agitation, are men who want crops without plowing up the ground, they want rain without thunder and lightning. They want the ocean without the awful roar of its many waters."[1]

Persistence is critical. The struggle to establish strong charter schools around the nation will take time. Minnesota advocates have been working at it for more than five years, and the Minnesota law still is not as strong as its sponsors envisioned when they first introduced the idea. But there is progress all around the country. Twenty-five states have adopted some form of charter legislation. About one-third of these of the laws give the concept a genuine trial. Hundreds of charter schools have been started, and evidence is growing that a number of them are helping youngsters.

Moreover, charter school legislation in some states is encouraging local school districts to improve existing programs and add new schools. And as mentioned previously, President Bill Clinton and U.S. Secretary of Education Richard Riley have endorsed the idea. In March 1996, Secretary Riley wrote to each charter school director in the country, explaining that President Clinton and he "have been working to familiarize the public with public charter schools and their potential to raise academic standards, empower educators, involve parents and communities in education and expand choice and accountability in public education."[2]

So charter school proponents should not be discouraged. In five years, the movement has come a long way. Governors, state legislators, and members of Congress representing both major political parties have endorsed and promoted charter school legislation. While respecting states and without imposing too many conditions, Congress has allocated millions of dollars to help people start charter schools.

In some places, the opposition is declining. In a few places, such as Houston, powerful educational groups such as the local Federation of Teachers are actually seeing the value of this idea. The National Education Association has allocated $1.5 million to help its members start charter schools. Progress is possible.

Recognize That Progress Requires Strong Pressure on Legislators

Progress will not come, however, without strong pressure from groups outside the major educational organizations. To pass strong charter school laws, advocates need allies—influential, committed people who promote the legislation. For example, one of the nation's strongest, most eloquent charter school proponents is Rose Bottom, the former Chicago public school educator who has helped ACORN chapters around the nation create new schools, including charter schools. In some states, similar major advocates for children and low-income families have played a critical role in promoting strong charter school legislation. In Colorado, for example, legislators point to vital encouragement and support from the Colorado Children's Campaign, headed by former governor's aide Barbara O'Brien. The Colorado Children's Campaign helped set up a statewide network of advocates who regularly contacted legislators and urged them to support the charter school concept. In Minnesota, low-income advocacy groups such as the Urban Coalition and ACORN have been strong supporters of charter school legislation. The Minnesota Minority Education Partnership has sponsored or cosponsored several meetings to spread the word about charter schools among communities of color who otherwise would not hear about the idea or would hear about it only from educational groups who oppose it.

These kinds of allies are invaluable. In 1995, Minnesota's Post-Secondary Enrollment Options Program was threatened by a coalition of secondary school principals and a few superintendents. The widely respected director of the Minnesota Children's Defense Fund, LuAnne Nyberg, and the equally respected education program officer of the Urban Coalition of Minneapolis–St. Paul, Elaine Salinas, wrote strong letters to legislators urging them to reject the proposed changes in the postsecondary law. For example, Nyberg urged legislators, "Please resist pressure to change one of Minnesota's most innovative and effective ways to serve students: the Post-Secondary Options Law. As a parent with youth and family advocate, I've seen real benefits to many low-income young people who have participated in this program."[3] A number of legislators cited these letters as one of the main reasons that crippling changes were not made to the postsecondary options act.

Support from children's and low-income advocacy groups makes it much more difficult for charter school opponents to insist that these schools will hurt youngsters from low-income families.

A second important potential source of support is business groups. These organizations are deeply concerned about the public education system. The California Business Roundtable has been an important ally for charter proponents in that state. The San Diego Chamber of Commerce has provided vital encouragement and assistance to charter schools in its community. The Minnesota Business Partnership, representing the chief executive officers of many large Minnesota corporations, has been a strong supporter of first public school choice legislation and then charter school legislation for more than a decade. Charter proponents in Delaware cite support from major business groups as one of the key reasons for the passage of that state's charter school legislation.[4]

In some states, educational groups have skillfully encouraged business groups to avoid getting into controversial areas such as public school choice and charter school legislation. In Washington State, for example, major business groups have focused on the creation of standards for achievement and seem to have forgotten the value of entrepreneurship and opportunity—the qualities that have added so much to the growth of the U.S. economy. These business groups have not been strong supporters of public school choice and charter legislation, and it is no accident that so far, Washington's state legislature has not passed any charter school legislation. State educational groups have been able to prevent even weak charter legislation from being adopted.

Recognize the Impact of Schools on Achievement

Charter school advocates will have to continue encouraging people to recognize that schools can have a significant positive impact on the achievement of students. The argument over the extent of school impact has been one of the strangest educational debates of the last quarter century. Virtually everyone agrees that there are some excellent schools that help young people, including those from low-income and otherwise challenging backgrounds, make important progress. Television, newspaper, and magazine stories periodically focus on these schools. But research is then trotted out by others in an attempt to show that compared to family background, schools have relatively little impact.

There are studies on both sides of this issue. But both test scores and student reports from outstanding schools like Bowling

Green Elementary in Sacramento and City Academy in St. Paul offer strong evidence that schools can make a big difference with youngsters from challenging backgrounds.

Charter advocates do not deny that there are important problems in the broader society. Of course, youngsters will, on average, do better if their mothers had good medical care during pregnancy. They will do better if families read to them while they were young children and praised them for their accomplishments. They will do better in school if they are not kept up at night by the sound of gunfire in the neighborhood and if they do not have to worry about gang members hassling them on the way to or from school. They will do better in school if their families tell them that school is important and if they see examples around them of people who get up in the morning, treat each other respectfully, and go to good jobs.

Tragically, millions of youngsters come to school without the advantages middle- and upper-class families take for granted. We would be better off as a nation if we reduced the problems that we know interfere with children's learning. Changes in society should accompany changes in the schools.

But we should not use problems outside schools as an excuse for lack of progress inside schools. There are clear, well-documented examples of schools that produce significant achievement gains among students from troubled communities and families. And these are not schools staffed by "supermen" and "superwomen" who cannot be emulated by others.

Researchers like James Comer of Yale University and Robert Slavin of Johns Hopkins University have demonstrated that there are clear and understandable ways to increase achievement of students from low-income inner-city and rural families. Each of them has developed ways to involve families, improve the curriculum, and provide specialized help to young people who need it. It is unquestionably hard work. But when schools reach out to parents, use more numerous active learning techniques, and help families understand how they can promote their children's learning, achievement improves significantly. This is encouraging.

The charter school movement builds on this kind of research as well as on the commitment and entrepreneurial spirit of our land. The youngsters at the New Visions School impressed Secretary of Education Richard Riley because they could show him higher test scores. But more importantly, they displayed a spirit of optimism and progress. That is what charter schools represent.

One of the most encouraging developments in this country has been the recognition among some advocacy groups that it is time for more accountability in education. There is too much denial in public education today of the impact that schools can and should have. Whether it comes from the San Diego Urban League, the Minneapolis–St. Paul Urban Coalition, or ACORN (Association of Community Organizations for Reform Now), the message is clear: schools are expected to help youngsters. We know schools can make a difference with our youngsters.

Recognize That an Educational System Must Reward Progress and Penalize Failure

Until we recognize that the current educational system neither rewards progress nor penalizes failure, we will not see any real progress toward educational reform. The Milo Cutters, Yvonne Chans, and Bob DeBoers of the world do not make excuses. They make commitments to improve student achievement—and meet those commitments or give up their jobs. But in most states and most communities, that kind of responsibility is not expected or rewarded.

Public schools in most states continue to receive funds regardless of how well or how poorly their students are doing. There is no real accountability for results, and many educators like that just fine because they have convinced themselves and others that they are doing the best job possible with the existing resources. But all over the country now, there are examples of schools that are doing a better job of helping young people, especially those from low-income backgrounds and families with limited ability to speak English.

We will make progress as we give new opportunities to the creative, committed, and talented educators who are willing to be held accountable for results. We must use this country's extraordinary entrepreneurial energy, which has produced products and services that people throughout the world want to own. Strong charter school laws will give new opportunities and encouragement to some of our most talented and energetic educators. We will have fewer frustrated educators, more involved families, and more successful students.

Appendix A: Charter Activity State by State

As of late 1998, thirty-three states and the District of Columbia have adopted some version of the charter school concept. However, this is an area of rapid development. Charter legislation has passed in some state every year since 1991, and many states have modified their legislation. In general, legislative revisions are moving closer to the charter idea by increasing the number of charter schools that can be created and making it possible for potential charter school operators to obtain sponsorship from organizations including, but not limited to, a local school board.

Any report of state-level charter legislation can become out of date rapidly. After reviewing the information to follow, check with your state department of education and state resource centers, which are the best sources of information about your state.

This section benefited from the advice and information gathered by a number of people, including Jerry Langley-Ripka (Center for School Change), Eric Hirsch (National Council of State Legislators), Jon Schroeder (Charter Friends Network), Ted Kolderie (Center for Policy Studies), and Stella Cheung (the Humphrey Institute). It represents the best information available in September 1998. However, as noted, things are changing rapidly, so this information should not be regarded as definitive.

In some cases, states were not sure exactly how many charters would open for the 1998–99 school year. This is because some schools had been approved but had not worked out final arrangements, such as obtaining a building or other facilities, at the time information was gathered.

Revised in 1998.

You may wish to check Internet web sites such as the federal site (www.uscharterschools.org), the site created by the National Council of State Legislators (www.ncsl.org/programs/educ/c1schls.htm), or the site developed by the Center for Education Reform (edreform.com/). However, like any other web sites, these may not have been updated recently or may contain inaccurate or debatable information.

The details of state legislation have a great impact on the number and type of charter schools a state can have; they also help determine the amount of incentive that existing schools and districts have to improve their programs. Various methods have been used to compare features of charter legislation across states. One widely used, comprehensive comparison of state charter school legislation, which was carried out by Louann Bierlein, classifies state laws from strongest to weakest using seven major criteria. The more of the following criteria that charter school legislation meets, the stronger it is considered to be:

- Both local and nonlocal board sponsorship is available, or an appeal process exists.
- Any individual or group can attempt to organize a charter proposal.
- Automatic exemptions from state laws and rules and from local policies are given.
- The school has fiscal autonomy, that is, complete control over funds generated by their student count and over staff salaries.
- The school has legal autonomy. Teachers are employees of the school, not the local district; the school, not the law, determines the level of legal autonomy.
- There are no (or very high) limits on the number of charter schools that can be formed.
- Some percentage of noncertified individuals can teach at the charter school without having to seek a waiver or alternative certification.

Using these criteria, the strongest charter laws are those in Arizona, California, Delaware, the District of Columbia, Massachusetts, Michigan, Minnesota, New Jersey, North Carolina, and Texas. In the middle are the charter laws of Colorado, Connecticut,

Idaho, Illinois, Louisiana, Missouri, Pennsylvania, South Carolina, and Wisconsin. The weakest laws are in Alaska, Arkansas, Florida, Georgia, Hawaii, Kansas, Mississippi, Nevada, New Hampshire, New Mexico, Ohio, Rhode Island, Utah, Virginia, and Wyoming.

I would add two criteria to Bierlein's list. First, it is important that students be allowed to move across district lines to attend the charter. This provision has been critical in Minnesota to a number of rural charter schools. Some of these rural charters attracted almost half of their students from families living outside their district of attendance.

The second measure of a charter law's strength is whether it stipulates that all the money that is allocated by the state or a local district follows the student. A number of states have responded to union, administrator, or school board pressure by giving charter schools less money per pupil than the typical public school. This is a bizarre situation. Charter schools are subject to much more rigorous accountability for results but are given less money per pupil to achieve these results.

These comparison tools may be of use in comparing your own state law or proposed law.

Alaska (1995)

Alaska adopted its charter legislation in 1995. The legislation permits up to thirty charter schools. All Alaska charter schools must be approved by both the local school board in which they operate and the state board of education. The Alaska legislation does not exempt charter schools from most state rules and regulations. It permits local boards to waive local requirements. Most charter advocates consider this to be one of the nation's weaker charter laws. Fifteen charters operated in 1997–98. One additional school is expected to open in the fall of 1998.

Contact: Marjorie Menzi, Alaska Department of Education, 801 West 10th Street, Juneau, AK 99801, (907) 465-8720.

Arizona (1994)

Arizona's 1994 law has produced some of the strongest response. The law permits three different organizations to sponsor charter schools: local districts, the state board of education, or a new state chartering agency. The state board of education and the state board for charter schools are permitted to approve no more than 25 charters each, per year, for a total of 50. Approximately 240 charter schools operated in Arizona in the 1997–98 school year, with about 27 more expected to open in the fall of 1998.

Contact: Arizona State Board for Charter Schools, 1535 West Jefferson Street, Phoenix, AZ 85007 (602) 542-3411; Mary Gifford, Goldwater Institute, 201 N. Central Avenue, Phoenix, AZ 85004, (602) 256-7018 (provides a variety of information about charter schools).

Arkansas (1995)

This may be the nation's weakest charter law. Only existing public schools may apply for charter status. These schools must have the approval of both their local school board and the state board of education. The petition requesting a charter must also be approved by the local teachers union if the school district has a bargaining agreement with this organization. The petition must be approved by at least two-thirds of the certified teachers at the school requesting the proposal and by at least two-thirds of the parents present at a meeting called for the purpose of deciding whether to move ahead on the petition. The state board of education can waive rules and regulations at the request of a charter school. There is no limit on the number of charter schools that may be established in Arkansas.

Contact: Margaret Crank, Arkansas Department of Education, Four State Capitol Mall, Little Rock, AR 72201, (501) 682-4251.

California (1992)

California's original legislation permitted up to 100 charter schools. The state board of education then decided that it had the power to waive that law; by the 1997–98 school year, 130 charters were operating. Officials expected another 12 charters to open in the fall of 1998. In 1998, the legislature made several important changes to the law, including permitting the number of charters to increase to 250 for the coming school year and permitting an additional 100 schools during each of the following years. Charters must be approved by a local school board, by a county school district, or by the state board on appeal from a local district.

California has dozens of charter public schools that were converted to charter status. Some of these conversions, such as Vaughn Street and Fenton in Los Angeles and Bowling Green in Sacramento, are among the most encouraging examples in the country of what can be accomplished when existing public schools convert to charter status.

Contact: David Patterson, California Department of Education, 560 J Street, Suite 170, Sacramento, CA 95814, (916) 327-5929; Sue Steelman Bragato, California Network of Educational Charters (CANEC), 1139 San Carlos Avenue, #304, San Carlos, CA 94070, (650) 654-6003 (a strong support organization organized primarily by people who work in charter schools; also provides information and hosts the largest state-based charter school conference in the country); Eric Premack (a researcher who has helped document and advise charter schools in California and is an excellent source of information, especially about the business side of operating a charter), Charter Schools Development Center, Institute for Educational Reform, California State University, 6000 J Street, Sacramento, CA 95819, (916) 278-4600; Pamela Riley, Pacific Research Institute, Center for Innovation in Education, 755 Sansome Street, Suite 450, San Francisco, CA 94111, (415) 989-0833 (conservative-oriented policy group; has sponsored conferences and has several publications about charter schools).

Colorado (1993)

Colorado's charter school legislation was adopted in 1993, with the strong support of Governor Roy Romer. There were fifty Colorado charter schools in 1997–98; about ten more are expected to open in September 1998. People wishing to create a charter school in Colorado must specify which state rules and regulations the initiator wishes to have waived. It is then up to the state board of education to determine which rules and regulations it *will* waive.

Colorado's legislation requires that people who want to start charter schools seek approval from their local school board. If the local board rejects the proposal, it can be appealed to the state board of education, which can then turn down the appeal. Or the state board can require that a school board work out its differences with the applicant rather than having the state sponsor the charter (an option developed in Minnesota). Requiring a local school board to accept the charter has led to extreme frustration in Denver. The state board turned down several appeals from Denver but mandated that the district sponsor a charter developed by a veteran Denver teacher. The district refused and has filed a suit challenging the charter legislation's constitutionality.

Contact: Bill Windler, Colorado Department of Education, 201 E. Colfax, Denver, CO 80202, (303) 866-6631 (publishes periodic newsletter about charter schools; has produced an excellent report on how charter schools assess student achievement); Jim Griffin, Colorado League of Charter Schools, 7700 W. Woodward Drive, Lakewood, CO 80227, (303) 989-5356.

Connecticut (1996)

Connecticut adopted its law in May 1996. The Connecticut law permits up to twenty-four charter schools; up to twelve must be authorized by local school boards, and up to twelve may be authorized by the state board of education. Schools authorized by local school boards must conform to local labor-management agreements. Schools sponsored by the state do not have to follow local bargaining agreements. According to Connecticut State Department officials, twelve charter schools operated in the 1997–98 school year, and sixteen will operate in 1998–99.

In one of the strangest provisions of any charter legislation in the country, the original legislation says that more than 1,000 students may attend charter schools sponsored by the state. This later was modified to permit up to 1,500 students to attend state-sponsored charter schools.

Contact: Jennifer Niles, c/o Connecticut State Department of Education, PO Box 2219, Hartford, CT 06145-2219, (860) 566-1233; (at the statewide resource center) Bill Jawitz, (860) 645-1234.

Delaware (1995)

Delaware's law permits creation of an unlimited number of charters but stipulates that no more than five can be created in the first three years of the legislation (that is, no more than five additional in the 1996–1997 and 1997–98 school years). Delaware charter schools must enroll students in at least two grades and have at least two hundred students (except during its first two years, when it must have at least one hundred students). Charter schools serving at-risk or special education students must enroll at least one hundred students. Charter schools may be approved by either a local school board or the Delaware State Board of Education. Three charters operated in the 1997–98 school year, and three or four more are expected to open in the fall of 1998.

Contact: Larry Gabbert, Department of Public Instruction, c/o Townsend Building, PO Box 1402, Dover, DE 19903, (302) 739-4583; Suzanne Donovan, Innovation in Education Initiative, Inc., 931 Church Hill Road, Milford, DE 19963, (302) 424-1545.

District of Columbia (1996)

Congress authorized charter schools to operate in the District of Columbia beginning in the 1996–97 school year. Up to ten were authorized for the first year, with up to twenty new charters available in each of the following years. Three charters operated in the 1997–98 school year, and about sixteen additional charters are expected to open in the fall of 1998. Charter schools may be approved by either the local school board or a special charter school authorizing group.

Contact: Shirley Monastra, D.C. Committee on Public Education, 1155 15th Street NW, #301, Washington, DC 20005, (202) 835-9011.

Florida (1996)

Florida's law allows school districts and public state universities to sponsor charter schools. The legislation limits the number of charter schools each district may sponsor but gives the district the right to appeal to the state board of education to increase this number. Charter schools may be either new schools or conversions of existing schools.

If a local district turns down a charter proposal, the charter proponents may appeal to the state board of education, which then forwards its recommendation to the local school board. The local board is asked to follow the state board's recommendation regarding the charter proposal unless the local board "determined by competent substantial evidence that approving the state board's recommendation would be contrary to law or contrary to the best interest of the pupils or the community." A local district not following the state board's recommendations is required to explain its decision in writing. Florida had thirty-three charters operating in the 1997–98 school year and expects about seventy-five to be operating in the 1998–99 school year. The director of the Florida Office of Public School Choice and Charter Schools is Tracey Bailey, a former National Teacher of the Year.

Contact: Tracey Bailey, Florida Department of Education, Room 522, Turlington Building, 325 W. Gaines Street, Tallahassee, FL 32399, (850) 414-0780; Lynn Lavely, Florida Charter School Resource Center, University of South Florida, Tampa, FL 33620, (813) 974-3700 (sponsors conferences and provides a variety of workshops).

Georgia (1993)

Georgia's original legislation permitted the conversion of existing public schools. In 1998 this was changed to permit the creation of new charter schools. The local school board in the town where a school is to operate must approve either a conversion or a new charter school. As of 1997–98, Georgia had twenty-one charter schools operating and expected twenty-seven to be operating in the 1998–99 school year.

Contact: John Rhodes, Georgia Department of Education, Twin Towers East, Suite 2052, Atlanta, GA 30334, (404) 657-7637.

Hawaii (1994)

Hawaii is a single school district. An existing public school may ask the board of education (which functions as both a local and the state's only school board) for permission to operate as a "student centered school." Before submitting the proposal, it must be approved by 60 percent of the school's administration, support staff, teaching personnel, and parents. Charter schools are exempt from most school code regulations but are not released from collective bargaining, civil rights, health and safety, and performance standards. Hawaii permits up to twenty-five charter schools. As of late 1998, two schools were operating as charter schools.

Contact: Art Kaneshiro, Hawaii Department of Education, 1270 Queen Emma Street #409, Honolulu, HI 96813, (808) 586-3124.

Idaho (1998)

The Idaho legislature authorized the creation of up to twelve charter schools per year for the next five years, beginning in September 1998. Schools can be either new or converted programs. Charters are given only by local school boards. However, if a local board turns down a charter proposal, its authors may appeal to the state. The state may choose to ask the local board to sponsor the charter.

As of late 1998, one charter had been approved by the Arco school board and several other schools were being developed. *Contact:* Carolyn Mauer, Idaho Department of Education, 650 West State Street, Boise, ID 83702, (208) 332-6974; Laurel and Jim Tangen-Foster, 106 North Van Buren, Moscow, ID 83843, (208) 882-6321.

Illinois (1996)

Illinois permits up to forty-five charter schools. Fifteen may be created in the city of Chicago; fifteen may be created in the suburbs around Chicago, and fifteen may be created in the rest of the state. As of late 1998, Chicago had authorized all fifteen of the charters it was permitted to start. Peoria had opened a charter for unsuccessful students who were assigned to the school (contrary to one of the basic principles of the charter movement). Several other charters had been authorized by local districts. Eight charter schools were open in the 1997–98 school year, and officials expect about four more to open in the fall of 1998. In the late spring of 1998, the state board of education approved the Thomas Jefferson Charter, which had appealed to the state after it was rejected by some suburban districts. Some of those districts announced that they would sue the state to block the opening of this school.

Contact: Gail Lieberman, Illinois State Board of Education, 100 North First Street, Springfield, IL (217) 782-5053; John Ayers or Margaret Lin, Leadership for Quality Education, One First National Plaza, Suite 3120, Chicago, IL 60603, (312) 853-1210.

Kansas (1994)

Kansas legislation allows up to fifteen charter schools. They must be approved by the local and state boards of education. There is no appeal process if a local board turns down the proposal. One charter school operated in the 1997–98 school year, and about fifteen are expected to be functioning in the 1998–99 school year.

Contact: Phyllis Kelly, Kansas State Board of Education, 120 South East 10th Avenue, Topeka, KS 66612, (785) 296-3069.

Louisiana (1995)

Louisiana charter schools originally authorized only eight charter schools, to be sponsored by local school boards. After some experience, the legislature authorized up to forty-two charters and permits an appeal to the state board of education. A charter may be a new school or a converted public school. In the case of a conversion, at least two-thirds of the full-time faculty and instructional staff members must sign a conversion petition, along with at least two-thirds of the parents present at a public meeting to discuss the idea. Six charters were operating in 1997–98, and four or five more are expected to open in the fall of 1998.

Contact: Kathy Mathene, Louisiana State Board of Elementary and Secondary Education, PO Box 96064, Capitol Station, Baton Rouge, LA 70804, (504) 219-4540.

Massachusetts (1994)

The Massachusetts legislature originally authorized up to twenty-five charter schools. Originally, applicants applied directly to the Massachusetts Executive Office of Education. Recently the law was changed to permit twelve additional state-authorized charter schools (called commonwealth schools) and thirteen new "Horace Mann" charters. These are charters authorized by local school boards, using a contract approved by the local teachers union. Twenty-four state-approved charters operated in the 1997–98 school year. As of fall 1998, the state expected about thirty state-approved charter schools and several district-approved charters to be in operation.

Contact: Scott Hamilton, Massachusetts Department of Education, One Ashburton Place, Room 1403, Boston, MA 02108, (617) 727-0075; Linda Brown, Charter School Resource Center, Pioneer Institute, 85 Devonshire Street, 8th floor, Boston, MA 02109-3506, (617) 723-2277 (one of the nation's pre-eminent charter resource centers; has published various materials about charter schools, including a periodic newsletter and handbook about starting a charter school in Massachusetts); Karen Byars (has organized parents and educators to help support charter legislation), Action for Children's Education, 124 Mt. Auburn Street, Cambridge, MA 02138, (978) 635-1800.

Michigan (1993)

Governor John Engler proposed charter schools as one portion of a larger school reform package. The Michigan legislation allows individual local districts, regional district cooperatives, and public universities to sponsor charter schools, which the state calls public school academies. Several charter schools were approved and opened in September 1994. In November of 1994 a district court ruled the charter law unconstitutional. In December of 1994, the Michigan legislature amended the law so that charters now are under the supervision of the Michigan State Board of Education.

Michigan public universities may sponsor a total of seventy-five charter schools (public school academies). Recent legislation prohibited "class four" and "class five" school districts—small districts and K–8 districts—from sponsoring charter schools.

As of 1997–98, 107 charter schools were operating in Michigan. The state expected this to increase to about 137 by September of 1998.

Central Michigan University has taken a leading role in the state's charter movement. The university has developed an extensive set of materials explaining the chartering process and describing how it will evaluate charter school proposals. For information about the CMU chartering process, contact James N. Goenner at CMU, (517) 774-3315.

Other charters are being sponsored by local districts and intermediate districts. Several other public universities are preparing to sponsor charter schools.

Contact: Joan May, Public School Academy Program, Michigan Department of Education, PO Box 30008, Lansing, MI 48909, (517) 373-3345; Jim Goenner, Michigan Resource Center for Charter Schools, 220A Ronan Hall, Central Michigan University, Mount Pleasant, MI 48859, (517) 774-2590; Anna Amato (has helped people start charter schools in the Detroit area), 6536 Woodmont Avenue, Detroit, MI 48228, (313) 581-7914; Dan Quisenberry, Michigan Association of Public School Academies, 124 West Allegan Street, Suite 750, Lansing, MI 48933, (517) 374-9167.

Minnesota (1991)

The nation's first charter law has been revised several times. Originally it permitted only eight charters. Now there is no limit. Originally it permitted only local boards to authorize charters. Now it allows local boards, colleges, universities, and, on appeal, the state board of education (if a local board turns down the proposal but at least two local board members vote for it). More than a dozen of Minnesota's charters have had their contracts renewed, beginning with City Academy, the nation's first operating charter school. Thirty-eight charters are operating in the fall of 1998. Several others are authorized to begin in 1999, and still others are under development.

Contact: Bill Allen, Minnesota Department of Children, Families and Learning, 550 Cedar Street, St. Paul, MN 55101 (612) 296-4231; Nancy Smith, New Twin Cities Charter School Project, c/o Humphrey Institute, University of Minnesota, 301 19th Avenue South, Minneapolis, MN 55455, (612) 625-7552; Joe Nathan (also at the Humphrey Institute), (612) 626-1834.

Missouri (1998)

The Missouri legislature adopted charter legislation in 1998. The law will focus on St. Louis and Kansas City. Missouri will allow these two large city school boards, along with public colleges, universities, and community colleges in the cities and adjacent counties, to authorize charter schools. If a charter proposal is turned down, its authors may appeal to the state board of education, which may approve and authorize the school. If a sponsor grants three or more charters, at least one-third of the charters granted by the sponsor shall be to schools that actively recruit dropouts or high-risk students in their student body.

Contact: Laura Friedman, Charter Schools Resource Center, 35 North Central Avenue, Suite 335, St. Louis, MS 63105, (314) 726-6474; Missouri Department of Education, 205 Jefferson Street, Jefferson City, MS 65102, (573) 751-3175.

Mississippi (1997)

Mississippi's legislature authorized one of the nation's weakest charters. It permits conversion of up to six existing public schools into charter schools. As of late 1998, one conversion had taken place.

Contact: Mississippi Department of Education, PO Box 771, Jackson, MS 39201, (601) 359-3501.

Nevada (1997)

Nevada's law permits twenty-one charters throughout the state. Only local boards have the authority to authorize charter schools, and local boards must first get permission from the state board of education to do so. The law permits only new schools—no conversions. As of fall, 1998, there was one charter school operating in Nevada—the "I Can Do Anything" School in Reno.

Contact: Holly Walton Buchanan, Nevada Department of Education, 700 East 5th Street, Reno, NV (702) 687-9186; Ricci Elkins, Nevada Charter School Project, PO Box 20758, Reno, NV 98515, (702) 626-2720.

New Hampshire (1995)

A charter school may be started by a group of two or more New Hampshire–certified teachers, a group of ten or more parents, or a nonprofit organization. Charter schools may be new or converted public schools. A conversion of an existing school must be approved by a majority of prospective teachers in a district with more than one school or two-thirds of the teachers in a single school district. A conversion also must be approved by both the superintendent and principal.

Any group wishing to start a charter school must ask the local town for permission. A public vote decides whether a charter proposal will be considered for that community. If the vote is no, the proposal cannot go forward. If the vote is yes, the proposal must be submitted to the local school board of the district in which the school wishes to locate. The school board must review the proposal and forward its recommendation (to approve or deny) to the state board of education, which decides whether to grant the charter. One or two charters may be opening in the fall of 1998.

Contact: Department of Education, 101 Pleasant St. Concord, NH 03301, (603) 271-3879; Sue Hollins, Charter School Resource Center, 5 Grauger Circle, Hanover, NH 03755, (603) 643-6115.

New Jersey (1996)

New Jersey is home for one of the nation's strongest charter laws. The legislation permits up to 135 charter schools, with a minimum of 3 per county. All of these schools must be approved by the state commissioner of education, who is expected to talk both with those proposing the charter and the local district in which the charter is located before making a decision about whether to sponsor the school.

In a last-minute compromise, the legislature agreed that newly created charter schools would not have to follow local labor-management agreements but that charter schools converted from existing public schools would have to follow local labor-management agreements.

In the 1997–98 school year, thirteen charter schools opened. In the 1998–99 year, about fifteen additional charters were expected to begin serving students.

Contact: Scott Moffitt, N.J. State Department of Education, 225 West State Street, CN 500, Trenton, NJ 08625–0500, (609) 984-5517; Sarah Tantillo, Charter School Resource Center, 303-309 Washington Street, 5th floor, Newark, NJ 07102, (973) 621-6467.

New Mexico (1993)

New Mexico's law allows up to five charter schools to be established. Only existing public schools are allowed to convert. At least

65 percent of an existing school's faculty must vote in favor of the charter application, and there must be documented parent involvement and support for the idea. Teachers remain employees of their local districts. All five slots have been taken, that is, five schools are operating as charters. Some parents have asked legislators to permit the creation of new charter schools, but so far this has not been done.

Contact: New Mexico Department of Education, 300 Don Gaspar, Santa Fe, NM 87501, (505) 827-6576.

North Carolina (1996)

North Carolina has one of the nation's strongest charter laws. Local school boards, the state board of education, and the University of North Carolina are permitted to sponsor charters. The law also permits creating new schools and converting existing schools.

During 1997–98, the first year charters could operate, there were thirty-three schools. The department anticipates that approximately twenty-six additional charter schools will begin operation in the 1998–99 school year.

Contact: Charter School Office, North Carolina Department of Public Instruction, Education Building, 301 North Wilmington Street, Raleigh, NC 27601, (919) 715-1730; Thelma Glynn, North Carolina Charter School Resource Center, 4711 Hope Valley Road #321, Durham, NC, (919) 682-4320 (www.ncharters.org); Vernon Robinson, North Carolina Education Reform Foundation, (919) 781-1066 (www.successnet.net/ncerf/)

Ohio (1997)

The Ohio legislature authorized an unlimited number of charters in several of the state's largest cities, including Akron, Canton, Cincinnati, Cleveland, Columbus, Dayton, and Youngstown. A special pilot charter project is operating in Lucas County (Toledo area). The law permits new schools and conversions. Local school boards authorize the charters. No charters opened in the 1997–98 school year. State officials estimate that between ten and fourteen charters will open in the 1998–99 school year.

Contact: Ohio Department of Education, 65 South Front Street, Columbus, OH 43215, (614) 466-2937 or (888) 510-394; Lucas County Education Service Center, 415 Emerald Avenue, Toledo, OH (419) 246-3137.

Pennsylvania (1997)

Pennsylvania adopted a charter law that has some unusual features. A year before it passed legislation authorizing charter schools, the legislature had allocated funds to help individuals and groups plan charter schools. Then in 1997, with clear evidence that people all over the state wanted to create charter schools, the legislature voted to let them do so, authorizing an unlimited number of schools.

Until the 1999–2000 school year, only local school boards may sponsor charter schools. Beginning in the 1999–2000 school year, advocates may appeal to the state if a local board turns them down. An appeal to the state requires gathering at least one thousand signatures of district residents, or 2 percent of the district residents, whichever is fewer.

During the 1997–98 school year, there were six charters operating in Pennsylvania. Tim Daniels of the state department of education expects that about twenty-five additional charters will begin operation in the 1998–99 school year.

Contact: Tim Daniels, Pennsylvania Department of Education, 333 Market Street, Harrisburg, PA 17126, (717) 705–2343 or Charter School Project, 712 Rockwell Hall, Duquesne University, Pittsburgh, PA 15282, (412) 396–4492; Rhonda Lauer, c/o FOUNDATIONS, 821 East Gate Drive, Mount Laurel, NJ 08054, (609) 727-8000 (a resource center for people in Eastern Pennsylvania, as well as New Jersey).

Rhode Island (1995)

Rhode Island gives groups of public school personnel the opportunity to create new schools and enables existing public schools to convert to charter status. If the charter is to be a conversion, at least two-thirds of the personnel in the school must approve it, along with a majority of the parents or guardians of the students currently assigned to the school. If the school is to be a new school, at least two-thirds the number of teachers expected to teach and one-half the number of parents of eligible children must support the school. A charter school proposal first goes to a local school board and then to the state board of regents (comparable to a state board of education). The regents have the ultimate decision as to whether the charter is granted. The legislation requires the local school board and local teachers unions to share their views about the charter with the state board of regents. Charter applicants must ask for waivers of specific rules and regulations in their proposal. Charter school employees remain members of the collective bargaining unit for teachers in the district.

No more than ten charters, serving no more than 2 percent of the state's school-age population, shall be granted prior to July 1, 1996, and an additional ten charters, serving no more than 4 percent of the state's school-age population, may be granted before July 1, 1997. Rhode Island had one charter school operating in 1998–99 and anticipated one more opening for the 1998–99 school year.

Contact: Rhode Island Department of Education, 22 Hayes, Providence, RI 02908, (401) 222-4600, X 2015.

South Carolina (1996)

South Carolina's law permits only local school boards to authorize charter schools. But new starts and converted public schools are permitted. Four charters operated in the 1997–98 school year, and one additional school was expected to open in the fall of 1998.

Contact: South Carolina Department of Education, 1429 Senate Street, Columbia, SC 29201, (803) 734-4110.

Texas (1995)

Texas passed a charter provision as part of a larger school reform package in 1995. The legislature has since modified the law. Originally the legislature authorized the state to sponsor up to 20 charters. This has been changed so that the state may sponsor up to 120 schools. And the state may sponsor an unlimited number of charters that plan to have at least 75 percent of their student be at risk of failure.

The state also allows local districts to establish new schools that are called campus or program charters. These schools are exempt from most state education laws and rules. Seventeen district-sponsored charter schools were operating in the 1998–99 school year.

Students may use the "open enrollment" provision of the 1995 Texas law to move across district lines to attend a charter.

During the 1997–98 school year, nineteen charter schools authorized by the state were operating. The department of education anticipates a total of approximately sixty state-sponsored charter schools will operate in the 1998–99 school year. Brooks Flemister, the charter school administrator, also reported that the state has received more than 160 applications for the remaining charters it can award.

Contact: Texas Education Agency, Travis Building, 1701 North Congress Avenue, Austin, TX 78701, (512) 463-9575; Patsy O'Neill, Charter School Resource Center, 40 NE Loop 410, Suite 408, San Antonio, TX 78278, (210) 348-7890 (www.charterstexas.org).

Utah (1998)

The Utah legislature recently authorized the creation of up to eight charters. These may be new schools or conversions of existing schools. The state board of education has the responsibility for sponsoring charters in Utah. Local school boards will review charter proposals that come from their areas and make recommendations or suggestions to the state board. The Utah department reported that five charter proposals were submitted to the state by August of 1998 and that the state is considering them for possible implementation in 1999.

Contact: Utah Office of Education, 250 East 500 South, Salt Lake City, UT 84111, (801) 538-7650.

Virginia (1998)

In late spring of 1998, the Virginia legislature adopted charter legislation. Only local school boards are permitted to sponsor charters. The law says that until June 1, 2000, there may be no more than two charters granted per district. Beginning June 1,

2000, the number of charter schools in a district shall not exceed 10 percent of the total number of schools in a district or two schools, whichever is greater. The department does not anticipate any charter schools opening before fall of 1999. People in several Virginia communities have started talking about the possibilities of charters.

Contact: Virginia Department of Education, PO Box 2120, Richmond, VA 23218, (804) 786-5392.

Wisconsin (1993)

Wisconsin has modified its charter legislation several times. Since 1993 the legislature has increased the number of charters permitted and allowed charters more autonomy from local labor-management agreements. Only local school boards have the power to authorize charter schools, except in Milwaukee. The city council was given the power by the 1998 legislature to authorize charter schools. Wisconsin had eighteen charter schools operating in the 1997–98 school year and anticipated another four to eight opening for the 1998–99 school year.

Contact: Wisconsin Department of Public Instruction, PO Box 7841, Madison, WI 53707, (608) 266-5728; Cindy Zautcke, Wisconsin Charter School Resource Center, c/o Marquette University, PO Box 1881, Milwaukee, WI 53201–1881, (414) 288-1540.

Wyoming (1995)

Wyoming's law is one of the nation's weakest. It permits only local school boards to sponsor charter schools, which can be new schools or conversions. In order to establish a charter school, a person must get a petition signed by at least 10 percent of the teachers employed by the school district or at least 50 percent of the teachers employed at one school within the district. The petition also must be signed by at least 10 percent of the parents of all pupils in the district or by at least 50 percent of the parents of all pupils enrolled at one school in the district. As of mid-1998, there were no charter schools in Wyoming.

Contact: Wyoming Department of Education, 2300 Capitol Avenue, 2nd floor, Cheyenne, WY 82002, (307) 777-6268.

Contacts in States Without Charter Laws

Seventeen states currently do not have charter laws. However, in a number of these states, people are actively trying to help pass charter legislation. Following is a list of contact people in those states:

Indiana: Senator Teresa Lubbers, (317) 232-9808

Iowa: Representative Philip Wise, (319) 524-3643 or Representative Steven Warnstadt, (319) 258-3705

Maine: Emanuel Pariser, Community School, Camden, ME, (207) 763-3156

New York: Debbie Lazarus, Mid-Hudson Advocates for Charter Schools, 37 East Pond Road, Woodridge, NY 12789; Nick Paradiso, NY Charter School Resource Center, PO Box 985, Clifton Park, NY 12065, (518) 383-6907 (www.nycharterschools.org)

Oklahoma: Representative John Bryant, (918) 523-9040

Oregon: Richard Meinhard, Center for Education Change, 3957 East Burnside, Portland, OR 97214, (503) 234-4600; Representative Ron Sunseri, (503) 986-1422 and Senator Tom Hartung, (503) 629-8985.

South Dakota: Senator Barbara Everist, (605) 339-2952; Representative Scott Eccarius, (605) 341-8645

Tennessee: Dale Berryhill, Charter School Resource Center of Tennessee, 6363 Poplar Avenue, Suite 410, Memphis, TN 38119, (901) 844-0046

Vermont: Senator Jeb Spaulding, (802) 725-1219

Washington: Senator Steve Johnson, (253) 8782-6435; Frank Dooling, 14308 10th Avenue S, Tacoma, WA 98444 (Dooling also manages the American On-Line charter area, which is discussed in Appendix C.)

Appendix B:
Model Charter School Law

The following can serve as a model charter school bill that a bill drafter in any state can use to produce proposed legislation. This model bill relies on findings from considerable experience around the country.

This model was developed by Ted Kolderie.

Model Bill Provisions	*Comments*
Section 1: Background. This section allows the creation of charter schools. Charter schools are declared to be part of the state's program of public education.	*Essentially, in charter school legislation, the state says it is all right for more than one organization to be offering public education in the community—or put another way, that it is all right for somebody other than the local board of education to start and run a public school.*
Section 2: Purpose. The purpose of this law is to 1. Improve student learning. 2. Encourage the use of different and innovative learning and teaching methods. 3. Increase choice of learning opportunities for pupils.	*The movement for charter schools is not really about the charter schools themselves. It is about systemic change—about the state creating the dynamics that will make the system a self-improving system.*

4. Establish a new form of accountability for public schools.
5. Require the measurement of learning and create more effective, innovative measurement/assessment tools.
6. Make the school the unit for improvement.
7. Create new professional opportunities for teachers, including the opportunity to own the learning program at the school site.

Section 3: New schools, existing schools.

1. Charter schools may be formed either
   a. By creating a new school. A proposal for a new charter school may be made by an individual, a group of individuals, or an organization. Individuals are most commonly teachers or parents. Organizations could be, for example, community groups, universities, community colleges, hospitals, zoos, or museums.
   b. By converting an existing school. In the case of an existing public school, the proposers

One process can probably handle both new schools and conversions, even though in a conversion, two additional questions will have to be answered. The sponsor will have to decide whether enough support exists among teachers and parents for it to grant a charter. (The law should leave this as a matter of judgment on the sponsor's part.) And where a public school is converting to a charter school, the district will need to provide for students and teachers who choose not to remain after the change.

A question is whether a charter school may be created out of an existing nonpublic school. Answers vary. Some states prohibit

will be the principal,
teachers, and/or
parents at the school.
2. A board of education,
on its own motion, may
convert all or some of its
schools to charter status.

*this. Some, such as Minnesota,
feel it is all right for a school, as
it is for a student, to transfer from
the private to the public system.*

Section 4. Sponsor. The
organizers may apply to, and
the school may be sponsored
by, any of the following:

1. The board of a school
   district.
2. The state board of education (or if not the board,
   the state superintendent).
3. The board of a public
   postsecondary institution.
4. The board of a unit of
   general local government,
   such as a city or a county.
5. A new state body created
   to sponsor or oversee
   charter schools.
6. Such other responsible
   public body as the legislature may designate.

*The opportunity for an applicant
to go either to a local board or to
some other responsible public body
for its charter is the single most
important provision if charter
school legislation is to have the
dynamics the legislature wants.
The idea is not to bypass local
boards but to encourage them to
respond more positively within the
district framework to teachers and
parents who want changes and
improvements and to say to those
interested in a new school (as
local boards do in states with
such laws), "Charter with us!"*

*More and more, states have pro-
vided multiple routes to founding
a charter school.*

**Section 5. Number of
schools.** The number of
charter schools shall not be
limited.

*The state wants everybody to im-
prove. So the law should expose
every district to the possibility that
a charter school may appear in its
area. Small "pilot" programs that
authorize only a handful of charter schools fail this test. Some
states do "cap" the allowable
number of charter schools at any*

given time and then raise the cap over time. But again, a state that wants the maximum stimulus to change and improvement will not limit the opportunity for charter schools to appear.

Section 6. Eligible pupils.

1. Charter schools shall be open to any student residing in the state.

   Charter schools will be different schools. So students get to choose whether to come.

2. A charter school shall enroll an eligible pupil who submits a timely application, unless the number of applications exceeds the capacity of a program, class, grade level, or building. In that case, all applicants shall have an equal chance of being admitted (that is, pupils shall be accepted by lot).

   Letting students cross a district line to get to a charter school provides a larger enrollment base for innovations and diffuses the financial impact.

3. A charter school may elect to specialize in
   a. Pupils in an age group or grade level.
   b. Pupils considered "at risk."
   c. Residents of a specific geographical area where the population percentage of people of color is greater than the percentage of people of color in the congressional district in which the geographical area is

   The idea is to let the school target certain populations (often those not doing well in the conventional system) and, in general, to require it to meet the test of a common public school. It may not "cream" able kids or "nice" kids or create a white neighborhood school.

located, as long as the school reflects the racial and ethnic diversity of the area.

4. The school may not limit admission to pupils on the basis of intellectual ability, measure of achievement, or aptitude or athletic ability.

5. Private schools converting to public status under the charter school law may not give preference in admissions to prior students.

Section 7. The school as a legal entity. The charter school, new or existing, shall organize under one of the forms of organization available under the laws of the state: for example, nonprofit, cooperative, partnership, public benefit corporation, and the like. Or a new form may be established for charter schools.

The law may require the charter school to become a legal entity or may simply permit that step. The law should not require the school to remain a part of the local district. This is critical to provide the autonomy the school requires for its success.

Section 8. Requirements for public education.

1. The school must not be affiliated with a nonpublic sectarian school or religious institution. The school must be nonsectarian in its programs, admission policies, employment

This section and section 6 contain the provisions that distinguish charter schools from voucher programs and public education from private. In private education, a school can pick and choose its students, can teach

practices, and all other operations.
2. The school must admit students as provided in section 6.
3. The school is accountable to public authority for performance as provided in section 9.
4. The school may not charge tuition.
5. The school must meet all applicable state and local health, safety, and civil rights requirements.
6. The school may not discriminate.
7. The school is subject to financial audits in the same manner as a school district.

religion, can charge tuition, and is not accountable to public authority for student performance.

The idea, though, is basically to shift away from an auditor's mentality—away from a control system based on process to a control system based on performance.

Section 9. The charter document. The state will simply require that the major issues in the operation of the school be thought through in advance and written into the charter document, which must be signed by the school and the sponsor.

1. The school and the sponsor must come to a written agreement on the following:
   a. The educational program: the school's

It is a good idea (it is California's approach, for example) simply to list the questions that school and sponsor must answer and to be open to whatever answer they want to give. Some states do narrow charter schools' discretion, to require certified teachers or to specify the term of the agreement, for example.

mission, the students to be served, the ages and grades to be included, and the focus of the curriculum.

b. The outcomes to be achieved and the method of measurement that will be used, including how the school will meet state-required outcomes.

c. The admissions procedures and dismissal procedures under state law.

d. The ways by which the school will achieve a racial and ethnic balance reflective of the community it serves.

e. The manner in which the program and fiscal audit will be conducted.

f. How the school will be insured.

g. The term of the agreement.

Setting a term is essential, to establish that this is a school that will be continued only on an affirmative showing of student and fiscal performance. The setting of a term establishes the public character of the charter school and its accountability to public authority.

h. The facilities to be used and their location.

i. The qualifications to be required of the teachers.

j. The arrangements for covering teachers and

other staff for health, retirement, and other benefits.

2. The sponsor must require that the school include, as an addendum to the charter document, a plan covering the following items, although the school and the sponsor need not reach agreement at this time on the terms for these items:

   a. The governance structure of the school.

   b. The management and administration of the school.

   c. In the case of an existing school being converted to charter status, alternative arrangements for current students who choose not to attend the school and for current teachers who choose not to teach in the school after conversion.

   d. The learning methods to be used.

   e. Any distinctive learning techniques to be employed.

   f. Internal financial controls.

Section 10. Causes for non-renewal or termination.

1. At the end of the term, the sponsor may choose not to renew the agreement on any of the following grounds:
    a. Failure to meet the requirements for student performance stated in the agreement.
    b. Failure to meet generally accepted standards of fiscal management.
    c. Violation of law.
    d. Other good cause shown.
2. During the term of the agreement, the sponsor may act to terminate the agreement on any of the grounds listed above. At least 60 days before not renewing or terminating a contract, the sponsor shall notify the board of directors of the school of the proposed action in writing. The notice shall state the grounds for the proposed action in reasonable detail and that the school's board of directors may request, in writing, an informal school hearing before the sponsor within 14 days of receiving the

notice. A termination shall be effective only at the conclusion of a school year.

3. The school may appeal the sponsor's decision to terminate or not renew the agreement to the state board of education.

4. When an agreement is not renewed or is terminated, the school shall be dissolved under the provisions of the statute under which the school was organized.

5. If an agreement is not renewed or is terminated, a student who attended the school may apply to and shall be enrolled in another public school. Normal application deadlines will be disregarded under these circumstances.

Section 11. Exemption from statutes and rules. Except as provided in this section, a charter school is exempt from all statutes and rules applicable to a school board or school district, although it may elect to comply with one or more provisions of statutes or rules.

In return for accepting the accountability represented by the requirements placed on the charter school to get its charter affirmatively renewed at regular intervals and to attract and hold its student and parent community, the charter school has the other "rules" for public schools waived up front. This "superwaiver" is better (and fairer) than requiring each charter school to petition for the waivers it needs, one at a time.

Section 12. Teachers.

1. The charter school will select its teachers, and the teachers will select the school.

   A charter school that aims to have a distinctive character must be able to maintain the integrity of its teacher group. So the idea is both for the teachers to choose the school and for the school to choose its teachers.

2. If the teachers choose to be employees of the school, they shall have the rights of teachers in public education to organize and bargain collectively. Bargaining units at the school will be separate from other units, such as the district unit.

   Model charter school legislation breaks with the long-held assumption that if you want to be a teacher, you have to be an employee. It opens up a new option for teachers: to form a separate group that will provide the learning program under an agreement with the school. This will give teachers full control of the professional issues they have been unable to win through bargaining as employees.

3. Alternatively, the teachers may choose to be part of a professional group that operates the instructional program under an agreement with the school, forming a partnership or producer cooperative that they collectively own.

4. Teachers leaving a current position in a public school district to teach in a charter school may take leave to teach. While on leave, they retain their seniority

and continue to be covered by the benefit programs of the district in which they had been working.

5. Teachers not previously teaching in a public school district may be made eligible for the state teacher retirement program. Alternatively, the state may add to the financing of the school an amount equal to the employer contribution for teacher retirement so that the school may set up its own program.

Section 13. Revenue. The state will provide the charter school with the full amount of revenue for each student that would be available if the student were enrolled in a regular school.

States vary considerably in their provisions for financing K–12 education. Generally, the idea is for the charter school to receive the same amount that would have been available for each student under traditional arrangements and to receive that revenue directly from the state.

1. The state will pay directly to the school the average amount per pupil spent statewide for operating purposes, plus weightings and categoricals.

Think about it this way. The state now requires each community to pay each year a certain proportion of its wealth toward the cost of educating its children. With whatever dollars this levy raises, the community pays for the education of as many kids as those dollars will cover. The state pays in full for all the remaining kids.

This lets us think of district enrollment as a box full of kids: the bottom layer (say 60 percent) all green, fully paid by the community; topped off by a 40 percent layer all gold, fully paid by the state. Thus, the notion that there is a "local" portion and a "state" portion of educational funding never applies to the funding of an individual student.

A student moving to a charter school is assumed to be a kid off the top of the box—fully state paid. The state pays the full amount—say, $4,000—to the charter school, where the student now is in attendance, rather than to the district, where the student is no longer in attendance.

This view will fit a state with a foundation formula, where the state is contributing some part of the revenue, at least, for every district. Most states have some kind of foundation formula.

School districts always object when a charter law is proposed that a charter school will "take away our money." But the system of financing schools is pupil driven. When enrollment goes up, the district has more money; when enrollment goes down, it has less money. Kids moving to a charter school are another kind of enrollment change. The state payment changes accordingly. The district adjusts, just as it would if the students moved to another district or another state.

2. A charter school may receive other state and federal aid, grants, and revenue as though it were a district.

   Section 11 applies here, too.

3. The school may receive gifts and grants from private sources in whatever manner is available to districts.
4. Special education will be, as now, an obligation of the district of residence. The charter school must comply with the requirements of law with respect to pupils with disabilities, as though it were a district.

Section 14. Immunity.

1. The charter school may sue and be sued.
2. The sponsor of a charter school, members of the board of the sponsor organization in their official capacity, and employees of a sponsor are immune from civil or criminal liability with respect to all activities related to a charter school they approve or sponsor.

   Accidents happen: people sue. Someone has to buy insurance. It should be the school.

Section 15. Length of school year. The charter school shall provide instruction for at least the number of days required by state law. It may provide instruction for more days if not prohibited by state law.

Section 16. Leased space. A school district may lease space or sell services to a charter school. A charter school may lease space or secure services from another public body, nonprofit organization, or private organization or individual.

Perhaps the district could lease space at a price reflecting its operating costs for that space.

Section 17. Transportation. Transportation for pupils enrolled at a charter school shall be provided by the district in which the school is located for students residing in the district in which the school is located, and to and from the border of the district for nonresident students. Districts may provide transportation for nonresident students.

Most laws simply establish the principle that transportation to the public charter school will be provided through the district in which the school is located. Students coming from another district are usually responsible for getting themselves to the border of the district in which their school is located. School bus professionals are quite creative and practical about working out arrangements from that point on.

Section 18. Initial costs. A sponsor may authorize a school before the applicant has secured space, equipment, personnel, and so forth, if the applicant indicates authorization is

necessary for the school to
raise working capital.

Section 19. Information.

The state department of
education must disseminate
information to the public,
directly and through sponsors, both on how to form
and operate a charter school
and on how to enroll in
charter schools once they
are created.

Section 20. General authority.

A charter school may not levy
taxes or issue bonds secured
by tax revenues.

Appendix C:
Additional Resources

National Resources

American On-Line Charter area—the first on-line charter resource—is managed by Frank Dooling. The service has a great deal of material, including an on-line chat room about many issues. Pull down the menu to "keyword" and then type in "charter."

Joan Buckley, American Federation of Teachers, 555 New Jersey Ave. NW, Washington, DC 20001, (202) 393-8642. This is a good source for information about AFT activity in the area.

Center for Education Reform, 1001 Connecticut Ave. NW, Suite 204, Washington, DC 20036, (202) 822-9000 (good web site: [http://edreform.com]). The Center publishes a periodic newsletter with a conservative bent and other materials about school reform and charter schools and has published two excellent directories of charter public schools, state by state.

Charter Friends Network, Jon Schroeder, (651) 644-5270, [www.charterfriends.org]. Schroeder works with the state charter resource and support groups. He is an excellent source of information about who, in which states, is helping individuals create charter schools and who is trying to help legislatures to adopt charter laws.

Revised in 1998.

Charter School Research web site, created by Syracuse University graduate student Jude Hollins is: [http://csr.syr.edu]. The site offers a vast array of information and a daily chat about various items related to charter issues.

Federal Charter School Evaluation: [http://www.rppintl.com/]. This site will give you the latest information about results from the federally funded evaluation of charter schools.

Thomas Fordham Foundation: [http://www.edexcellence.net]. The site offers various publications related to many school reform issues, including charter schools. The foundation has done several important studies on charter schools, with a somewhat conservative viewpoint.

Ted Kolderie, Center for Policy Studies, 59 West Fourth Street, St. Paul, MN 55102, (612) 224-9703. The Center publishes periodic essays primarily geared to people who want to understand the rationale for and recent policy developments with the charter concept.

Joe Nathan, Center for School Change, Humphrey Institute, University of Minnesota, 301 19th Ave. S, Minneapolis, MN 55455, (612) 626-1834, (e-mail) JNathan@hhh.umn.edu. The Center publishes periodic reports about the charter school concept, some of them useful for policy makers, some of them useful for people trying to create charter schools.

National Council of State Legislators web site: [www.ncsl.org/programs/educ/c1schls.htm].

National Education Association Charter School Project, NEA, 1201 16th Street NW, Washington, DC 20036, (202) 877-7200.

Progressive Policy Institute, 518 C Street NE, Washington, DC 20002. The Institute produces various publications from the centrist Democratic viewpoint.

U.S. Department of Education web site: [www.uscharterschools.org]. The site contains a vast array of information.

Canadian Charter School Developments

Ron Babiuk, c/o Alberta Education, Edmonton Regional Office, 11160 Jasper Avenue, Edmonton, Alberta, Canada T5K 01.2 (403) 427-2952. This is a good source of information about charters in Alberta, the only Canadian province to adopt the idea so far.

Joe Freedman, M.D., President, Society for Advancing Educational Research, 57 Allan Close, Red Deer, Alberta, Canada T4R 1A4, (403) 340-0406. Freedman has written a book about the charter idea and has produced a videotape on the subject. He knows about charter efforts throughout Canada.

Stephen B. Lawton, Chair, Department of Educational Administration, Ontario Institute for Studies in Education, 252 Bloor Street West, Toronto and Ontario, Canada M5S 1V6.

Notes

Preface to the Paperback Edition

1. H. Abdullah, "Rights Hero Seeks to Open School in Detroit," *New York Times,* June 30, 1997, p. A12.
2. R. Hernandez, "Pressure Grows for Schools Led by the Parents," *New York Times,* Feb. 28, 1998, p. A1.
3. G. Vanourek, B. V. Manno, C. E. Finn, Jr., and L. A. Bierlein, *Charter Schools in Action,* Final Report, Part 1 (Washington: Hudson Institute, June 1997).
4. Center for Applied Research and Educational Improvement, *Minnesota Charter Schools Evaluation,* Interim Report (Minneapolis: University of Minnesota, Dec. 1996).
5. S. Cheung, M. E. Murphy, and J. Nathan, "Making a Difference?" *Charter Schools, Evaluation and Student Performance* (Minneapolis: University of Minnesota Humphrey Institute Center for School Change, Mar. 1998).
6. K. Matheson, presentation at the Idaho School Superintendents Association, Boise, Feb. 21, 1998.
7. John Gardner, conversation with the author, June 16, 1998.
8. E. Rofes, "How Are School Districts Responding to Charter Laws and Charter Schools?" (Berkeley, Graduate School of Education Policy Analysis for California Education [PACE], n.d).
9. Deborah Meier and Paul Schwarz, personal correspondence, Sept. 3, 1998.
10. S. Cheung, M. E. Murphy, and J. Nathan, "Making a Difference?" *Charter Schools, Evaluation and Student Performance* (Minneapolis: University of Minnesota Humphrey Institute Center for School Change, Mar. 1998).
11. P. Wohlstetter, and N. C. Griffin, "First Lessons: Charter Schools as Learning Communities" (Pittsburgh: Consortium for Policy Research in Education, RB–22, Sept. 1997).
12. C. Mandala, "How Level a Playing Field? The Search for Equity in Charter School Funding" (Minneapolis: Humphrey Institute Center for School Change, July 1998).

13. J. J. Gallagher, "Education Alone is a Weak Treatment, *Education Week,* July 8, 1998, p. 60.
14. P. Wellstone, "Remarks Delivered to the Minnesota Legislature," Feb. 17, 1997.
15. W. Clinton, "Opening and Closing Remarks by the President in Roundtable Discussion on Charter Schools," Sept. 20, 1997, White House Press Office.
16. R. Rothstein, "Charter Conundrum," *American Prospect,* July-Aug., 1998, pp. 46–60.

Preface
Epigraph: V. Hugo, *Histoire d'un Crime; Conclusion:* p. 649
  1. T. Kolderie, *The States Will Have to Withdraw the Exclusive Franchise* (St. Paul, Minn.: Center for Policy Studies, July 1990).
  2. S. M. Elam, L. C. Rose, and L. M. Gallup, "25th Annual Phil Delta Kappa Gallup Poll of the Public's Attitudes Toward the Public Schools, *Phi Delta Kappan,* Oct. 1993, p. 151.

Introduction
  1. T. Kolderie, July 1990.
  2. A. Urbanski, "Public Schools of Choice and Education Reform," in J. Nathan (ed.), *Public Schools by Choice: Expanding Opportunities for Parents, Students and Teachers* (Minneapolis, Minn.: Free Spirit Press, 1989), p. 230.
  3. R. Wood, "SAIL: A Pioneer for Schools of Choice in Florida," in J. Nathan (ed.), *Public Schools by Choice: Expanding Opportunities for Parents, Students and Teachers* (Minneapolis, Minn.: Free Spirit Press, 1989), p. 202.
  4. C. Glenn, "Parent Choice and American Values," in J. Nathan (ed.), *Public Schools by Choice: Expanding Opportunities for Parents, Students and Teachers* (Minneapolis, Minn.: Free Spirit Press, 1989), p. 53.
  5. M. Friedman, "The Voucher Idea," *New York Times Magazine,* Sept. 23, 1973; J. Coons and S. Sugarmen, *Education by Choice: The Case for Family Control* (Berkeley: University of California Press, 1978); J. E. Chubb and T. M. Moe, *Politics, Markets and America's Schools* (Washington, D.C.: Brookings Institution, 1990).
  6. L. Steel and R. Levine, *Educational Innovation in Multiracial Contexts: The Growth of Magnet Schools in American Education,* prepared for the U.S. Department of Education, contract #LC90043001 (Palo Alto, Calif.: American Institutes for Research, 1994).
  7. T. J. Hughes, "Magnets' Pull Weakens in Suburbs," *St. Louis Post-Dispatch,* Feb. 25, 1988, p. 8A.

8. S. Davenport and D. Moore, *The New Improved Sorting Machine* (Chicago: Designs for Change, 1988).

9. A. A. Summers and A. W. Johnson, "Review of the Evidence of Effects of School-Based Management Plans," paper presented at the Conference on Improving the Performance of America's Schools: Economic Choices (Board of Science, Technology and Economic Policy, National Research Council, National Academy of Sciences), Washington, D.C., Oct. 12–13, 1994.

10. National Commission on Excellence in Education, *A Nation at Risk* (Washington, D.C.: U.S. Department of Education, 1983).

11. A. Bestor, *The Educational Wasteland* (Urbana: University of Illinois), 1953; H. Rickover, *Education and Freedom* (New York: Dutton, 1959).

12. Rickover, 1959, quoted in Edward R. Murrow, "Foreword," p. 6.

13. J. Kozol, *Death at an Early Age* (Boston: Houghton Mifflin, 1967).

14. J. Johnson and J. Immerwahr, *First Things First: What Americans Expect from the Public Schools* (New York: Public Agenda Foundation, 1994), p. 15.

15. National Education Goals Panel, *National Education Goals Report* (Washington, D.C.: U.S. Government Printing Office, 1995), p. 36.

16. National Education Goals Panel, *National Education Goals Report*, p. 33.

17. National Education Goals Panel, *National Education Goals Report*, p. 33.

18. I.V.S. Mullis and others, *Trends in Academic Progress* (Washington, D.C.: U.S. Department of Education, Nov. 1991), p. 170.

19. S. Farkas and J. Johnson, *Given the Circumstances: Teachers Talk About Public Education Today* (New York: Public Agenda Foundation, 1996), p. 24.

20. S. G. Friedman, *Small Victories* (New York: HarperCollins, 1990), pp. 212–213.

21. J. Nathan, *Free to Teach: Achieving Equity and Excellence in Schools* (Rev. ed.). (Cleveland: Pilgrim Press, 1989). (Originally published 1983.)

22. H. Kohl, *Thirty-Six Children* (New York: Signet, 1968), p. 177.

23. R. A. Schmuck and P. A. Schmuck, *Small Districts and Big Problems* (Newbury Park, Calif.: Corwin Press, 1992), p. 10.

24. J. Comer "Educating Poor Minority Children," *Scientific American*, Nov. 1988, pp. 42–48; R. E. Slavin, N. A. Madden, L. Dolan, and B. A. Wasik, *Every Child, Every School: Success for All* (Thousand Oaks, Calif.: Corwin Press, 1996); S. Fliegel, *Miracle in East Harlem: The Fight for Choice in Pubic Education* (New York: Random House, 1993); D. W. Meier, "Choice Can Save Public Education," *The Nation*, Mar. 4, 1991, pp. 253, 266–271; H. Levin, *Accelerated Schools* (newsletter available from Accelerated Schools Project, 109 CERAS, Stanford University, Stanford, CA 94305).

25. Dan Daly, interview with the author, Feb. 21, 1996.

26. Richard Farias, interview with the author, Mar. 10, 1996.
27. Frank Esposito, letter to the author, Mar. 10, 1996.

Chapter One

1. Information about the City Academy is derived from a series of site visits by the author from 1994 to 1996 and the author's interviews with Milo Cutter and with Terry Kraabel, Dec. 1995.
2. C. R. Yusten, memo to St. Paul Board of Education Teaching and Learning Committee, Oct. 23, 1995.
3. Information about O'Farrell Community School is derived from a site visit by the author in April 1995 and the author's interview with Robert Stein, in February 1996, unless otherwise indicated.
4. R. Stein, "O'Farrell Charter School," *Phi Delta Kappan*, Sept. 1996.
5. Stein, "O'Farrell Charter School," Sept. 1996.
6. Information about Minnesota New Country School is derived from a series of site visits by the author from Sept. 1995 to Apr. 1996.
7. Wayne Jennings, interview with the author, Feb. 1996.
8. Information about Academy Charter School is derived from a site visit by the author in Oct. 1994 and discussion with Melinda Windler and Karen Woods, July 1996.
9. P. Grippe, interview with the author, July 1996.
10. Information about the Hickman Charter School is derived from the author's interview with Richard Ferriera, Mar. 23, 1996.
11. Information about New Visions School is derived from a series of site visits by the author in 1995 and 1996; from the author's interview with Bob DeBoer, Mar. 15, 1996; and from New Visions School, *New Visions School: First Year Charter School Summary Results, 1994–95* (Minneapolis, Minn.: New Visions School, n.d.).
12. New Visions School, *New Visions School*, n.d., p. 2.
13. Information about PS1 is derived from a site visit by the author in May 1996 and from the author's interview with Rexford Brown, May 19, 1996.

Chapter Two

1. Meier, "Choice Can Save Public Education," 1991, p. 266.
2. Nathan, *Free to Teach*, 1989.
3. "Draft '86 Public Schools of Choice Bill," p. 3.
4. D. Sedio, director of the Advanced High School Students office at the University of Minnesota, Minneapolis, unpublished report, University of Minnesota, 1994.
5. J. Nathan and W. Jennings, *Access to Opportunity: Experiences of Minnesota Students in Four Statewide Choice Programs, 1989–90* (University of Minnesota: Hubert H. Humphrey Institute of Public Affairs, 1990), p. i.

6. Minnesota Education Association, "Video News Release," (St. Paul, Minn.: Minnesota Education Association, Apr. 1985). (Videotape.)

7. S. Dornfield, "Public Schools Rank High," *St. Paul Pioneer Press,* Mar. 3, 1995, p. 1A.

8. R. Hotakainen, "55 percent in State Want Students to Spend More Time in School," *Minneapolis Star-Tribune,* Aug. 12, 1992, p. B1.

9. Minnesota Education Association, *Open Enrollment: A Minnesota Choice* (St. Paul: Minnesota Education Association, n.d.), p. 2.

10. T. Mazzoni and B. Sullivan, "Legislating Educational Choice in Minnesota: Politics and Prospects," in W. L. Boyd and H. J. Walberg, *Choice in Education: Potential and Problems* (Berkeley, Calif.: McCutchan, 1990); N. C. Roberts and P. J. King, *Transforming Public Policy: Dynamics of Policy Entrepreneurship and Innovation* (San Francisco: Jossey-Bass, 1996).

11. K. Jorgenson and E. Ward, "Rothsay Program Makes a Difference," *ECSU Review,* Nov. 1993, p. 6.

12. The five student stories that follow are from unpublished letters sent to Darryl Sedio, director of the Advanced High School Students office at the University of Minnesota, Minneapolis.

13. Ember Reichgott-Junge spoke to the author in numerous interviews from April 1989 to July 1996 about her role in passing the charter school legislation.

14. S. Fliegel, presentation at the Minnesota Foundation's Itasca Conference, Oct. 4, 1988; see also S. Fliegel, *Miracle in East Harlem* (New York: Times Books, 1993).

15. R. Budde, *Education by Charter: Restructuring School Districts* (Andover, Mass.: Regional Laboratory for Educational Improvement of the Northeast and Islands, 1988).

16. R. Budde, "Education by Charter—Key to New Model of School District." Presentation at the annual meeting of the Society for General Systems Research, 1975. (Mimeographed.)

17. Budde, *Education by Charter,* 1988; R. Budde, "Education by Charter," *Phi Delta Kappan,* Mar. 1989, pp. 518–520.

18. A. Shanker, "National Press Club Speech," Mar. 31, 1988, Washington, D.C., pp. 17–18.

19. A. Shanker, "Convention Plots New Course—A Charter for Change," *New York Times* (paid advertisement), July 10, 1988, p. E7.

20. R. Budde, interview with the author, Jan. 1996.

21. A. Shanker, " Charter Schools: Option for Other 80 percent," *School Administrator,* Nov. 1988, p. 72.

22. Becky Kelson, interview with the author, Mar. 1996.

23. Terry Lydell, interview with the author, Feb. 1996.

24. Peter Vanderpoel, interview with the author, Feb. 1996.

25. L. Ellison, *Seeing with Magic Glasses* (Arlington, Va.: Great Ocean, 1993).

26. Launa Ellison, interviews with the author, June 1991 and Feb. 1996; see also Ellison, *Seeing with Magic Glasses,* 1993.

27. "Why MEA Opposes Chartered Schools," St. Paul: Minnesota Education Association, no date.

Chapter Three

1. Kolderie, *The States Will Have to Withdraw the Exclusive Franchise,* 1990, p. 3.

2. J. I. Goodlad, "What Some Schools and Classrooms Teach," *Educational Leadership,* Apr. 1983, p. 15.

3. L. Hinz and J. Nathan, *A Survey of Minnesota's Teachers of the Year* (Minneapolis: University of Minnesota Hubert H. Humphrey Institute of Public Affairs Center for School Change, Dec. 1992).

4. This example draws upon a series of interviews with participating teachers. I also attended the school board meeting where the decisions took place.

5. Twentieth Century Fund Task Force on School Governance, *Report of the Twentieth Century Task Force on School Governance* (New York: Twentieth Century Fund, 1992), p. 2.

6. Ms. R's story comes from my personal knowledge of the event and interviews with Ms. R.

7. J. McKay, "The Forces Most Destructive of Public Education," *The School Administrator,* May 1996, pp. 12–13.

8. Kolderie, *The States Will Have to Withdraw the Exclusive Franchise,* July 1990.

9. W. Celis III, "Beyond the P.T.A.: Parents Seek More Power," *New York Times,* Oct. 24, 1994, p. A1.

10. S. M. Wilson, P. L. Peterson, D. L. Ball, and D. K. Cohen, "Learning by All," *Phi Delta Kappan,* Mar. 1996, p. 469.

11. Twentieth Century Fund Task Force on School Governance, *Report of the Twentieth Century Task Force on School Governance,* pp. 1–2.

12. J. Nathan and J. Ysseldyke, "School Choice in Minnesota," *Phi Delta Kappan,* May 1994, pp. 682–688.

13. Pete Holden, interview with the author, Mar. 1996.

14. Bob Vaadeland, interview with the author, Mar. 1996.

15. Office of the Legislative Auditor, Program Evaluation Division, *Post-Secondary Enrollment Options Program* (St. Paul, Minn.: Office of the Legislative Auditor, Mar. 1996), p. 108.

16. L. Myatt and L. Nathan, "Fenway Pilot School," *Phi Delta Kappan,* forthcoming.

17. Myatt and Nathan, "Fenway Pilot School," forthcoming.

18. M. A. Raywid, "The Struggles and Joys of Trailblazing: A Tale of Two Charter Schools," *Phi Delta Kappan,* Mar. 1995, pp. 555–560.

19. Raywid, "The Struggles and Joys of Trailblazing," 1995, p. 557.
20. Raywid, "The Struggles and Joys of Trailblazing," 1995, p. 560.
21. Raywid, "The Struggles and Joys of Trailblazing," 1995, p. 560.
22. Information about the charter school experience in Detroit is derived from David Snead's "Charter School Presentation" given at a conference held at Wayne State University, Detroit, Oct. 5, 1994, and the author's interview with David Snead, Nov. 1995.
23. Snead, "Charter School Presentation," 1994.
24. Snead, interview, 1995.
25. Carol Carryer, interview with author, Apr. 1996.
26. C. Wallis, "A Class of Their Own," *Time,* Oct. 31, 1994, p. 61.
27. J. Peyser, *Changing the Monopoly Structure of Public Education: Dialogue* (Boston: Pioneer Institute, Mar. 1996), p. 5.
28. B. Krodel, "Charter School Is Likely," *Duluth News Tribune,* July 10, 1996, pp. 1A, 8A.
29. R. Quinn, "Viewpoint," *Colorado Association of School Boards Agenda,* Aug. 1993, p. 2.

Chapter Four

1. T. Toch, "Why Teachers Don't Teach," *U.S. News & World Report,* Feb. 26, 1996, p. 63.
2. P. Wohlstetter, R. Wenning, and K. L. Briggs, "Charter Schools in the United States: The Question of Autonomy," *Education Policy,* Dec. 1995, p. 350.
3. Gary Hart, interview with the author, Jan. 5, 1996.
4. M. E. Sweeney, *Planning a Charter School* (Denver: Angel Press, 1994), p. 13.
5. Jennifer Power, "Charting Education Reform." Unpublished paper, Hubert H. Humphrey Institute, Minneapolis: 1996.
6. Steve Wilson, interview with the author, May 1996.
7. Wohlstetter, Wenning, and Briggs, "Charter Schools in the United States," Dec. 1995, p. 350.
8. Michigan Education Association, *Michigan—The Far Right's New Frontier* (East Lansing: Michigan Education Association, n.d.), p. 2.
9. Michigan Education Association, *Michigan—The Far Right's New Frontier,* n.d., p. 19.
10. C. Furrer, letter to Senator Ember Reichgott, Apr. 11, 1991.
11. R. E. Astrup, "Charter Schools: A Dissenting View," *Education Week,* Sept. 23, 1992, p. 29.
12. Minnesota Federation of Teachers, Executive Council Meeting Minutes, Apr. 20, 1991.
13. Ricci Elkins, interview with the author, Mar. 1996.

14. E. Reichgott-Junge, "Charter Schools Will Work Better Than Private School Vouchers," *Minneapolis Star-Tribune,* Jan. 23, 1996, p. A11.

15. Discussion in a meeting the author attended in New Orleans with union representatives and Senator Picard.

16. D. Lilly, "State Eyes Charter School Options," *Seattle Times,* Feb. 28, 1996.

17. Editorial Board, "House Mangles Charter School Bill," *Tacoma Times,* Mar. 3, 1996, p. E4.

18. Editorial Board, "Charter Schools: Will the Legislature Flunk?" *Aberdeen (Washington) Daily World,* Mar. 4, 1996, p. A1.

19. J. Bross, "Allow Innovation," *Longview (Washington) Daily News,* Mar. 4, 1996, p. A1.

20. R. Anderson, "Cautious Course Smothers Charter-School Alternative," *Seattle Times,* Mar. 3, 1996, p. B6.

21. Brenda Matthews, interview with the author, July 1996.

22. K. B. Carter, "Charter School Bill Clears Legislature, Goes to Whitman," *Star-Ledger,* Jan. 5, 1996.

23. J. Preston, "Trenton Senate Votes to Subsidize Charter Schools," *New York Times,* Dec. 22, 1995, p. A1.

24. Dennis Michael Mah, interview with the author, Mar. 11, 1996; D. M. Mah, *Annual Report for 1993–94 Bowling Green Charter School* (Sacramento, Calif.: Bowling Green Charter School, July 18, 1994).

25. Eric Premack, interview with the author, Mar. 1996; California Teachers Association, "Region 2 Leaders Conference Exposes Misuse of Charter Act," *CTA Action,* Nov. 1995.

26. A. Stern, "SVSU Students in Crosshairs of MEA Threat," *Saginaw News,* June 3, 1994, p. A1.

27. Stern, "SVSU Students in Crosshairs of MEA Threat," June 3, 1994, p. A1.

28. Stern, "SVSU Students in Crosshairs of MEA Threat," June 3, 1994, p. A1.

29. Jim Goenner, interview with the author, Feb. 1996.

30. C. Reister, "GVSU's Ties to Charters Make It Target," *Grand Rapids Press,* Feb. 25, 1996, p. A1.

31. Goenner, interview, Feb. 1996.

32. B. Wheaton, "Because of Ties to Charter Schools, Teachers Union Doesn't Want Grant," *Record Eagle,* Feb. 5, 1996.

33. A. Shanker, "Goals Not Gimmicks" (paid advertisement), *New York Times,* Nov. 7, 1993, p. E7.

34. A. Shanker, "Charter Schools" (paid advertisement), *New York Times,* June 26, 1994, p. E9.

35. Shanker, "Charter Schools," 1994, p. E9.

36. A. Shanker, "Risky Business" (paid advertisement), *New York Times,* Feb. 16, 1996, p. E7.

37. American Federation of Teachers, "AFT Report Recommends Changes in Charter School Laws," (press release). Washington: AFT, 1996, p. 1.

38. American Federation of Teachers, "AFT Report Recommends Changes in Charter School Laws," (press release). Washington: AFT, 1996, p. 2.

39. Louann A. Bierlein, "Existing Charter School Laws: Analysis of 'Stronger Components.'" Baton Rouge, July 27, 1995.

40. American Federation of Teachers, "AFT Report Recommends Changes in Charter School Laws," (press release). Washington: AFT, 1996, p. 2

41. D. DeLee, letter to U.S. Senator David Durenberger from the National Education Association, Washington, D.C., Jan. 16, 1992.

42. A. DiLorenzo, "National Education Association's Charter School Initiative," *CANEC Connections,* Feb. 1996, p. 6.

43. DiLorenzo, "National Education Association's Charter School Initiative," 1996, p. 6.

44. Andrea DiLorenzo, interview with the author, Jan. 1996.

45. J. Berglund, "Life Inside a Charter School," *MEA (Minnesota Education Association) Advocate,* Dec. 17, 1993, pp. 10–11.

46. R. Houde, "Teacher Believes in Charter Schools," *MFT (Minnesota Federation of Teachers) Action,* Oct. 13, 1993, p. 4.

47. Gayle Fallon, interview with the author, Mar. 1996.

48. Richard Farias, interviews with the author, Mar. 1996 and May 1996.

49. J. Johnson and J. Immerwahr, *First Things First: What Americans Expect from the Public Schools,* 1994, p. 36.

50. Johnson and Immerwahr, *First Things First,* 1994, p. 40.

51. Johnson and Immerwahr, *First Things First,* 1994, p. 43.

Chapter Five

1. A. Medler and J. Nathan, *Charter Schools: What Are They Up To?* (Denver, Colo.: Education Commission of the States, and Minneapolis, Minn.: University of Minnesota Hubert H. Humphrey Institute of Public Affairs Center for School Change, 1995), p. v.

2. Curriculum Committee, O'Farrell Community School, "The O'Farrell Standard" (San Diego: O'Farrell Community School, revised 1993–94).

3. J. Hall, "Options for Youth Charter School Self-Study," La Crescenta, California: Options for Youth Charter School, Jan. 1996.

4. Sweeney, *Planning a Charter School,* 1994, p. 24.

5. Academy Charter School, *Mission Statement* (Castle Rock, Colo.: Academy Charter School), n.p.

6. J. Nathan, J. Power, and M. Bruce, *Deserved, Defensible Diplomas: Lessons from High Schools with Competency-Based Graduation Requirements* (Minneapolis: University of Minnesota Hubert H. Humphrey Institute of Public Affairs Center for School Change, May 1995).

Chapter Six

1. Medler and Nathan, *Charter Schools: What Are They Up To?* 1995.
2. L. Bierlein, *Charter Schools: Initial Findings* (Denver, Colo.: Education Commission of the States, Feb. 1996), p. 4.
3. J. Power and J. Nathan, *Characteristics of Students Attending Minnesota Charter Schools,* unpublished report, University of Minnesota Hubert H. Humphrey Institute of Public Affairs Center for School Change, 1996, p. 1.
4. M. A. Raywid, "Choice Inequitable? As Compared to What?" *Changing Schools,* Feb. 1996, pp. 19–21.
5. T. Vitullo-Martin, *Diversity in the Characteristics of Students Enrolled in Charter Schools* (East Lansing: Michigan Center for Charter Schools, Nov. 1994).
6. Bierlein, *Charter Schools,* 1996, p. 5.
7. Goenner, interview, Feb. 1996.

Chapter Seven

1. B. Windler, "Is your Charter School Governance System Working?" *Charter School Bulletin* (Colorado State Department of Education), Mar. 1996, p. 1.
2. Windler, "Is your Charter School Governance System Working?" 1996, p. 1.
3. D. Berliner and B. Biddle, *The Manufactured Crisis: Myths, Fraud and the Attack on America's Public Schools* (New York: Addison-Wesley, 1996).
4. B. Fuller, *Who Gains, Who Loses from School Choice: A Research Summary* (Denver, Colo.: National Conference of State Legislators, n.d.).
5. H. J. Becker, K. Nakagawa, and R. Corwin, *Parent Involvement Contracts in California's Charter Schools: Strategy for Educational Improvement or Method of Exclusion?* (Los Alamitos, Calif.: Southwest Regional Laboratory, Apr. 1995, p. 8.).
6. J. Epstein, "School/Family/Community Partnerships: Caring for the Children We Share," *Phi Delta Kappan,* May 1995, pp. 701–712.
7. Farkas and Johnson, *Given the Circumstances,* 1996.
8. Becker, Nakagawa, and Corwin, *Parent Involvement Contracts in California's Charter Schools,* Apr. 1995.
9. J. P. McDonald, B. Rogers, and T. Sizer, *Standards and School Reform—Asking the Essential Questions,* Studies on Exhibitions, no. 8 (Providence: RI: Coalition of Essential Schools, April 1993), p. 9.
10. Medler and Nathan, *Charter Schools: What Are They Up To?* 1995.
11. McDonald, Rogers, and Sizer, *Standards and School Reform,* April 1993, p. 9.

12. Catterall and Associates, *Options for Youth Charter School*, Oct. 1995, p. 11.
13. McDonald, Rogers, and Sizer, *Standards and School Reform*, April 1993, p. 9.
14. McDonald, Rogers, and Sizer, *Standards and School Reform*, April 1993, p. 10.
15. P. Westrup, *Bowling Green Charter Elementary Year End Report for 1994–95* (Sacramento, Calif.: Bowling Green Charter School, Oct. 10, 1995).
16. C. E. Finn, Jr., L. Bierlein, and B. V. Manno, *Charter Schools in Action: A First Look* (Washington, D.C.: Hudson Institute, Jan. 1996), p. 4.
17. A. Wabnik, "Chartering a New Course," *Arizona Daily Star,* Dec. 24, 1995, p. 1A.
18. Don Jacobson, interview with the author, Mar. 10, 1996.
19. Yvonne Chan, interview with the author, June 1996.
20. Medler and Nathan, *Charter Schools: What Are They Up To?* 1995, p. 19.
21. Finn, Bierlein, and Manno, *Charter Schools in Action,* Jan. 1996.

Chapter Eight
1. E. Premack, *Profile of California's Charter Schools, 1994–95* (San Diego: Greater San Diego Chamber of Commerce, Mar. 1996), p. 21.
2. D. M. Mah, *Annual Report for 1993–94 Bowling Green Charter School,* 1994; and Westrup, *Bowling Green Charter Elementary Year End Report for 1994–95,* 1995.
3. C. Horlock, *Summary of Demographic and Accountability Information, Washington Charter School: 1991–95* (Palm Desert, Calif.: Washington Charter School, 1995), p. 2.
4. Palmer, "New Visions School Statistical Analysis," n.d., p. 12.
5. Premack, *Profile of California's Charter Schools, 1994–95* (Mar. 1996), p. 37.
6. Catterall and Associates, *Options for Youth Charter School,* Oct. 1995, p. 34.
7. Melinda Windler, interview with the author, May 1995.
8. Cutter, interview, Dec. 1995; C. R. Yusten, memo to St. Paul Board of Education Teaching and Learning Committee, Oct. 23, 1995.
9. American Federation of Teachers, "State Voucher Threats Heat Up," *American Teacher,* May–June 1995, p. 3.
10. Medler and Nathan, *Charter Schools: What Are They Up To?* 1995.
11. Finn, Bierlein, and Manno, *Charter Schools in Action,* Jan. 1996), p. 2.
12. Pioneer Institute, *Charter Schools: A Reality Check* (Boston: Pioneer Institute, n.d.), pp. 1–2.
13. S. Dennison, "Charters Charm Frustrated Teachers," *Wilmington Sunday News Journal,* Nov. 19, 1995, p. 1B.

14. A. Ellis, "Charter Schools Redefining Future of Public Education," *Rocky Mountain News,* June 9, 1994, p. 50A.
15. Bierlein, *Charter Schools,* 1996.
16. Matthews, interview, July 1996.
17. Frank Esposito, personal correspondence and interview with the author, June 1996.
18. Office of the Legislative Auditor, Program Evaluation Division, 1996.
19. Medler and Nathan, *Charter Schools: What Are They Up To?* 1995.
20. Medler and Nathan, *Charter Schools: What Are They Up To?* 1995.
21. P. Applebome, "Start of Charter School Shows Flaws in Concept," *New York Times,* Mar. 6, 1996, p. B8.
22. Finn, Bierlein, and Manno, *Charter Schools in Action,* Jan. 1996), p. 5.
23. Applebome, "Start of Charter School Shows Flaws in Concept," 1996, p. B8.
24. Medler and Nathan, *Charter Schools: What Are They Up To?* 1995.
25. Gerald Bracey, conversation with the author, May 1996.
26. P. Wohlstetter and L. Anderson, "What Can U.S. Charter Schools Learn from England's Grant Maintained Schools," *Phi Delta Kappan,* Feb. 1994, pp. 486–491.
27. Fuller, *Who Gains, Who Loses from School Choice,* n.d., pp. 1–2.
28. Ralph Ellison, *Invisible Man,* New York: Random House, 1952, p. 3.
29. Raywid, "Choice Inequitable? As Compared to What?" Feb. 1996.

Chapter Nine

1. F. Douglass, quoted in J. W. Blassingame, *Frederick Douglass: The Clarion Voice,* in E. M. Beck (ed.), *Bartlett's Familiar Quotations* (15th ed.) (Boston: Little, Brown, 1980), p. 556.
2. R. Riley, letter to charter school leaders (Washington: U.S. Department of Education, Mar. 8, 1996).
3. L. Nyberg, letter to members of the Minnesota Senate, Apr. 21, 1995.
4. J. Nathan and J. Power, *Policy-Makers View the Charter School Movement* (Minneapolis: University of Minnesota Hubert H. Humphrey Institute of Public Affairs Center for School Change, 1996).

The Author

Joe Nathan is senior fellow at the University of Minnesota Hubert H. Humphrey Institute of Public Affairs and director of the Center for School Change. Initiated with a $2.3 million grant from the Grand Rapids, Minnesota–based Blandin Foundation, the center works with communities and schools to make significant improvements in public education and was recently awarded a total of $4 million to help continue its work from the Blandin Foundation, the Annenberg Foundation, and the University of Minnesota.

Nathan holds a B.A. degree (1970) in government and international relations from Carleton College and an M.A. degree (1977) and a Ph.D. degree (1981) in educational administration from the University of Minnesota. His areas of specialization include parent involvement, school choice, charter schools, youth service, and the use of technology in schools. He has been an aide, teacher, and administrator with the Wichita, Minneapolis, and St. Paul Public Schools. He has been president of PTA at his children's public school and a member of the Minnesota State PTA Board. His first book, *Free to Teach: Achieving Equity and Excellence in Schools* (1983) was distributed by Senator David Durenberger to each U.S. Senator. His second book, *Micro-Myths: Exploring the Limits of Learning with Computers* (1985), was selected by the National School Boards Association as one of ten "must reading" books in 1985. Nathan is also the editor of *Public Schools by Choice: Expanding Opportunities for Parents, Students and Teachers* (1989), writes a weekly column for the *St. Paul Pioneer Press, Rochester Post-Bulletin,* and *Duluth News Tribune,* and has written guest columns for such newspapers as the *Wall Street Journal, USA Today,* and the *Christian Science Monitor* and for various educational magazines. He has served on the board of the Minnesota Educational Computer Corporation and the editorial board of *Phi Delta Kappan* magazine, and he has taught graduate courses at the University of St. Thomas and University of Minnesota.

Nathan served as coordinator of the National Governor's Association 1986 project, *Time for Results: The Governors' 1991 Report on Education.* He has testified on educational reform before fourteen state legislatures, including the Arkansas State Legislature at the request of then-Governor Bill Clinton, and at several Congressional hearings. He served as a member of President Bush's Educational Policy Advisory Group and of Minnesota governor Arne Carlson's Action for Children Commission, and appeared on many national network radio and television programs. His work has been described in a number of national popular and educational periodicals.

Nathan is married to a public school teacher. Their three children attend the St. Paul public schools.

Index